HINDU PHILOSOPHY

HINDU PHILOSOPHY

By THEOS BERNARD, PH.D.

GREENWOOD PRESS, PUBLISHERS
NEW YORK 1968

15 EAST 40TH STREET, NEW YORK, N. Y.

Reprinted with the permission of
The Philosophical Library, Inc.

LIBRARY OF CONGRESS catalogue card number: 68-21323

Printed in the United States of America

TO
MY TEACHER

PREFACE

This book is an attempt to outline the essence of the six classic systems of Hindū Philosophy, namely; Nyāya, Vaiśeṣika, Sāṁkhya, Yoga, Mīmāṁsā, and Vedānta. All other schools of thought are but variations of these six. I felt it necessary to present only one additional school, namely Kāśmīr Śaivism which gives the most detailed analysis of the Ultimate Principle; however, it can hardly be fully understood until the other six systems are comprehended.

To understand correctly Hindū Philosophy, it is paramount that one realize that the basis of all the schools is the same. Together they form a graduated interpretation of the Ultimate Reality. Each school is based on the same metaphysical doctrine, while discussing some particular aspect of the whole. For example: Nyāya discusses the means by which knowledge may be had of the Ultimate Reality; Vaiśeṣika, the things to be known about that Ultimate Reality; Sāṁkhya, the evolution of metaphysical doctrine; Yoga, the metaphysical doctrine in relation to the individual; Mīmāṁsā, the rules and method of interpreting the doctrine; Vedānta, the relationship between God, Matter, and the world; and Kāśmīr Śaivism, the nature of the Ultimate Spirit and the Cause of the Initial Impulse. This outline is intended merely to show the interrelationship of these schools and how each assumes the doctrines of the other while it solves its special problem.

In this introduction to the classic philosophical schools of India, there is no attempt to prove or disprove but rather to present the system of each school—many eminent scholars have ably discussed the philosophical implications in full detail. My problem has been one of deciding what would be omitted rather than what should be included. Only the essentials of each system are presented.

According to the classic schools of Hindū Philosophy, the method by which the individual can evolve himself during this life is through the practice of Yoga. This is the universal technique recommended to enable man to acquire actual insight into the true nature of things. All schools agree that until the faith is fortified with understanding, little progress can be made, for knowledge without application is like medicine that is not taken.

To aid those who do not have a knowledge of Sanskrit, each term, in most cases, is defined when it is introduced, giving the seed concept of the word, so that the intended metaphysical idea can be more readily grasped. For future reference a glossary of all important terms has been provided in the hope that it may aid those who wish to read some of the recommended bibliographical material. In the use of the English translation of these technical Sanskrit terms, one is cautioned not to take them literally, for it is impossible to adequately translate them. Various writers have used different translations which will be the source of confusion at first. However, if one learns to use the technical term, he will soon grasp its full connotation.

This work is a synthesis rather than an original contribution. In its preparation, I have relied extensively upon the writings of recognized authorities on Hindū Philosophy. For the sake of simplification, I have avoided extensive use of quotations and footnotes, and I have made use of the traditional chronology throughout without comment.

In conclusion, I wish to express my gratitude to those authors, listed in the bibliography, from whose works I have drawn. Special mention should be made of two outstanding guides: *Indian Philosophy* by S. Radhakrishnan, and *A History of Indian Philosophy* by S. Dasgupta. I am also indebted to Professor Herbert W. Schneider, for many helpful recommendations in the preparation of the manuscript, and to Professor Louis H. Grey, for his constructive criticism and technical assistance.

THEOS BERNARD.

TABLE OF CONTENTS

INTRODUCTION

There is innate in the human heart a metaphysical hunger to know and understand what lies beyond the mysterious and illusive veil of nature. This is true from savage to savant. Each in his own way, according to his own capacity, tries to fathom the eternal mystery of life. From the beginning of time, teachers have endeavoured to bridge the gap between the seen and the unseen and to show cause for the inescapable experiences of sorrow and suffering that engulf mankind. But the questions still remain: What is the nature of Reality? What is the nature of human existence? What is the cause of pleasure and pain? How can Liberation be attained?

The solutions and explanations offered by man range from the simplest superstitions to the most subtle philosophical speculations. In the West, man's perceptual knowledge of the external world has been his measuring rod, his basis for theorizing. The primitive who is unable to see beyond the physical manifestation of forces displayed by nature constructs an animism or a pantheism; the scientist examining the depths of matter with his microscope and sweeping the heavens with his telescope postulates a materialism. Nowhere is there any record. Mystery still remains.

Since the dawn of Western Civilization, there have been few achievements in the realm of philosophy that have been able to outlive the scientific findings of a single century. With the advent of every new discovery, we have to revise our scheme of things. The entire sea of science is strewn with theories that have had to be abandoned because the inventive genius of man has been able to bring to light new facts that would not fit into the previous theories. The latest ideas are always called improvements and "evolution."

The West refuses to accept the postulate that the world of mind and matter is but an appearance of a deeper reality which lies beyond the perception of our senses, regardless of how magnified these may be by powerful instruments of precision. One of the reasons for this is due to the preconceived notion that man cannot know metaphysical truths by direct experience; therefore, at best, metaphysical truths can only be speculations, inferences, or ungrounded faith. Even if it were possible, the West maintains that no man has ever attained such supreme knowledge. Another attitude is that all systems of thought must be mutually contradictive, and that, if one of them be true, the rest must be false. There is little place left for various interpretations of a single philosophy to suit different minds.

In the Orient, it has been accepted that man can know metaphysical truths by direct experience. He need not depend upon speculation, inference, or faith. The literature is replete with the writings of men who are said to know the whole truth of Nature and human existence, and the teachings of these men have been set forth in the philosophical systems of ancient India.

Purpose of Hindū Philosophy

All systems of Hindū Philosophy are in complete agreement that the purpose of philosophy is the extinction of sorrow and suffering and that the method is by the acquisition of knowledge of the true nature of things which aims to free man from the bondage of ignorance which all teachers agree is the cause of human suffering.

Hindū Philosophy does not attempt to train one to discern metaphysical truths; it offers a way of thinking which enables one rationally to understand the reality experienced by self-fulfilled personalities, and thereby to lead one to the realization of Truth. In this light, philosophy is seen as an art of life and not a theory about the universe, for it is the means of attaining the highest aspirations of man. It is not for the discovery, but for the understanding of Truth.

There are said to be three stages by which the student can arrive at this realization of the true nature of things. They are: (1) Faith; (2) Understanding; and (3) Realization. The first stage is that of accepting the laws of nature as taught by the great minds of the past. In the next stage, through the process of analysis, the student arrives at a rational and logical conviction; however, reasoning and speculation about transcendental principles can never lead to more than probability, for there can never be certainty in reason as a means of discovering transcendental truths. At best, reasoning is merely a means of understanding the principles of nature and it is the purpose of philosophy to guide and aid the reasoning of the student. The last stage enables the individual actually to become one with the Ultimate Reality. This is accomplished through the practice of Yoga. The techniques and methods used for the attainment of this end have been treated at length in a previous book [1] by the author.

These stages are not unlike those employed in teaching geometry. First the student is given the proposition that the sum of the angles of a triangle is equal to two right angles. This must be accepted as axiomatic, until it is finally demonstrated through reason to be an actual fact. Still it is only a rational conviction which does not necessarily carry certainty. The truth of this proposition can be verified only by actually cutting out from a piece of paper a triangle and measuring the angles, thereby actually experiencing beyond any measure of doubt that the sum total of the three angles is 180 degrees or the equivalent of two right angles. This last procedure of obtaining direct knowledge or realization of a geometrical truth might be said to correspond to the realization of transcendental truth through Yoga.

Test of Philosophy

Philosophy is one of life's noblest pursuits; although its wisdom is the reward of few, it ought to be the aspiration of all. If a philosophy is going to satisfy the intellectual life of the modern world, its conclusions must be able to withstand the acid test of analysis in the dry light of reason. Nothing can be taken for granted; the necessity of every assumption must be established. It must be capable of explaining all things from the Great Absolute to a blade of grass; it

[1] *Haṭha Yoga,* New York, Columbia University Press, 1944.

must not contradict the facts of experience, conceptual or perceptual. Its hypothesis must satisfy all the demands of our nature; it must account for all types of experience: waking, dreaming, sleeping, and those moments which are claimed by the religious ascetic during his deep contemplation. It must be realistic as well as idealistic; it must not be a brutal materialism, worshipping facts and figures and ignoring values, idealizing science and denying spirituality. Nor must it be predominantly a philosophy of values which evades and ignores all connection with facts. It must be comprehensive enough to account for every new discovery of science; it must embrace all the concepts of religion and other philosophical systems. All ideas must receive recognition and find their proper place within the border of its synthesis; every fact of the universe, every aspect of life, every content of experience must immediately fall within the scope of its mould. The March of Science must justify it at every step.

It is not enough merely to interpret reality as perceived by the senses; it must explain both sides of reality, the change and the unchangeable, being and becoming, permanent and impermanent, animate and inanimate. The emphasis on one or the other of these two aspects brings about many of the radical differences in philosophy. The need is to unite them in a deep abiding harmony. All these conditions have been satisfied by the philosophical systems of India.

The Darśanas

According to Indian tradition there is only one Ultimate Reality, but there are six fundamental interpretations of that Reality. These are called the Ṣaḍ Darśanas or "six insights," because they give man sight of the sensible verities and enable him to understand in the light of reason the super-sensible Truth attainable only through the revealed scriptures or through the experience of ṛṣis (sages). The word darśana comes from the root *dṛś,* "to see," and is the Sanskrit term used for philosophy. The six darśanas constitute the classic philosophical systems of India. They are Nyāya, Vaiśeṣika, Sāṁkhya,

Yoga, Mīmāṁsā, and Vedānta. They are not the creation of any one mind nor the discovery of any single individual. The real founders are unknown, and there is considerable controversy as to when they were first reduced to writing, but neither of these conditions detracts from the value of their principles. Together they form a graduated interpretation of the Ultimate Reality, so interrelated that the hypothesis and method of each is dependent upon the other. In no way are they contradictory or antagonistic to one another, for they all lead to the same practical end, knowledge of the Absolute and Liberation of the Soul.

They have many characteristics in common. They all grew out of the Upaniṣads, the philosophical portion of the Veda which is accepted as the supreme authority; they are delivered in the Sūtra style, that is as aphorisms; as such, they are extremely concise, avoiding all unnecessary repetition and employing a rigid economy of words, making it difficult to understand them correctly in their original form without the use of commentaries, for they use many of the same terms, but each system gives its own meaning to the use of the term. They rest their conclusions on several common concepts: all accept the eternal cycle of Nature which is without beginning and end, and which consists of vast periods of creation, maintenance, and dissolution; all accept the principle of regeneration of the soul that maintains that life and death are but two phases of a single cycle to which the soul is bound and to which it clings because of ignorance of the true nature of things; all accept Dharma as the moral law of the universe that accounts for these eternal cycles of Nature, as well as the destiny of the human soul; all agree that knowledge is the path to freedom and that Yoga is the method to attain final liberation.

For the purpose of study, the six Darśanas have been classified into three divisions:

Nyāya	Vaiśeṣika
Sāṁkhya	Yoga
Mīmāṁsā	Vedānta

The first division lays down the methodology of science and elaborates the concepts of physics and chemistry to show how manifestation of phenomena comes into being; the second division sets forth an account of cosmic evolution on purely logical principles; and the third division critically analyses the basic principles, developing them in greater detail and furnishing arguments to substantiate, as well as making incidental contributions on points of special interest.

Nyāya was founded by Gotama. It is purely a system of logic, concerned with the means of acquiring right knowledge which it classifies under sixteen topics.

Vaiśeṣika was founded by Kaṇāda. It classifies all knowledge of the objective world under nine realities and discusses how the various combinations of these nine basic realities bring all things into being.

Sāṁkhya was founded by Kapila who is considered the Father of Hindū Philosophy. This system comprehends the universe as a sum total of twenty-five categories. In no way does it discard the basic realities of the previous system. It only shows that they are not final, in the same way that the breaking down of the atom to electrons and protons did not discard the existence of the atom, but only showed that it was not the last possible reduction of matter. It shows that all derived things in this world are not produced from the nine realities, but from two realities, Spirit and Matter, which are considered as the Ultimate Realities. It discards the creation of the Vaiśeṣika system and shows that all things are evolved out of preexisting material which is the static background of the universe and which simply unfolds itself as a rose unfolds from its seed.

Yoga was founded by Patañjali. This is the individual aspect of the system laid down by the Sāṁkhya doctrine. Here the concern is with the ways and means by which the individual can know Reality by direct experience.

Mīmāṁsā was founded by Jaimini. It is concerned chiefly with the correct interpretation of Vedic ritual and texts.

Vedānta was founded by Bādarāyaṇa. It is an inquiry into the nature of the Ultimate Principle (Brahman). It does not discard the finding of Sāṁkhya, but it endeavours to show that there can be only one Ultimate Reality which makes its appearance to the sense as an illusion (māyā). Its analysis of the process of cosmic evolution is virtually the same as the Sāṁkhya with only those differences which must logically follow from its original premise. It shows how the world with its infinite variety is only an appearance, and that all things are one and the same, only appearing differently.

Influence

Three schools have developed from the interpretation of the opening sūtra of the *Vedāntasūtra,* the classic text of the Vedānta system written by *Bādarāyaṇa:*

"Now, therefore, enquiry should be made into Brahman [the Ultimate Principle]." [2] They are: The Advaita (non-dualism), Viśiṣṭādvaita (qualified non-dualism), and Dvaita (dualism), founded respectively by Śaṁkara (8th cent.), Rāmānuja (11th cent.), Madhva (12th cent.). Fundamentally they have a single conception which they individually develop to suit particular minds. The Advaita school contends that all phenomenal existence is an illusion, called māyā in Sanskrit, and that only the Ultimate Principle (Brahman) is real; the Viśiṣṭādvaita system maintains that there is only One Reality, but that in the objective world it manifests itself as a duality; the Dvaita school treats the evolutionary scheme in the same way as Sāṁkhya. Its only contribution is the way in which it deals with the Supreme Deity. Special mention should be made of the leaders of these three schools.

Śaṁkara

The name Śaṁkara has become almost synonymous with Vedānta, for his commentary on the *Vedāntasūtra* is the foundation for the largest and most popular religious sect of modern Hindūism called Vedānta. In his mind, the *Sūtras* of Bādarāyaṇa unfold into the fullness of their magnificence, liberating the subtlest insight man can obtain into the eternal scheme of things. He is the undefeated cham-

[2] *Vedāntasūtra,* i, I, 1.

of the *Sūtras*; he leaves not a stone of doubt unturned; he embraces every tenet as the sun embraces the diversified objects of this earth. Within his exposition all conflicts and doubts find harmonious equipoise; for he is the master of reason and resolves every difference to the ultimate source from which all things come. Here the teachings of the Upaniṣads find their greatest advocate, exponent and interpreter.

His achievements were many, but his greatest was in the field of speculation, in constructing his system of Monism, called Advaita in Sanskrit, meaning "non-dualism," the central position of which is that all is One, only the Ultimate Principle has any actual existence, everything else is an illusion (māyā). The literature expounding the details of the arguments which he advances to sustain his position is extensive and readily accessible. He believed this system to be the best way to reconcile the teachings of his times with the traditional literature. Much of his intellectual attainment was a reaction against the ascetic tendency of Buddhism and the devotional tendencies stressed by the Mīmāṁsā school. Here his effort was to save the Vedic texts from any exaggerated viewpoint and to bring them into the light of reason. He tried to revive the age of intellectual speculation which abounded when the Upaniṣads were compiled and when the earlier systems of thought reached the fullness of their glory. He was impelled by the spiritual direction of his age to formulate a philosophy and to lay the foundations of a religion which could satisfy the ethical demands and spiritual needs of his people better than the systems of Buddhism, Mīmāṁsā, and Bhakti. In the course of his life he accepted every faith that had the power to elevate man and refine his nature, thus learning from all. He was one of the great philosophers of his day, the sage of his century, the saint of his race.

Indian literature is barren of biographical accounts of their spiritual and philosophical leaders of the past; therefore, very little is known of the life of Śaṁkara. It is generally held that he lived between A.D. 788 and 820, but tradition records that he flourished about 200 B.C.; however, all accounts are in accord that his life was short but vital, crowded with accomplishment and enshrined with profound philosophical insight, and that he left this world at the age of thirty-two. For what little detail there is on his life, we are indebted to his disciples Mādhava, who wrote *Śaṁkaradigvijaya,* and Ānandagiri, who left us his *Śaṁkaravijaya.* Other students wrote brief accounts, but these are considered the most outstanding.

Śaṁkara is believed to have been born at Kāladi, on the west coast of the peninsula in the Malabar. His family was of the learned but hardworking Nambūdri sect of Brahmans. Their family-deity, according to tradition, was Śiva, and Śaṁkara was a Śākta by birth. Early in his youth he went to a Vedic school presided over by Govinda, the pupil of Gauḍapāda. Here he learned the principles of the philosophy which he later made famous. At the age of eight, he is said to have revealed his genius, and early in his youth he gave up the world to become a saṅnyāsin. At no time did he become a passionate recluse, for he wandered throughout India, teaching and discussing his beliefs. Everywhere he challenged the leaders of other schools to philosophical debate. He founded four maṭhas or monasteries, the chief of which is the one at Śṛṅgeri in the Mysore Province of Southern India. The others are at Pūri in the East, Dvārakā in the West, and Badarināth in the North in the Himalayas. He is believed to have died in the Himalayan village of Kedārnāth.

In the course of his life he wrote many texts, the most important being his commentaries on the *Prasthānatraya* which consists of the Upaniṣads, *Bhagavadgītā,* and *Vedāntasūtra.* His general position is revealed in his *Vivekacūdāmaṇi* and *Upadeśasahasrī.* Besides these he leaves many other works that mirror the power of his mind and the genius of his soul. They are: *Āptavajrasūcī, Ātmabodha, Mohamudgara, Daśaślokī, Aparokṣānubhūti,* and commentaries on *Viṣṇusahasranāma* and *Sanatsujātīya.*

Rāmānuja

The uncompromising logic of Śaṁkara initiated a strong reaction led by the equally famed teacher Rāmānuja who is credited with having brought the soul back to philosophy. Both were outstanding spokesmen of their times, but they were poles apart in character. Śaṁkara was the great logician, while Rāmānuja was the great intuitionalist, surrendering to his feelings and setting forth his religious views. Rāmānuja stressed the theistic aspect of the Upaniṣads, while Śaṁkara held strictly to the intellectual. Śaṁkara locked thought in the vacuum chamber of the mind and closed the doors to the light of intuition. It was the purpose of Rāmānuja to reconcile the *Vedāntasūtra,* Upaniṣads, and the *Bhagavadgītā* with the faith and beliefs of the Vaiṣı ava saints.

The system founded by the famed Vaiṣṇava leader Rāmānuja is called Viśiṣṭādvaita, or qualified non-dualism. He admits that the Ultimate Principle is real and exists, but he qualifies his position by arguing that souls are also real, though their reality is dependent upon this Ultimate Principle. He maintains that the Spiritual Principle is the basis of the world, which is not an illusion, as is argued by Śaṁkara. Rāmānuja insists on the continued existence of the individual soul after its release from worldly chains. He holds that the Ultimate Principle, the world, and souls, form a single unity with the souls and world existing only as the body of the Ultimate Principle. He agrees that, in the end, there is nothing but the Ultimate Principle, but maintains that during the period of manifestation, the world and souls are separate in order to serve the Ultimate Principle.

His aim is to proclaim the doctrine of salvation through bhakti or devotion, regarding it as the central teaching of the Upaniṣads, *Bhagavadgītā,* and *Vedāntasūtra.* The effectiveness of his arguments is seen by the movements that have stemmed from his teachings as led by Madhva (12th cent.), Vallabha (15th cent.), Caitanya (15th cent.), Rāmānanda (13th cent.), Kabīr (14th cent.), and Nānak (15th cent.).

Though both Śaṁkara and Rāmānuja were motivated by the same problem, used the same assumptions for their methods, their results were amazingly different. As Śaṁkara was restrained by the rules of logic, Rāmānuja was driven by the fever of the religious instinct.

Rāmānuja embraces all in religious feeling, while Śamkara unites all in the realm of reason. Rāmānuja's philosophical spirit was not altogether wanting, but his religious need was greater; so he tried to reconcile the demands of religious feeling with the claims of logical thinking and thereby bridge the gulf between religion and philosophy.

Rāmānuja was born A.D. 1027 in Śṛperuṁbudūr, a town located a few miles west of Madras. He lost his father early; studied Vedānta under Yādavaprakāśa of Conjeevaram; and was initiated by Perianaṁbi, the learned disciple of Ālavandār. Marital incompatibility proved to him that renunciation was a necessary condition for attaining his highest aspirations of human perfection; so he gave up the world and became a saṅnyāsin, settling down at Śrīraṅgam. His life was dedicated to study and converting large numbers to Vaiṣṇavism which he accomplished during his tours of South India where he restored many Vaiṣṇava temples. His great commentary (*Śrībhāṣya*) on the *Vedāntasūtra* is the classic text for the Vaiṣṇavas today. Other works attributed to him are *Vedāntasāra, Vedārthasamgraha, Vedāntadīpa*, and a commentary on the *Bhagavadgītā*. Tradition has it that he lived to be 120 years of age.

Madhva

The opposite interpretation of Śaṁkara is set forth by the Kanarese Brahman Madhva. His system is popularly known as the Dvaita, or dualistic system. He denies that the Ultimate Principle is the cause of the world, and contends that the soul is a separate principle having an independent existence of its own, and is only associated with the Ultimate Principle. He stands firm for unqualified dualism, whereas Śaṁkara upholds a pure monism.

The orthodox biographical account of the life and work of Madhva is *Nārayaṇācārya's Madhvavijaya* and *Maṇimañjari*. Madhva is also known by the names Pūrṇaprajnā and Ānandatīrtha. He was born in the year 1199 in a village near Udipi of the South Kanara district about sixty miles north of Mangalore. At an early age he became proficient in Vedic learning and soon became a saṁnyāsin. After spending several years in prayer and meditation, study and discussion, he went forth to teach and preach. He founded a temple for Kṛṣṇa at Udipi, where he taught until his death at the age of seventy-nine.

The standard treatises of his school are the commentary which he composed on the *Vedāntasūtra* and a work called *Anuvyākhyāna* in which he justifies his interpretation. Other works that help to elucidate his central position are his commentaries on the *Bhagavadgītā* and the Upaniṣads, his epitome of the *Mahābhārata* called *Mahabhāratatātparyanirṇaya,* and his gloss on the *Bhāgavatapurāṇa.* These are considered his most important, although he wrote many others. Much can be gleaned from the study of Jayatīrtha's commentary on Madhva's *Sūtrabhāṣya* and that on Madhva's *Anuvyākhyāna* called *Nyāyasudhā.* Still another work of importance is Vyāsatīrtha's gloss on Jayatīrtha's commentary called *Tātparyacandrikā.*

The influence of these three leaders, Śamkara, Rāmānuja, and Madhva, has been far reaching, in fact, their history is still in progress; however, there are many other outstanding commentators who have contributed valuable material to the history of thought. A few of them are Bhāskara (10th cent.), Nimbārka (11th cent.), Yadavaprakāśa (11th cent.), Keśava (13th cent.), Nīlakaṇṭha (also known as Śrīkaṇṭha (14th cent.), Caitanya (15th cent.), Vallabha (15th cent.), Vijñānabhikṣu (16th cent.), and Baladeva (18th cent.).

Kāśmīr Śaivism

No account of the philosophical systems of India would be complete without Kāśmīr Śaivism, for its analysis of Nature is more comprehensive than any of the six Darśanas; therefore, it must be included. It is a system of Ideal Monism founded by Vasugupta in the ninth century. Its central position is that there is only one Ultimate Principle, but that this principle has two aspects, one transcendental and the other immanent. Its analysis of the process of cosmic evolution postulates thirty-six categories (tattvas). What the other systems assume, Kāśmīr Śaivism explains, for it shows the origin of Spirit and Matter; it discusses the nature of the Ultimate Principle; and it explains the cause of the initial impulse in Nature.

Kāśmīr Śaivism is a philosophical system based on the Śivasūtra which is one of the texts of that vast body of Indian literature called the Tantras. There is probably no body of traditional literature that has suffered such widespread criticism, from Western and Eastern scholars alike, as the Tantras, due mainly to their esoteric character which made it impossible for scholars to obtain adequate information of their true content. The ban on their investigation was finally removed by the fruitful labours of the late Sir John Woodroffe, the first to defend the outraged Tantras, and now the field of Tāntrik literature can be intelligently investigated. For a correct and complete understanding of Indian culture, it is imperative that this body of traditional literature is properly understood; therefore, a brief outline of their position in the history of Hindū thought will be helpful.

The Tantras

The word Tantra is derived from the root *tan,* "to spread," and the agential suffix *tra,* "to save," meaning that knowledge which is "spread to save." It is a generic term under which a whole culture of a certain epoch of Indian history found expression. According to their own definition, Tantra denotes that body of religious scriptures (śāstra) which is stated to have been revealed by Śiva as a specific scripture for the fourth and present age (Kali Yuga). They are without authorship, for they are revealed by divine inspiration to ṛṣis (sages) who record them for the benefit of men living during this age.

According to Indian tradition there are four ages, collectively called a Mahāyuga, namely, the Satya Yuga (also called Kṛta Yuga), or golden age; the Tretā Yuga (age), in which righteousness (dharma) decreased by one-fourth; the Dvāpara Yuga (age), in which righteousness (dharma) decreased by one-half; and the present Kali Yuga (age) (lit. the age of quarrel), in which righteousness (dharma) has decreased three-fourths, considered the most evil of all ages. According to this doctrine each age has its appropriate scripture (śāstra), designed to meet the requirements and needs of men of each age in their effort to attain liberation.

The Hindū Śāstras (scriptures) are classified into Śruti, Smṛti, Purāṇa, and Tantra; the last three assume the first as their base, in fact, they are merely special presentments of it for the respective ages: Śruti for the Satya Yuga; Smṛti for the Tretā Yuga; Purāṇa for the Dvāpara Yuga; and Tantra for the Kali Yuga. The orthodox view is that the means used during the Satya Yuga became void of power; therefore, a new interpretation had to be given for each age in order to meet the needs of environment and the temperament and capacity of men living in each age. Śruti is that knowledge which is seen by the ṛṣis (sages), therefore without authorship; Smṛti is that knowledge which has been remembered by the ṛṣis (sages); the Purāṇas preserved the teachings and doctrines of the Veda for the declining intelligence and spirituality of men by means of mythology and stories; the Tantra is the universal scripture (śāstra) for this age and is therefore considered as a Yuga Śāstra. It is only a reinterpretation of the Veda for modern man and therefore is frequently called the Fifth Veda (the Mahābhārata is also frequently called by this name).

A Tantra is generally cast in the form of a dialogue between Śiva, the deification of the Ultimate Principle, and his female consort, Pārvatī, the active aspect of the Ultimate Principle. When Pārvatī asks the questions and Śiva answers them, the treatise is called an Āgama, that which has come down; when Śiva asks the questions and Pārvatī answers them, the treatise is called a Nigama. The Tantras are said to be the truest exegesis of the Vedas, and their origin is certainly as ancient as those of some of the classical Upaniṣads.

The Tantras not only issued from the same source as did the Upaniṣads, but it is said that they have been as widespread in India. According to tradition, India had been divided into three regions called Krāntās. These Krāntās were Viṣṇukrāntā, Rathakrāntā, and Aśvakrāntā. Viṣṇukrāntā extended from the Vindhya Mountain in

Cattala (Chittagong), thus including Bengal; Rathakrāntā, from the same mountain to Mahācīna (Tibet), including Nepal; and Aśvakrāntā, from the same mountain to "the great ocean," apparently including the rest of India. Sixty-four Tantras had been assigned to each region, and all of them could be classified according to the three interpretations of philosophy, Abheda, Bedha, and Bhedābheda, that is, non-dualism, dualism, and dualism and non-dualism.

A Tantra is said to consist of seven marks or topics: (1) creation, (2) destruction of the universe, (3) worship, (4) spiritual exercises (Yoga), (5) rituals and ceremonies, (6) six actions, and (7) meditation. They were the encyclopedias of knowledge of their time, for they dealt with all subjects from the creation of the universe to the regulation of society, and they have always been the repository of esoteric spiritual beliefs and practices, especially the spiritual science of Yoga.

There is much controversy over their antiquity which usually reflects a lack of full knowledge of their tradition and a failure to distinguish between the record and the doctrine. The Kali age is still in progress; therefore, it is believed, that new Tantras will continue to appear as ṛṣis (sages) record their intuitional insights on the needs of modern man, but the appearance of these records in no way dates the doctrine which they express, for the doctrine has existed in the minds of man since time immemorial.

The Tantras have many common characteristics. They all accept the Veda and are in no way hostile to the six Darśanas. Their purpose is to provide a way for the salvation of man during the present age (Kali Yuga). Their principles are of universal application without regard to time or place, temperament or capacity, as is witnessed by the many religious sects that have received inspiration from their teachings. They maintain that mere philosophical speculation on the ultimate nature of things is not enough to satisfy the spiritual hunger of the soul, no more than a description of a banquet is sufficient to satisfy the physical hunger of the body. Therefore, they provide not only the principles of speculation, but also the basis for experience; they not only argue, but they experiment. They provide a rational foundation for the spiritual exercises that will liberate man during one lifetime. These practices are referred to as Sādhana, derived from the root *sādh*, "to succeed," that is, that success which leads to final emancipation of the soul. Their philosophy furnishes the reasons required to make the mind firm in its faith so that it will not despair in the early stages when all seems so hopeless. Other philosophies offer a theoretical explanation of the ultimate nature of reality which brings peace of mind, but the Tantras provide a basis for the actual absorption of the essence of man into the essence of Reality. Throughout their structure, the emphasis is placed on the practical aspect of knowledge.

The Tantras are aware of the fact that the world of name and form with its sorrow and suffering cannot be dissolved by logic alone. They teach that only by growth and development can the obstacles of life be surmounted. They accept the world around us as it is, exalting everything, discarding nothing, relegating everything to its rightful place, and providing a spiritual prescription for an orderly life according to the Laws of Nature.

The many errors of interpretation which the Tantras have suffered are perhaps due to the fragmentary character of available material, the technical character of their terminology, the subtle and metaphysical character of their teachings, and the lack of general knowledge of the traditional background upon which they are based. Some of these problems may be solved when scholars bring to light the rich and untouched wealth of knowledge to be had in Tibetan literature, for in Tibet today that which has become tradition in India is still living.

The Tantras are commonly called Āgama, and these are divided into three main groups according to which deity is worshipped: Śiva, Śakti, or Viṣṇu. Together they form the three principal divisions of modern Hindūism, namely Śaivism, Śāktism, and Vaiṣṇavism. All of them have their seeds of origin in the hoary antiquity of time, and they have passed through many transitions according to the interpretations of their many leaders. As they exist today, they are considered as the outstanding religious systems of India and have their beginnings in the early period of the Christian era. Numerous schools have stemmed from each of these, but it will suffice to mention briefly the three principal fountainheads.

Śaivism

Śaivism worships Śiva as the supreme being, regarding him as the source and essence of the universe. The temples dedicated to him are characterized by the Liṅga (phallus) which is symbolic of the attributes of Śiva. The sect as it is known today is said to date from some time between the fifth and sixth centuries. It elaborated a distinctive philosophy called the *Śaivasiddhānta* about the eleventh century. This is based on the tradition of the Vedas and the Āgamas. Other works that have influenced the growth and development of Śaivism are the Tamil *Tolkāppiaṁ* and the Sanskrit Mahābhārata and *Śvetāśvatara Upaniṣad.* Their other sources are twenty-eight Śaiva Āgamas, the hymns of the Śaiva saints, and the works of theologians.

The chief of the twenty-eight Āgamas is Kāmika, including the section dealing with knowledge called *Mṛgendra Āgama.* These are referred to by the Tamil saints Māṇikkavāsagar (7th cent.) and Sundarar. The most outstanding compiler of devotional literature was Naṁbi Āṇḍār Naṁbi (1000 A.D.), and his hymns are collectively called *Tirumurai.* Other important works are Sekkirar's *Periapuraṇam* (11th cent.), describing the lives of the sixty-three Śaiva saints and giving some other valuable information; Meykaṇḍer's *Śivajñānabodham* (13th cent.), the standard exposition of the *Śaivasiddhānta;* Arulnandi Śivācārya's *Śivajñānasiddhiyar;* and Umāpati's *Śivaprakāśam* and *Tiruarulpayan* (14th cent.). A systematic reconciliation of the two-fold tradition of the Veda and Āgama was undertaken by Nīlakaṇṭha (14th cent.), who wrote a commentary on the *Vedāntasūtra,* interpreting that work in the light of the Śaiva system.

Śaivism is divided into two principal schools, the Northern school, known as Kaśmīr Śaivism (to be discussed later), and the Southern school, known as the Liṅgāyat sects, characterized by wearing a

Liṅga around their necks. The first great leader of the Southern school was Lakulīśa, believed to have been the last incarnation of Maheśvara and the founder of the sect of Pāśupatas. The influence of Śaivism grew by its conflict with Buddhism and Jainism in the age of the great Pallavas king. The fact that it flourished in the Gupta era is attested by the Mathurā pillar inscription of Candragupta II Vikramāditya (380 A.D.). The famed Cola kings were likewise Śaivas and did everything to further its influence.

Śāktism

This cult takes its name from its worship of Śakti, which is represented as the embodiment of the power that supports all that lives and which upholds the universe. Śakti is portrayed as the female aspect of the Ultimate Principle, for it is this force that brings all manifestations into being; it is, therefore, deified as the wife of Śiva. Around this principle an intricate system of ritual has developed. Its literature is specifically called the Tantras. All the followers claim great antiquity for their literature, teachings, and principles, tracing their origin to the Vedas. The literature tells of many famed personages believed to have attained enlightenment through the practice of the rites taught by the Śāktas.

Vaiṣṇavism

The chief characteristic of Vaiṣṇavism is the intense devotion to the personal god Viṣṇu, who is accepted not only as the preserver, but also as the creator and destroyer of the universe. As such, Vaiṣṇavism is a form of monotheism, for it sets aside the original triune equality of Brahmā, Viṣṇu, and Śiva in favour of the one god Viṣṇu, often called Hari. His two manifestations in human form are said to be Rāma and Kṛṣṇa.

Vaiṣṇavism is very tolerant, for it is always ready to adapt itself to other creeds when winning over other religions. It has no formal organization or selected leader; it is always guided by the most outstanding mind its teachings and doctrines can develop. Its first great leader is generally conceded to have been Nātha Muni (824–924 A.D.), who was formally anointed in the Śrīraṅgam temple in South India. With him began a new era of Vaiṣṇavism. Then followed Yāmunācārya and Rāmānuja (1017–1137 A.D.). It was Rāmānuja who laid down the lines of its doctrine by elaborating the system of Viśiṣṭādvaita. Vaiṣṇavaite theology is based on the Vedas, Āgamas, Purāṇas, and Prabandham, which consist of the hymns of the poet-saints called Ālvārs. The distinctive features of Vaiṣṇavism are found in the Pañcarātra religion mentioned in the Mahābhārata.

With the death of Rāmānuja came a period of sectarian split among the Vaiṣṇavas which finally ended about the thirteenth century in the permanent division in their ranks into two sects of Tenkalais (Southern school) and the Vadakalais (Northern school). The former regards the Tamil Prabandham as canonical, and is indifferent to the Sanskrit tradition; the latter accepts both the Tamil and the Sanskrit tradition as equally authoritative.

The founder of the Vaḍakalai (Northern school) was Vedānta Deśika, also known as Veṇkaṭanātha (13th cent.). He was one of the greatest successors of Rāmānuja. Other outstanding leaders who have received their inspiration from the teachings of Rāmānuja are Nimbārka (11th cent.), Mādhva (12th cent.), Rāmānanda (13th cent.), Kabīr (14th cent.), Nānak (15th cent.), Vallabha (15th cent.), and Caitanya (15th cent.).

NYĀYA

The Nyāya is the science of logical proof, and furnishes a correct method of philosophical inquiry into the objects and subjects of human knowledge. It is said to be the means to true knowledge about the soul and the realization of the destiny of man according to the laws of nature. The term Nyāya is a Sanskrit word which signifies "going into a subject," that is, an analytical investigation of the subject through the process of logical reason. Vātsyāyana, the classic commentator on the Nyāya-Sūtra, defines it as a "critical examination of the objects of knowledge by means of the canons of logical proof." The Nyāya is also called Tarkavidyā, "science of reasoning," or Vādavidyā, "science of discussion."

The founder of the Nyāya was Gautama (Gotama) who is frequently referred to in the literature as Akṣapāda, "Eye-footed," and Dīrghatapas, "Long-penance." It was customary to call one by a name which gave a descriptive characterization of the individual. In this instance, Gautama probably received these names from his long penances during his periods of study and from the fact that he was customarily seen with his eyes directed toward his feet when walking, which is a natural way to carry the head when contemplating during the course of a stroll. In fact, it is the way one is trained to walk.

There is considerable argument about the exact date of Gautama but the outstanding authorities place him about 550 B.C., making him almost a contemporary of Buddha. According to tradition, Gautama, the founder of the Nyāya, was born at Gautamasthāna, and each year a fair is held in this village in his honour on the 9th day of the lunar month of Caitra (March-April). The village is located 28 miles northeast of Darbhanga. Two miles east is a village called Ahalyāsthāna where a stone slab lies between two trees which is believed to mark the resting place of his wife, Ahalyā. Gautama is said to have spent most of his life with his wife Ahalyā, in a hermitage situated on the banks of the Kṣīrodadhi River on the outskirts of the city of Mithilā, the modern Darbhanga in North Behar. He is also reputed to have lived for a time at Godnā at the confluence of the Ganges and Sarayū. For his retirement he went to Prabhāsa, the well-known sacred place of pilgrimage in Kathiawar on the west sea-coast. He had a son, Śatānanda, who became a priest in the royal family of Janaka much in the same way as the father of Gautama was a priest in the royal family of Kuruśṛṅjaya.

Before the time of Gautama, the principles of the Nyāya existed as an undifferentiated body of philosophical thought bearing on things that can be known and on the means of acquiring such knowledge. Gautama merely formulated the generally accepted principles of the time. This was in keeping with the traditional beliefs about the evolution of man during the present age (Kali Yuga) which was just starting. During this age, it is believed that the conditions and nature of man were to undergo certain changes which necessitated the compilation of traditional knowledge necessary for the spiritual progress of man. Therefore, the outstanding minds of that time reduced to writing what had before existed only in the memory of man. Gautama was the first to reduce the principles for the examination of Truth into their present form; therefore, he is considered as the father of the Nyāya.

Purpose

The purpose of the Nyāya is said to enable us to attain the highest end of life, salvation, release, freedom as it is variously referred to. For this purpose it classifies the different ways in which knowledge is acquired. It teaches that the world consists of the uninterrupted flow of misapprehension, faults, activity, birth and pain. By the cessation of the flow of this chain of consequences will we be freed. The way to break this chain is to obtain a fuller understanding of the true nature of things. When this has been accomplished the faults which consist of a delusion causing us to like and dislike a thing will no longer exist. When this disappears, there will no longer be any desire which is the stimulus for all action. It is claimed that this will free us from rebirth, the cause of all sorrow and suffering, and enable us to achieve the supreme end of life.

This exalted goal is said to be attained by thoroughly realizing the four subjects established in the *Nyāyasūtra*, namely: (1) the thing to be avoided (i.e., pain), (2) its cause (i.e., desire and ignorance), (3) absolute avoidance, (4) and the means of such avoidance (i.e., true knowledge) which is to be secured. These four steps are considered the prime pre-requisites for the attainment of life's highest reward.

The teachings of the Nyāya are believed to enable us to discern the true from the false, and at the same time, to be our greatest protection when our knowledge is still in the process of growth and has not yet matured into the ripened fruit of enlightenment. Today in the search for truth, the doctrine of each new teacher raises doubt as to which is the right path. The seeker of truth centuries before the advent of the Christian era was likewise confronted with the same problem of trying to discern the true from the false. For this very purpose, certain teachings of the Nyāya were laid down so that there would be a rational basis for recognizing the Truth. The only difference between those of the past and ourselves was that in those days there were a thousand teachers to every one met today.

Scope

In its scope, the Nyāya is a critical treatment of the problems of the Spirit. It tries to solve the problems of philosophy by studying the general plan and method of critical inquiry. It explores the traditional beliefs of its time and argues vigorously against all prejudiced and irrational scepticism. It is said that wherever there is mental activity controlled by the purpose of acquiring knowledge of reality, there is a topic for logic. This capacity for truth seeking is innate in human nature and is not created by logic; however, logic enables it to accomplish its aims. Its sole purpose is the reclamation of the soul by providing the means of studying, listening and judging, for this is said to be the way to mature wisdom which is acquired by the removal of doubt, or to confirm that which has been passed down through tradition. The Nyāya is founded on the belief that only by the thorough examination of the modes and sources of correct knowledge can the ends of life be truly accomplished; therefore, what has been supplied to us by the traditional teachings and by evidences of the senses must be submitted to critical inquiry.

The Nyāya considers the psychological aspect of obtaining knowledge and treats at length the ways by which the mind is carried forward and impelled to produce fresh results and also points out the pitfalls. As such, it is the science of proof and of the estimation of evidence. The logical and physical departments become the predominant features. It accepts the standard systems of philosophical thought and sets for its task the examination of the fundamental problems of reality. Its concern is the means of knowledge and not the nature of knowledge. It devotes its inquiry into the objects of perception, leaving the problems of origin and manifestation for the other systems. As such, it lays down the rules of syllogistic reasoning for the purpose of examining the objects of perceptions. It is the operative cause of valid knowledge and classifies the different ways in which knowledge is acquired.

Philosophy

The opening verse of the *Nyāyasūtra* says that Supreme Felicity is attained by knowledge of the true nature of the sixteen categories, namely:

1. Means of right knowledge (pramāṇa)
2. Object of right knowledge (prameya)
3. Doubt (saṁśaya)
4. Purpose (prayojana)
5. Familiar example (dṛṣṭanta)

6. Established tenet (siddhānta)
7. Members of a syllogism (avayava)
8. Confutation (tarka)
9. Ascertainment (nirṇaya)
10. Discussion (vāda)
11. Controversy (jalpa)
12. Cavil (vitaṇḍā)
13. Fallacy (hetvābhāsa)
14. Equivocation (chala)
15. Futility (jāti)
16. Disagreement in principle (nigrahasthāna)

These sixteen topics are to be used to discover truth. The first nine deal more strictly with logic, while the last seven have the function of preventing and destroying error.

Gautama in the compilation of his work has used the method of "enumeration," "definition" and "critical examination." The first book deals with the "enumeration" and "definition" of his sixteen categories, and the remaining four books are reserved for "critical examination." Since it is the purpose of this book to set forth only the principles of each system in order to enable the student to have a systematized outline for further study, only the first book of Gautama's will be discussed. This in no way will omit anything that is materially important.

1. "THE MEANS OF RIGHT KNOWLEDGE [pramāṇa] are perception [pratyakṣa], inference [anumāna], comparison [upamāna], and verbal testimony [śabda]." [1]

Each school of thought has its theory of knowledge. Perception (pratyakṣa) is the only means admitted by the Cārvakas; verbal testimony (śabda) is the only means admitted by the Mīmāmsās; perception (pratyakṣa) and inference (anumāna) are admitted by the Vaiśeṣikas and Bauddhas (Buddhists); perception (pratyakṣa), inference (anumāna) and verbal testimony (śabda) are accepted by the Sāṁkhyas; to the four recognized by the Naiyāyikas, a fifth, called presumption (arthāpatti), is used by the Prābhākaras; a sixth, called non-existence (abhāva), is added by the Bhāṭṭas and Vedan-

[1] *Nyāyasūtra*, i, I, 3.

tins; a seventh and eighth, called probability (sambhava) and tradition (aitihya) are added by the Paurāṇikas.

Presumption (arthāpatti) is the deduction of one thing from the declaration of another thing, e.g., from the declaration that 'unless there is cloud, there is no rain,' we deduce that 'there is rain, if there is cloud.' Non-existence (abhāva) is the deduction of the existence of one of two opposite things from the non-existence of the other; e.g., the non-existence of the sun established the existence of the stars. Probability (sambhava) consists in cognizing the existence of a thing from that of another thing in which it is included. Tradition (aitihya) is an assertion which has come down from the past without any indication of the source from which it first originated.

Nyāya comprehends these additional means of valid knowledge, because presumption, non-existence and probability are included in inference, and tradition is included in verbal testimony. Since no new category is raised by them, they cannot be considered as independent means of right knowledge; therefore, there is no need to consider them separately.

PERCEPTION (pratyakṣa) is defined as that knowledge which arises from the contact of a sense with its object, and which is determinate, unnameable and non-erratic. Determinate is distinguished from indeterminate knowledge in the instance of a man who, looking from a distance, cannot ascertain whether there is smoke or dust. The unnameable brings to our attention the fact that the name of a thing has no connection with the knowledge of a thing derived through our perception. The non-erratic means that we cannot derive knowledge of water by the perception of a mirage which is an illusion or erratic. Perceptional knowledge must be real, actual, discreet, specific, particular and not vague, visionary or general.

INFERENCE (anumāna) is defined as that knowledge which is preceded by perception. It may be a priori, from cause to effect; e.g., on seeing clouds, one infers that it is going to rain; or it may be a posteriori, from effect to cause; e.g., on seeing a river swollen, one infers that there has been rain. It may also be what is termed 'commonly seen,' which is knowledge of one thing derived from the perception of another thing with which it is commonly seen; e.g., on seeing rain, one infers that there are clouds.

COMPARISON (upamāna) is defined as knowledge of a thing derived from its similarity to another thing previously well known. For example, one is told that a water-buffalo resembles a cow. Then one goes into a region where the water-buffalo lives, and on seeing an animal resembling a cow, one concludes that it must be a water-buffalo.

VERBAL TESTIMONY (śabda) is defined as the instructive assertion of a reliable person, that is, one who is possessed of true knowledge and is truthful. This may be about things which can be seen or about intangible realities. The first can be verified, but one must depend upon inference to ascertain the verity of the last.

The sphere of perception is the present; that of inference is the past, present, and future; while comparison is an instrument of perception, enabling one to know an object designated by a name. It has been said that it is by means of these four sources of right knowledge that the affairs of men are conducted.

2. "THE OBJECTS OF RIGHT KNOWLEDGE [prameya] are the soul [ātman], body [śarīra], senses [indriya], objects [artha], intelligence [buddhi], intellect [manas], activity [pravṛtti], fault [doṣa], re-birth [pretyabhāva], fruit [phala], pain [duḥkha], and release [apavarga]." [2]

There are innumerable objects that might serve as the objects of right knowledge, but these twelve are especially listed because knowledge of truth about them is said to dispel all delusions and lead to salvation; while false knowledge concerning these topics holds man in the bondage of human sorrow and suffering. It is not the object of Nyāya to explain all that is known about these several topics, that is left for the more speculative systems.

The marks of the SOUL (ātman) are said to be desire (icchha), aversion (dveṣa), effort (prayatna), pleasure (sukha), pain (duḥkha), and knowledge (jñāna). That is, the substance called soul is said to

[2] *Ibid.*, i, I, 9.

be the abode of these qualities. Since the soul is one of the intangible realities, it cannot be apprehended through the contact of the senses; therefore, it must be known either from verbal testimony or by means of inference from the presence of these marks.

THE BODY (śarīra) is said to be the site of motion (ceṣṭā), of the senses (indriyas) and of the objects (arthas) of pleasure and pain. As such, the body is the field of the soul's experiences as it strives to reach what is desirable and avoid what is undesirable, all of which are made known through the senses, the instruments through which the soul comes in contact with the outer world.

The SENSES (indriyas) and their objects (arthas) are the nose (ghrāṇa), the tongue (rasanā), the eyes (cakṣus), the skin (tvak), and the ears (śrotrāṇi). Here are meant the powers of smell, taste, sight, touch and hearing. They are associated respectively with the five elements: earth (pṛthivī), water (āpas), fire (tejas), air (vāyu), and ether (ākāśa). Their respective objects (arthas) are odour (gandha), flavour (rasa), colour (rūpa), sensation (sparśa), and sound (śabda). The senses and their objects provide five varieties of perception yielding special kinds of knowledge according to the objects which they illumine. They will be explained in more detail when discussing Sāṁkhya.

INTELLIGENCE (buddhi) is the power of forming and retaining conceptions and general notions, the faculty of the mind to discern, judge, comprehend, apprehend, and understand the meaning of right knowledge. It is that power of man which enables him to contemplate the eternal.

The mark of the INTELLECT (manas) is the capacity for reflection, inference, testimony, doubt, ready wit, dream, cognition, conjecture, memory, desire, and feeling of pleasure and pain. Another indication of the intellect is its incapacity to perceive two things at the same time even though the senses are in contact with their objects. In contrast with the faculty of intelligence, the intellect seeks factual knowledge which is worldly, while the intelligence aims at wisdom which is divine.

ACTIVITY (pravṛtti) is that which sets the mind, body, and

voice in motion, which may be either good or bad. It is the effect of these actions, stimulated by desire because of false knowledge, that holds man in bondage.

FAULTS (doṣa) are the cause of all action. They are (1) *Attraction,* which consists of lust, greed, craving, longing, and covetousness; (2) *Aversion,* which consists of anger, envy, jealousy, and implacability; (3) *Delusion,* which consists of false knowledge, doubt, pride, and carelessness. The mark of attraction is attachment; of aversion, is the want of forbearance; of delusion, is misapprehension. The worst of these is delusion because it breeds attraction and aversion, which make one forget that there is nothing agreeable or disagreeable to the soul; therefore, there is no reason to like or dislike objects.

The reason for the appearance of the faults is due to the incapacity to distinguish the parts from the whole, that is, the real from the unreal; e.g., the shapely form of a beautiful woman provokes lust, while the sight of blood is repelling. And so it is with everything throughout nature; there is the twofold aspect, the real and the unreal. Because of this false conception of the true nature of things, desires are born which, in turn, stimulate action. Here it must be remembered that the hatred of pain is none the less hatred; and until all such reactions are removed by true knowledge, one will remain attached to the illusionary world of name and form.

True knowledge for the reclamation of the soul is said to be acquired by constant study and reflection on the teachings of philosophy. In this way wisdom can be matured until all doubt has been removed, and the mind will then awaken to the unseen reality within. Aids mentioned which lead to this end are lectures on philosophical topics by individuals well versed in the śāstras (ancient wisdom) and discussions with teachers and fellow-students who are sincerely seeking true knowledge.

REBIRTH (pretyabhāva) means the reappearance of the animating principle in physical form after having passed away. Birth consists of the connection of the soul with the body, sense-organs, and mind. Therefore, birth is not the production of anything new, but only reassociation; while death is not the destruction of anything, but only separation. To deny this would be to destroy the moral law that everyone will receive his just dues. At the same time it would leave meaningless the teachings of some of the greatest minds who have ever lived.

FRUIT (phala) is the product of all activity. It may be in the form of either pleasure or pain, depending upon the nature of its cause. It is of two kinds, that which appears immediately as seen in the labours of a carpenter, or that which appears after a lapse of time as seen in the planting of seed by a farmer. The same principles operate in man, for the body is merely a field where the harvest of the soul will be reaped according to past conduct. The fruit of right conduct in the world of affairs may appear as companionship, progeny and wealth, which are merely the sources out of which joy may be experienced.

PAIN (duḥkha) is an impediment that hinders the progress of the soul. The body is said to be the abode of pain; the senses are the instruments of pain; the intellect is the agent of pain; birth, then, is association with pain; therefore, life is a passing experience of sorrow and suffering. Pleasure is but an interval, for all pleasures are attended with suffering of non-fulfillment which produces constant mental suffering. It can, therefore, be said that he who is addicted to the pursuit of pleasure is in reality given to the pursuit of pain, for there is no pleasure, in the attainment and enjoyment of which, pain in some form or other is not present.

RELEASE (apavarga) is defined as absolute deliverance from pain. Only the soul which is no longer associated with the body, sense-organs and intellect is freed from pain. This will come to pass when one sees that all pleasures of the world are tinged with pain, and that the body, senses, and intellect are the vehicles of pain. When the mind is awakened to the true nature of things by right knowledge, pain will fade away as the darkness of the night before the rising sun. The faults will have disappeared, and there will be no longer any incentive to action, which, in turn, will free the soul from future rebirths. The Śāstras teach that man must learn to discriminate: (1) that rebirth, fruit, and pain are the things to be known; (2) that action and faults are to be avoided; (3) that release is to be attained; and (4) that knowledge of Truth is the means of its attainment. It is by constantly turning over the thoughts of these teachings in one's mind that the vision of true knowledge appears.

True knowledge is developed first by learning to withdraw the senses from their contact with their respective objects in the outer world. When this has been accomplished, they must be held steadfast by retentive effort, and then the mind will unite with the soul when knowledge of the Truth will begin to dawn. This is made to happen by a strong desire to know the Truth. By habitual cultivation of this state, the mind learns to repose in the soul, and cognition of the eternal reality soon arises.

There are many objects which force themselves upon the consciousness with such intensity that the mind cannot achieve this state of abstraction, such as hunger, thirst, heat, cold, disease, and the elements. The practices of Yoga have been devised to enable one to overcome even these obstacles. This capacity for the practice of Yoga comes from the accumulation of previous effort in past lives, for it is said that the virtue born of the practice of Yoga accompanies one even into another life. Preparation for the practice of Yoga is the study of philosophy.

3. "DOUBT [saṁśaya] which is a conflicting judgment about the precise character of an object, arises from the recognition of properties common to many objects, or of properties not common to any of the objects, from conflicting testimony, and from irregularity of perception and non-perception." [3]

Doubt must not be confused with error, which is false knowledge, while doubt is incomplete knowledge which serves as the incentive for investigation. False knowledge may produce conviction which puts the mind to sleep by removing all desire for further knowledge. Here error is defined as that which does not lead to successful action; for example, it is impossible to fulfill the expectations created by

[3] *Ibid.*, i, I, 23.

hallucinations. In other words, the ideal world of thought must correspond to the outer reality in order to be considered true. The rules of Nyāya are to be used when doubt has arisen in the mind, and it becomes necessary, therefore, to examine reality for confirmation.

The following examples will make clear the five kinds of doubt:

(1) Recognition of common properties; e.g., being unable to determine in the twilight whether an object is a post or a man, for the property of tallness belongs to both.

(2) Recognition of properties not common; e.g., being unable to determine whether a sound is eternal or non-eternal, for the property of sound does not abide in either men, animals, and plants which are non-eternal, nor in the elements, which are eternal.

(3) Conflicting testimony; e.g., being unable to decide whether the soul exists or does not exist from the mere study of philosophical writings which set forth convincing arguments on both sides.

(4) Irregularity of perception; e.g., being unable to determine whether water is perceived when it is seen in a tank where it actually exists, or when it is seen in a mirage where it really does not exist.

(5) Irregularity of non-perception; e.g., being unable to determine whether water exists in a vegetable, such as a carrot, where it really exists but cannot be perceived, or if it exists on dry land, where it does not exist and also cannot be perceived.

4. "PURPOSE [prayojana] is that with an eye to which one proceeds to act."

Purpose serves as the motive behind all action which may be to attain something or avoid something. Until there is purpose, there can be no successful action; therefore, a wise man never engages in purposeless action. It is said to pervade all living beings, all acts and all systems of right knowledge.[4]

5. "A FAMILIAR EXAMPLE [dṛṣṭānta] is the thing about which an ordinary man and an expert entertain the same opinion."[5]

Both scientists and ordinary men accept the general proposition that whenever there is rain there must be clouds; therefore, such an

[4] *Ibid.*, i, I, 24.
[5] *Ibid.*, i, I, 25.

example can be used as an example in the process of reasoning from the known to the unknown.

6. "An ESTABLISHED TENET [siddhānta] is a dogma resting on the authority of a certain school, hypothesis, or implication." [6]

There are four kinds of dogma:

(1) A dogma of all the schools is defined as a tenet which is not opposed by any school and which is claimed by at least one school; e.g., all schools accept earth, water, light, air, and ether as the basic five elements, and smell, taste, colour, touch, and sound as the objects of the five senses.

(2) A dogma peculiar to some school is defined as a tenet which is accepted by similar schools, but rejected by opposite schools; e.g., the Saṁkhya doctrine proceeds on the established premise that "a thing cannot come into existence out of nothing."

(3) An hypothetical dogma is defined as a tenet which, if accepted, leads to the acceptance of another tenet; e.g., the acceptance of the doctrine that there is a soul apart from the senses, because it can recognize one and the same object by seeing and touch, implies (a) that the senses are more than one; (b) that each of the senses has its particular object; (c) that the soul derives its knowledge through the channels of the senses; and (d) that a substance which is distinct from its qualities is the abode of them. Many other implications could be cited.

(4) An implied dogma is defined as a tenet which is not explicitly declared as such, but which follows from the examination of particulars concerning it, e.g., the discussion whether sound is eternal or non-eternal implies that sound is a substance.

7. "The MEMBERS [avayava] (of a syllogism) are proposition [pratijñā], reason [hetu], example [udāharaṇa], application [upanaya], and conclusion [nigamana]." [7]

The members are the logical steps used to establish the object of knowledge. Together they combine the four means of right knowledge:

(1) Proposition is the enunciation of the object of knowledge to be proved as set forth in the Śāstras or by *Verbal Testimony.*

[6] *Ibid.*, i, I, 26.
[7] *Ibid.*, i, I, 32.

(2) Reason is the vehicle of *Inference* used to prove the proposition.

(3) Example is an object of *Perception.*

(4) Application consists of *Comparison.*

(5) Conclusion shows the convergence of the four means of right knowledge toward the same object.

The application of the members of a syllogism can best be seen from the classic example:

1. Proposition	This hill is fiery.
2. Reason	Because it is smoky.
3. Example	Whatever is smoky is fiery, as a kitchen.
4. Application	So this hill is smoky.
5. Conclusion	Therefore, this hill is fiery.

These five members form the integral part of a syllogism designed to demonstrate the truth concerning a particular statement or object. In order to establish the object to be examined, later commentaries have introduced five additional members: however, they do not form any part of the actual argument. They are.

(1) Inquiry (jijñāsā), which is the investigation of the proposition; e.g., is this hill fiery in all its parts, or in a particular part?

(2) Doubt (saṁśaya), which is questioning the reason; e.g., that which is called smoke may be dust.

(3) Capacity (śakyaprāpti), which is to determine if the example warrants the conclusion; e.g., is there always smoke where there is fire? It is not seen in a moulten ball of steel.

(4) Purpose (prayojana), which is to ascertain if the object is something to be sought, avoided, or ignored.

(5) Removal of all doubt (saṁśayavyudāsa), which is to make certain that the opposite of the proposition is not true; e.g., it is settled beyond any measure of a doubt that wherever there is smoke there is fire.

The function of the Proposition is to connect with the substance the attribute to be demonstrated; for it enunciates the thing to be proved and renders the operation of the other members of the syllogism.

The function of the Reason is to state that the attribute to be demonstrated is the cause of demonstration; for it furnishes the means by which a thing is proved. It is brought forward in the Example and the Application; and by its predication, the re-statement of the Proposition in the Conclusion is possible. It may accomplish its purpose either by affirming the character of the Example or by denying it.

The function of the Example is to show that the two attributes are related in the same substratum as the thing to be demonstrated and the means of demonstration. It consists of a familiar instance which is known to possess the property to be established and which implies that this property is invariably contained in the reason given. The Example can be either affirmative or negative. A negative Example is a familiar instance which is known to be devoid of the property to be established and which implies that the absence of this property is invariably rejected in the reason given. As such, it furnishes the resemblance or difference as the means of the demonstration of the thing to be proved and makes Application possible through resemblance to it.

The function of the Application is to demonstrate that the attribute which is the means of demonstration co-exists with the attribute which is to be demonstrated. It consists of a statement which brings forward the attribute which the thing to be demonstrated possesses, to show that it is or is not in common with the Example. Without Application, the attribute, which is the cause of the demonstration, cannot be brought forward in the thing; and it cannot, in consequence, demonstrate the object.

The function of the Conclusion is to exclude all contrary conclusions against the Proposition to be proved. It brings together the Proposition, Reason, Example, and Application; otherwise, the various members cannot operate toward the same end and thereby produce proof. In other words, the Conclusion exhibits the capacity of all the members to operate as a unit and prove the truth of a single statement.

8. "CONFUTATION [tarka], which is carried on for ascertain-

ing the real character of a thing of which the character is not known, is reasoning which reveals the character by showing the absurdity of all contrary characters." [8]

Confutation is a conjecture for the sake of knowledge of truth in respect to an unknown object by elimination of all contrary suppositions; e.g., is the soul a product or a non-product? If the soul is a non-product, it will experience the fruit of its action and will on the eradication of the cause of re-birth, attain release; therefore, rebirth and release will be possible. If it is a product, these will not be possible, because the soul's connection with the body, mind, and senses will not be the result of its own action, nor will it experience the fruit of its own action. The phenomenon of re-birth and release is well known and established; therefore, the soul must be a nonproduct. Conjecture in this form is called Confutation. This is not knowledge of the truth which ascertains, determines and makes certain that the soul is such and such and nothing else. It leaves the supposition to which assent is given to hold the field undisputed; after which knowledge of the truth is produced through the application of the means of right knowledge. For this reason Confutation is said to be only in association with the other means of knowledge and is, therefore, mentioned separately.

9. "ASCERTAINMENT [nirṇaya] is the removal of doubts, and the determination of a question, by hearing two opposite sides." [9]

Ascertainment is the determination of the object by means of opposite views after a first impression which creates a doubt. The sequence of investigation is as follows: first impression, doubt, opposite views, application of the rules of reason, determination of the object, ascertainment, and knowledge of reality. Doubt is the result of first impression, and gives impetus to investigation in order to ascertain the truth. There is no need of ascertainment in the case of direct perception or in reading authoritative texts.

10. "DISCUSSION [vāda] is the adoption of one of two opposing sides. What is adopted is analyzed in the form of five members, and defended by the aid of any of the means of right knowl-

[8] *Ibid.*, i, I, 40.

[9] *Ibid.*, i, I, 41.

edge, while its opposite is assailed by confutation, without deviation from the established tenets." [10]

The purpose of Discussion is to arrive at the truth of the proposition under consideration. This may be by discussing the topic with anyone who is a sincere seeker of Truth. It is not necessary to establish one's belief. It is enough to desire merely to submit one's views for examination in order to ascertain the Truth. The discussion does not necessarily have to take into consideration the opposite opinion; it is enough to put any proposition to the test of logic. The usual procedure is to maintain the thesis by means of valid knowledge and to attack the counter-thesis by means of confutation.

11. "CONTROVERSY, POLEMICS [jalpa], which aims at gaining victory, is the defense or attack of a proposition in the manner aforesaid, by quibbles, futilities, and other processes which deserve rebuke." [11]

A polemist is one who engages in an argument for the sole purpose of victory. He has no desire to gain further knowledge of Truth, and therefore, will employ any device of debate in order to win. These are usually of a negative character, such as quibbling, putting up futile arguments, or resorting to one of the occasions for rebuke, such as evading the issue.

12. "CAVIL [vitaṇḍā] is a kind of wrangling, which consists in mere attacks on the opposite side." [12]

Here there is no desire to establish any proposition. The only interest is to heckle the speaker by carping and offering frivolous objections.

Polemics and Caviling, which are considered as forms of Discussion, may be used by one in search of Truth in order to protect one's growing knowledge which has not yet matured into a full blossomed conviction. Frequently the student will encounter objectionable personalities who have not attained true knowledge but who are overcome with their intellectual attainments in the field of philosophical thought. These people, not being possessed of a noble character, will violate all the rules of propriety, having no consideration for the

[10] *Ibid.*, i, II, 1. [11] *Ibid.*, i, II, 2. [12] *Ibid.*, i, II, 3.

beliefs of another. Under such circumstances the student is urged to make use of these devices in order to protect his growing mind in the same way that nature uses thorns on some plants to safeguard the growth of its fruit.

13. "FALLACIES OF A REASON [hetvābhāsa] are the erratic, the contradictory, the equal to the question, the unproved, and the mistimed."[13]

The classic examples given in the commentary on the text will best serve to illustrate what is intended. They are:

(1) *The Erratic* is defined as the reason which leads to more conclusions than one.

Proposition.	Sound is eternal,
Erratic Reason.	Because it is intangible,
Example.	Whatever is intangible is eternal, as atoms,
Application.	So is sound (intangible),
Conclusion.	Therefore, sound is eternal.

Again:

Proposition.	Sound is non-eternal,
Erratic Reason.	Because it is intangible.
Example.	Whatever is intangible is non-eternal, as intellect,
Conclusion.	Therefore, sound is non-eternal.

Here two opposite conclusions have been drawn from the same reason. This is due to the fact that there is no relationship between "intangible" and "eternal and non-eternal." In other words, the middle term "intangible" is not pervaded by the major terms "eternal and non-eternal"; therefore the reason is said to be Erratic.

(2) *The Contradictory* is defined as the reason which opposes what is to be established.

Proposition.	A pot is produced,
Contradictory Reason.	Because it is eternal.

Here the reason contradicts that which is to be proved, because that which is eternal is never produced. Eternal and produced are contradictory attributes and cannot abide together.

[13] *Ibid.*, i, II, 4.

(3) *Equal to the Question* (i.e. Petitio Principii) is defined as the reason which provokes the very question for the solution of which it was employed.

Proposition.	Sound is non-eternal,
Reason which is Equal to the Question.	Because it is not possessed of the attribute of eternality.

Here nothing new is contributed to the argument. The reason merely begs the question, for "non-eternal" is the same as "not possessed of the attribute of eternality." In other words, the subject matter of the topic is advanced as the reason for the desired inference. This stops the argument and makes the investigation of Truth impossible.

(4) *The Unproved* is defined as the reason which stands in need of proof, in the same way as the proposition does.

Proposition.	Shadow is a substance,
Unproved Reason.	Because it possesses motion.

Here it is necessary to prove the reason as well as the proposition; therefore, the reason cannot be used.

(5) *The Mistimed* is defined as the reason which is adduced when the time is passed in which it might hold good.

Proposition.	Sound is durable,
Mistimed Reason.	Because it is manifested by union, as a colour.

The colour of a pot manifests the instance when the pot is revealed by the light of a lamp; however, the colour was there before its recognition, and it remains after the lamp is taken away. This is not the case with sound, for it does not come into being until after a drum is struck with a drumstick. It did not exist before the drum was struck and it does not remain after the drum is struck; therefore, the analogy between colour and sound is not complete, and the reason is said to be mistimed.

14. "EQUIVOCATION (chala) is the opposition offered to a proposition by the assumption of an alternative meaning."[14]

Equivocations are of three sorts:

(1) Playing upon words (vācas). This consists of wilfully taking

[14] *Ibid.*, i, II, 10.

a term to mean something different from that intended by the speaker; e.g., taking the word quadruped to mean four-legged table instead of an animal.

(2) Generalizations (sāmānyās). This consists of asserting the impossibility of a particular because of the impossibility of the whole; e.g., to deny that a particular cow is black because all cows are not black.

(3) Metaphors (upacārās). This consists of denying the proper meaning of a word by taking it literally when it was used metaphorically; e.g., the grandstand cheered means that the people in the grandstand cheered and not the physical structure.

15. "FUTILITY [jāti] consists in offering objections founded on mere similarity or dissimilarity." [15]

The reply is said to be futile if it does not take into consideration the universal connection between the middle term and the major term. Mere similarity or dissimilarity is not sufficient. There are twenty-four kinds of futility which aim at showing an equality of the arguments of two sides. They are as follows:

(1) Balancing the homogeneity.
(2) Balancing the heterogeneity.
(3) Balancing the addition.
(4) Balancing the subtraction.
(5) Balancing the questionable.
(6) Balancing the unquestionable.
(7) Balancing the alternative.
(8) Balancing the reciprocity.
(9) Balancing the co-presence.
(10) Balancing the mutual absence.
(11) Balancing the infinite regression.
(12) Balancing the counter-example.
(13) Balancing the non-produced.
(14) Balancing the doubt.
(15) Balancing the controversy.
(16) Balancing the non-reason.
(17) Balancing the presumption.
(18) Balancing the non-difference.
(19) Balancing the non-demonstration.

[15] *Ibid.*, i, II, 18.

(20) Balancing the perception.
(21) Balancing the non-perception.
(22) Balancing the non-eternality.
(23) Balancing the eternality.
(24) Balancing the effect.

16. "DISAGREEMENT IN PRINCIPLE [nigrahasthāna] arises when one misunderstands, or does not understand at all." [16]

There is no purpose in arguing with one who reveals his utter lack of understanding of the subject of investigation; therefore, one is privileged to stop the argument. Twenty-two occasions of disagreement in principle are listed and discussed in the text, but it is beyond the scope of this volume to examine them in full detail. They are as follows:

(1) Hurting the proposition.
(2) Shifting the proposition.
(3) Opposing the proposition.
(4) Renouncing the proposition.
(5) Shifting the reason.
(6) Shifting the topic.
(7) The meaningless.
(8) The unintelligible.
(9) The incoherent.
(10) The inopportune.
(11) Saying too little.
(12) Saying too much.
(13) Repetition.
(14) Silence.
(15) Ignorance.
(16) Non-ingenuity.
(17) Evasion.
(18) Admission of an opinion.
(19) Overlooking the censurable.
(20) Censuring the non-censurable.
(21) Deviating from a tenet.
(22) The semblance of a reason.

[16] *Ibid.*, i, II, 19.

Literature

The *Nyāyasūtra* is divided into five books, each containing two chapters which were supposed to have been delivered in a series of ten lectures. It is not known for certain that Gautama is the author of the five books or if he actually committed them to writing, for during his time it was customary to transmit such knowledge by oral tradition. Nevertheless, the importance of this treatise is partly seen from the number of outstanding commentaries that it has received. The classic commentary is that of Vātsyāyana (450 A.D.). A few other important Hindu exponents and their works are: the *Vārttika* of Uddyotarka (6th cent.), *Tātparyaṭīkā* of Vācaspati Miśra (9th cent.), *Tātparyapariśuddhi* by Udayana (10th cent.), *Nyāyamañjari* by Jayanta (10th cent.), *Nyāyasāra* of Bhāsarvajña (10th cent.), and the *Tattvacintāmaṇi* of Gaṅgeśa (12th cent.).

Gaṅgeśa is considered the father of the modern school and his work is the standard text. His son, Vardhamāna, continued the tradition of his works. The school is called Navadvīpa and flourishes to this very day in Nudea, Bengal. The first great work of the Navadvīpa school was the *Tattvacintāmaṇivyākhyā* of Vāsudeva Sārvabhauma. It belongs to the end of the fifteenth century. One of the reasons for its success was due to the outstanding disciples of Vāsudeva, the most renowned being Caitanya, the famous Vaiṣṇava reformer. In the 17th century, Annaṁ Bhaṭṭa tried to evolve a consistent system from the ancient and modern schools of Nyāya. Today his *Tarkasaṁgraha* is a popular manual of the Nyāya school.

The traditional use and application of the teachings of the Nyāya have best been preserved for us today in Tibet, where the Nyāya holds its supreme position as being the foundation for all philosophical inquiry. Today in the great monastic universities of Lhasa, regardless of what a student may eventually undertake to study, he must devote about four years to mastering the teachings of the Nyāya. This knowledge has been passed down through Buddhist teachings from Asaṅga who is said to have introduced first the principles of Nyāya into the practice of Buddhistic circles. Another renowned teacher of Logic was Vasubandhu, who was the teacher of Dignāga. His famous pupil was Īśvarasena, the teacher of Dharmakīrti (7th cent.). Both Dignāga and Dharmakīrti were natives of Southern India and born from Brahman parents. Dignāga won his fame as a powerful logician in a famous debate with a Brahman named Sudurjaya at the Nālandā University, the centre of Buddhistic learning for almost a thousand years. The continuator of Dharmakīrti's teachings emerged a generation later in the person of Dharmottara, through the intermediate pupil, Devendrabuddhi. Today the teachings of Dharmakīrti are the standard text studied in Tibet; the Tibetans provide their own commentaries, but it is praiseworthy that these writings live today in their traditional form.

VAIŚEṢIKA

The term Vaiśeṣika is derived from the Sanskrit word *"viśeṣa,"* which means the characteristics that distinguish a particular thing from all other things. As a system of philosophy, the Vaiśeṣika teaches that knowledge of the nature of reality is obtained by knowing the special properties or essential differences which distinguish nine Eternal Realities (Dravyas): Earth (Pṛthivī), Water (Āpas), Fire (Tejas), Air (Vāyu), Ether (Ākāśa), Time (Kāla), Space (Dik), Soul (Ātman), and Mind (Manas).

The importance of the teachings of Vaiśeṣika as contrasted with other teachings is best illustrated by the classic example of the post and the thief. If we see a tall object in front of us when walking in the twilight, a doubt arises in our mind as to whether the tall object is a post or a thief, and because of this uncertainty we suffer from fear. This is due to the fact that we see only the common property of tallness which belongs to both post and thief. If we had knowledge of the properties which distinguish a post from a thief, there would be no doubt, and, consequently, no suffering of fear. The same condition obtains in regard to all objects in the world around us. When we have knowledge of the distinguishing characteristics of the reality, objects of perception will no longer awaken within us the feeling of attraction or aversion which is the source of all misery. This is why the teachings that reveal to us knowledge of this sort are called Vaiśeṣika.

The founder of the Vaiśeṣika was Kaṇāda, also known as Kaṇabhuj or Kaṇabhakṣa. These names are merely descriptive of his accomplishment, for his real name appears to have been Kāśyapa. The name Kaṇāda is derived from *kaṇa,* "atom" and *ad,* "to eat," literally, the "atom-eater." He is so named because he resolved reality to its smallest possible division, which is called *aṇu* in Sanskrit and commonly translated as "atom."

The system has also been called Aulūka which comes from ulūka, "owl." This name is said to be descriptive of Kaṇāda's habit of meditating all day and seeking his food during the night like an owl. It is the common practice of yogis to sleep by day and practice by night; so it is quite possible that Kaṇāda followed this routine of living.

Kaṇāda is not the originator of these teachings, for they have existed in the minds of the enlightened ones from time immemorial; however, he is credited with having given us the first systematic account of them. There is little available historical information on the personal life of Kaṇāda, and there is much speculation as to when he actually lived. The weight of authority places him in the third century B.C.

Purpose

The purpose of the *Vaiśeṣikasūtra* is best understood from the story of how it happened to be written. It is told that in times past a group of worthy disciples desiring to throw off the cloak of suffering that shrouds human existence entered the first stage of self-culture known as Hearing (Śravaṇa), which means to acquire information or understanding by merely listening to the teachings of the sacred writings. These are the various Śrutis (Vedas or revealed knowledge), Smṛitis (traditional knowledge, such as the philosophical teachings), Itihāsas (historical literature), and Purāṇas (teachings of the origin of the universe). The purāṇas have five purposes, i.e., Sargasca pratisargasca vaṁśomanvantarāṇica, vamśānucaritañcaiva, purāṇam pañca lakṣṇam. After an exhaustive search, they concluded that the fundamental means of escape from human bondage was to attain a direct vision of the reality of the Self. With the need further to elaborate their faith, they entered upon the second stage of self-culture, called Manana, which consists of discriminative understanding, rather than simple belief. With this purpose in mind, they approached the renowned sage, Kaṇāda, beseeching him to reveal to them rationally the means by which they could attain Self-Realization, and thereby be forever released from the coil of mortality. In response to their sincere desire to know the path which leads to Self-Realization, Kaṇāda, full of compassion, set forth the true nature of reality. His treatise, the *Vaiśeṣikasūtra,* is frequently called a Mokṣaśāstra, because it teaches the doctrine of liberation; and because it also teaches that Self-Knowledge and Self-Realization are the means of attaining liberation (Mokṣa), it is sometimes called an Adhyātmaśāstra, "treatise about the Supreme Spirit."

Liberation (Mokṣa) cannot be attained by the cessation of pain alone, for there is still the memory (Saṃskāra) of past pain and the ever present potentiality (Adṛṣṭa) of future pain. This potentiality is the resultant energy abiding in the soul as potential energy in consequence of previous action. This is said to be the cause of all suffering, because it urges the Real Self to seek or avoid the illusive phantoms of worldly existence. It is possible to neutralize this resultant energy by the practice of Yoga, the third stage of self-culture. But the prime prerequisite is claimed to be an intellectual insight into the true nature of reality.

Scope

The Vaiśeṣika accepts the universe as it is found extended in space and changing in time, displaying a medley of sounds, colours and forms of the phenomenal world. By the process of reason it organizes this chaotic mass into a coherent and intelligible whole, and exhibits a system that sets forth the cosmic plan which shows the interrelation of all its parts into a synthetic whole, operating with such perfection that its very conception is spiritually exhilarating.

The criterion of truth is the correspondence between the subjective world of thought and the objective world of form. Reality is pervaded by existence; therefore, to be real is to exist, and to exist is to be knowable; so when there is perfect harmony between the inner and outer world, the truth of reality is said to cast its light.

As a system of philosophical thought, the Vaiśeṣika is intended only for those interested in the phenomenal world as it pertains to the fulfillment of life's purpose. The principal question the Vaiśeṣika endeavours to answer is, "What are the basic realities of nature?" There is no desire to indulge in intellectual speculations about the origin of things, but only to seek the practical means of philosophical insight. The sole interest is to analyze and synthesize the world of experience, striving to explain rationally the true nature of things.

Kaṇāda reduces this objective world of infinite variety to nine ultimate realities, beyond which the mind cannot go and without which the objective world could not exist. He removes the illusions of life and lifts the veil of mystery from all forms, leaving reality naked in all its simplicity and beauty. As yarn is shown to be the reality of cloth which is only the appearance of a new form, Kaṇāda discloses the reality behind all the objects of experience, the concepts of thoughts, and all the movements of heavenly bodies. He reveals the workings of the invisible forces of nature and indelibly imprints upon the mind that the diversity of forms is nothing but a reflection of the nine basic realities which, if realized, will enable us to attain the goal of absolute freedom.

The method of observation by which the characteristics of the nine Eternal Realities can be known is stated in the *Vaiśeṣikasūtra*, as follows:

"The Supreme Good (results) from the knowledge, produced by a particular dharma, of the essence of the Predicables [Padārthas], Substance [Dravya], Attribute [Guṇa], Action [Karma], Genus [Sāmānya], Species [Viśeṣa], and Combination [Samavāya], by means of their resemblances and differences." [1]

Kaṇāda then shows that Attribute, Action, Genus, and Species exist because of their combination with Substance (Dravya), in which they inhere. These can no more exist without Substance (Dravya) than a shadow can exist without its substance, for they are not realities; therefore, they must inhere in something in order to manifest. In the same manner, Combination is shown to be inseparably connected with Substance (Dravya); as heat is associated

[1] *Vaiśeṣikasūtra,* i, I, 4.

with fire, one cannot exist without the other. Finally, Substance (Dravya) is shown to be the foundation of the universe and is resolved into the nine Eternal Realities.

In the teachings of the Vaiśeṣika are to be found references to the laws which have served as the means of all ancient knowledge of the composition and transformation of substances, the action of forces on moving bodies, and the sciences dealing with heat, light, sound, electricity, and magnetism. Even the basis for ethics, sociology and psychology are intimated; but it is beyond the scope of this volume to point out the philosophical foundations for these subjects.

Philosophy

The nine Eternal Realities according to the *Vaiśeṣikasūtra* are:

"Earth [Pṛthivī], Water [Āpas], Fire [Tejas], Air [Vāyu], Ether [Ākāśa], Time [Kāla], Space [Dik], Soul [Ātman], and Mind [Manas] (are) the only Substances [Dravyas]." [2]

The following discussion will show why the early teachers found it necessary to postulate these nine ultimate realities and no others in order to account for all known phenomena of Nature.

Paramāṇus

The first four Eternal Realities, Earth, Water, Fire, and Air are considered together under the term Paramāṇus, which are the ultimate elements out of which they are composed. Paramāṇu is a Sanskrit term composed of aṇu, meaning that beyond which there can be no division, and the superlative prefix *parama*; therefore, the term means the smallest possible division of matter, beyond which further division is impossible, or that whole which has no parts. The word has been translated into English as "atom" which does not give precisely the same meaning as Atom is understood today; however, if the definition as given to Aṇu is held in mind, no harm will be done in using the term "Atom."

[2] *Ibid.*, i, I, 5.

Logical necessity showed the ancient thinkers that it was not plausible to go beyond the concept of Aṇu, otherwise a small thing such as a grain of rice, would be of the same dimension as a large thing, such as Mount Everest; for both of them would possess an infinite number of parts. And since by logic it is impossible for something to come out of nothing, it was necessary to stop with some existent Reality; so the logical concept of Paramāṇus was postulated. By definition it is without parts, which means that it was not produced, and cannot be destroyed, since destruction involves the separation of parts; therefore, it is eternal. For the same reason it has no magnitude; therefore, it does not occupy any space and has no inside or outside. It is super-sensible, that is, transcendental in the same way that light is beyond the range of smell; therefore, it can be conceived only by the mind.

We do not doubt the actual existence of sensible matter of the objective world, for its very persistence establishes its existence. The fact that it is something apart from ourselves is proved from the fact that it does not yield to our influence as do ideas and thoughts of the mental world which we can call into being and banish at our will. The objective world is observed only when we come in relation to it, and it reveals the same forms to everyone, as for example, when everyone reports the same form on the observation of a chair; while the inner forms of ideas and thoughts of the subjective world cannot be observed by others; for example, only one individual can see a dream. If, then, the sensible world exists, it must be made of Paramāṇus, which are the logical ultimates of all things.

The emptiness of matter has been proved today by our own scientists employing western methods. They have been able to show us that a block of marble contains more space than solid substance. This has been established from the fact that all mass is composed of atoms, that is, the smallest possible division of particles which physicists have found to be nothing but a microcosmic reproduction of the macrocosm; for each atom contains a nucleus analogous to our sun, and around this nucleus revolve what are called electrons corresponding to our planets. The distances between the nucleus and constituents of an atom are proportionately the same as the planets of our solar system.

There are logical reasons, also, why all sensible matter must contain space. The fact that all mass is capable of being compressed means, by definition, that its parts must be apart in order to be pressed more closely together; for if its parts were contiguous, it would be solid, which, by definition, is that without an internal cavity, therefore, incapable of being compressed. Then, too, mass must be porous in order to be operated upon by heat, which is said to penetrate the substance in order to produce a transformation. To penetrate means to enter into, which is impossible of a solid thing. Then, too, all mass has magnitude, which is defined as the capacity to increase or decrease, which is impossible of things that are solid.

If all sensible matter did not contain empty space, we could not accept the axiom that the Universe is pervaded by some cosmic force or power, whether it be called God or Nature. All religions, beliefs, and philosophies are in accord that this cosmic force or power is omnipresent, that is, pervading all space and manifesting itself in all things. If the objective world of diversified forms known to our senses is to be pervaded by this cosmic force, it means that all sensible matter cannot be composed of hard, solid particles of extended matter with magnitude so related as not to have any intervening space. If this were the case, it would be impossible for all sensible matter to be pervaded, which is a principle universally accepted.

If science has shown us that matter is merely an extension of the invisible, the question arises, how can something of magnitude be produced from something without magnitude? This can best be illustrated by an example from mathematics, which deals in the realms of abstraction. Through a process of logical reason in the analysis of matter, we arrive at a place beyond which further division would involve us in the fallacy of *regressus ad infinitum,* which no reasonable person can admit. This ultimate position is designated a point, which is defined as that which has neither parts nor extent, but position only; therefore, it can be considered only from its position, which is a stress in the universal, all-pervading cosmic force out of which all things come. As such, it occupies no space, has no inside or outside; having no parts, it is not produced and cannot be destroyed, which involves the separation of parts; therefore, it is eternal, and it has no magnitude, that is, no length, breadth, or thickness. This positional reality is what is meant by the Sanskrit word Aṇu and the superlative of the term, Paramāṇu.

If, at least, two points (aṇus) associate themselves in such a manner as to combine along a common axis, the resultant effect is classified as a binary or a form consisting of two variables. This form is described as a line which is defined as a series of related positions or association of points so co-ordinated as to have a single axis. In Sanskrit this binary form is known as a Dvyaṇuka.

To produce the third element of thickness necessary for the creation of all visible phenomena having magnitude, it is necessary for at least three lines to associate themselves in such a manner that they will combine to form an integral whole, operating and functioning as a single system. This system is technically classified as a ternary form, that is a rational, integral, homogeneous function of a set of three variables. In Sanskrit it is designated as a Tryaṇuka or Trasareṇu. To produce this form, three lines must remain apart and relate themselves on different planes so as not to form a more extended line, e.g. . In this manner they produce an independent unit, operating as a separate system with its own sphere of influence apart from the individual points from which it is made. This combination of lines gives thickness to the former unit having only length and breadth, and thus produces all visible forms known to us in the objective world, varying only in the degree of intensity of the association forming either vaporous clouds or a glittering diamond.

In this manner, all the objects of the phenomenal world are produced. So, in the last analysis, everything is but an appearance of an intangible reality; that appearance is the magnitude called mass, which is only a means of measurement and not an actual reality. These new forms act independently from their fundamental constituent parts in the same way that a gyroscope exerts its own influence when it is operating.

The Paramāṇus are supersensible, that is, they are beyond the range of sense perception in the same way that all flavours are beyond the range of smell. Therefore, they cannot be classified according to such standards as weight, measure, shape, size, and such means as are customarily used. Their existence is known only by the manifestation of the attributes which inhere in them; therefore, they must be classified accordingly. There are certain attributes which they all have in common. For instance, when they are so associated as to produce the various forms of the objective world, they are all impenetrable; therefore, this attribute is called one of their General Qualities (Sāmānya Guṇa). But knowledge of General Qualities which are common to all things of magnitude does not enable us to isolate and comprehend the ultimate variables out of which all things are produced.

The fact that there is a diversity of forms assures us that there must be several different kinds of ultimate Paramāṇus; otherwise, everything would be of the same nature, varying only in form, such as the infinite variety of pottery forms that can be made out of clay. The fact that we perceive things that are made of gold means there must be another material cause. These different kinds of materials out of which things are made have attributes which distinguish them one from another, and these attributes are so intimately associated with their substance that their removal means the absence of their substance. For example, if the attribute of being golden is removed from a gold chain, there can be no chain, for gold is the substance of golden. Attributes of this description are termed Special Properties (Viśeṣās), that is, those qualities which are so inalienably associated with their substance that they cannot be removed without altering the nature of the substance in which they inhere. Therefore, it is by the Special Qualities (Viśeṣās) that the Paramāṇus must be classified. There are only four which we can use, namely:

1. Odour (Gandha)
2. Flavour (Rasa)

3. Form (Rūpa)
4. Touch (Sparśa) [3]

By means of these four Special Properties (Viśeṣās) the Paramāṇus can be classified and in no other way, for these qualities alone show the essential difference between the Paramāṇus. These four qualities as attributes cannot manifest themselves without a substance, and since they are essentially and basically different, the substance with which they are inalienably associated must likewise be different. Therefore, to classify the different kinds of substance it is necessary to find:

1. That form of matter from which odour (Gandha) cannot be eliminated.
2. That form of matter from which flavour (Rasa) cannot be eliminated.
3. That form of matter from which form (Rūpa) cannot be eliminated.
4. That form of matter from which touch (Sparśa) cannot be eliminated.

An examination of the objective world will clearly show us that there are certain forms of matter with which these four Special Properties (Viśeṣās) are so closely allied that, if the quality is removed, that particular form of matter can no longer obtain, in the same way that the removal of fragrance from perfume destroys perfume which is, by definition, a substance with an agreeable odour; and the removal of wetness from water, destroys water, which is wet by its very nature. In each case there is some form of extended matter which is the means by which each particular quality is enabled to manifest. In Sanskrit they have been technically called Pṛthivī (Earth), Āpas (Water), Tejas (Fire), and Vāyu (Air). They are collectively called Bhūtas in Sanskrit, "that which has been," and are considered as compound and produced forms of matter. Only the Paramāṇus are considered real because they are self-subsisting and unproduced. They may be classified as follows:

[3] Sparśa is a technical term generally translated as Touch and used to mean the sense of feeling as the impression left on the consciousness rather than its tactual meaning. As for example, one is touched by an act of kindness.

1. The Paramāṇus which originate odour.
2. The Paramāṇus which originate flavour.
3. The Paramāṇus which originate form.
4. The Paramāṇus which originate touch.

This classification does not mean that several of these Special Properties (Viśeṣās) cannot manifest themselves in a single form of matter; but only that each class of matter has one Special Property (Viśeṣa) which cannot be removed without bringing about a radical change in the nature of that particular form of matter.

The different classes of matter are described in the *Sūtras* as follows:

"Earth [Pṛthivī] possesses Odour [Gandha], Flavour [Rasa], Form [Rūpa], Touch [Sparśa]."

"Water [Āpas] possesses Flavour [Rasa], Form [Rūpa], and Touch [Sparśa] and is fluid and viscid."

"Fire possesses Form [Rūpa] and Touch [Sparśa]."

"Air [Vāyu] possesses Touch [Sparśa]." [4]

Classification of these categories shows that the range of each succeeding one is wider and more subtle than the preceding one. This is best illustrated by a concrete example:

1. An apple has odour, flavour, form and touch.
2. A glass of water has flavour, form and touch, but no odour.
3. A flame has form and touch, but no odour or flavour.
4. A gust of air has touch, but no odour, flavour or form.

This means that the element Air must be more subtle than the element Earth, for Air is able to pervade Earth as seen from the fact that Earth has Touch; but Earth does not pervade Air, which has only Touch.

These four categories of matter make themselves known to us by means of special senses which must be made from the same essential ingredients. The truth of this is based on the principle that the material cause can be found in the effect; for example, a cotton blanket must be made out of cotton. We know that each sense is capable of perceiving only one of the Special Properties (Viśeṣās);

[4] *Ibid.*, ii, I, 1–4.

for example the eye can see only forms, it can never smell odours or taste flavours, and, similarly, for the other senses. That which a sense is capable of perceiving is determined by that which it is capable of producing; for example, artificial pressure on the optic nerve produces light, never odours or flavours; the olfactory nerves always produce odours, never light or flavours; the taste buds always produce flavours, never light or odours. To produce these respective qualities means that they are made of the same ingredients; therefore, the senses are made from the same Paramāṇus that produce the respective Qualities. Because of this fact, we are able to resolve the entire objective world of sensible matter down to terms of Odour, Flavour, Form, and Touch.

Since nothing can be found from the unfathomable depths beyond the starry firmament above to the core of this celestial planet bounded by the four directions that is composed of anything besides these four basic Realities, they are considered as the foundation and ultimate constituents of all things in the objective world of sensible matter.

Ākāśa

The fifth Eternal Reality (Dravya) is called Ākāśa in Sanskrit which is derived from the root *kāś*, "to be visible, appear, to shine, be brilliant." Ākāśa is that in which things appear, that is, the open space of the sky or atmosphere, the Ether.

In the *Sūtrās* Ether is described as follows:

"These (characteristics) are not in Ether [Ākāśa)."[5]

By "these characteristics" is meant, Odour, Flavour, Colour and Touch, the characteristics of Earth, Water, Fire, and Air.

Ākāśa is postulated to account for the universal phenomenon of sound known to all of us. Perhaps it was observed that sound was not included when speaking of the senses. This was due to the fact that the Special Quality sound is not inalienably associated with any of the four Elements, Earth, Water, Fire, and Air. Sound can be

[5] *Ibid.*, ii, I, 5.

produced in any of them, but the removal of sound from any of them does not produce any alteration in their essential nature; therefore, another reality must be postulated in which sound can inhere.

That sound is an objective phenomenon is known from the fact that a single sound can be witnessed by several persons as being something apart from themselves, while a ringing in the head is known only to be one individual who feels it to be within himself—that is, his sound.

The existence of Ākāśa is proved by another reason. It has been shown that all discrete things are produced by Paramāṇus, which are pure points, when they stand apart, and thereby form a co-ordinating system of functioning variables; therefore, there must be some Reality to serve as the medium in which they unite to produce new forms. Ākāśa is postulated to account for this need.

Ākāśa must be a continuum which is in touch with all discrete things, that is, all-pervading; otherwise it would be made out of Paramāṇus as all other things, which is impossible, for still another medium would have to be postulated, and so on *ad infinitum*. Since an all-pervading continuum is an absolute logical necessity for the manifestation of discrete things, Ākāśa must be assumed to be that medium.

As a continuum, Ākāśa is absolutely continuous and selfsame, that is, of which no distinction of content can be affirmed except by reference to something else. Therefore, it is of infinite magnitude, which means that it has no parts, and is, therefore, indestructible and eternal. It is motionless, because it has infinite magnitude, implying that it is a whole without parts; therefore, it cannot be expanded or contracted, because all movement necessitates the displacement of parts.

As a continuum, Ākāśa is supersensible and cannot be perceived in the same way that the Paramāṇus cannot be perceived. This is due to the fact that all things are perceived by some form of contrast, which is impossible of a uniform continuum. However, it has a special property, sound, which is perceived by the special sense of hearing when this sense is conditioned by the Ākāśa. As the other senses were composed of the same essential ingredients as were the Paramāṇus which produced the qualities that the special senses perceived, so must the special sense of hearing be essentially the same as Ākāśa.

The five Realities thus far discussed are collectively called in Sanskrit Bhūtas, "that which has become," or that out of which all things come, the ultimate essence of Nature.

Kāla

The sixth Eternal Reality (Dravya) is called Kāla in Sanskrit. The etymology of this term is uncertain, but, according to one authority, it is said to come from the root *kal,* "to calculate or enumerate," that is, a fixed or right point of time; therefore, Kāla is translated as "Time." In the *Sūtras,* Time is described as follows:

" 'Posterior' in respect of that which is posterior, 'simultaneous,' 'slow,' 'quick,'—such (cognitions) are the marks of Time." [6]

The necessity of another reality arises from the notional ideas of present, past, and future produced by the continual coming and going of all manifest phenomena observed in the objective world of sensible matter. We know that some force must be the cause of this phenomenon, and this force must be something that effects all discrete things from the outside. If this force resided within things, there would be no reason for their mutual relations or for the existence of seasonal changes and other such periodic cycles.

This force must be all pervading, for it affects all things at all times. It cannot be Ākāśa, which is all-pervading, because whenever Ākāśa comes into special relationship with things, the phenomenon of sound, its special quality, is produced; but there is no manifestation of sound when the force which produces all change is operating, for no one ever heard the coming of the day and night or the passing of the seasons. These changes do not produce sound; therefore, the force which effects this orderly sequence of eternal events cannot

[6] *Ibid.,* ii, II, 6.

be Ākāśa. Still another reason why it cannot be Ākāśa is proved by the phenomenon of silence, which would be impossible, for this force is in contact with all things at all times; therefore, if it were Ākāśa, having the special quality of sound which is manifested whenever it is in special relationship with things, the universe would be in a constant roar, and there could be no silence in the ethereal realms above. Therefore, this force must have no special quality and must be only in a general relationship with all things.

It must be agreed then that there is some general principle which is the cause of all movement and which has only a general relation with all things, producing the ideas of present, past, and future. This thing is called Time (Kāla). It is a reality because we cannot conceive it to be dependent on anything for its existence.

Dik

The seventh Eternal Reality (Dravya) is called Dik in Sanskrit. This word is derived from the root *diś*, "to point out, show, exhibit." It is the direction, the quarter, region, or cardinal point, giving rise to the notions of east, west, north, and south. Space (Dik) is described in the *Sūtras* as follows:

"That which gives rise to such (cognition and usage) as 'This (is remote, etc.) from this,'—(the same is) the mark of Space [Dik]." [7]

The necessity for this reality arises from the fact that all things are seen to have an orderly relationship in the course of their movement, that is, they hold a relative position. If some force did not hold things apart during their career of existence, there could be no orderly succession of periodic events.

Ākāśa cannot be this force for the same reason that Ākāśa could not account for the phenomenon of Time (Kāla), even though it is all-pervading. Here again, it must be some universal force, all-pervading, without a special quality, having only a general relationship with things.

Kāla (Time) cannot be this force, because it must operate in the

[7] *Ibid.*, ii, II, 10.

opposite direction to Kāla (Time); that is, it must hold everything apart in order to enable things to have positional relationship with one another.

Therefore, a separate principle must be recognized to account for these factors, and this principle is Dik (Space). This term is customarily translated as "Space" which is confusing until the concept intended is clearly grasped. We tend to think of Ether (Ākāśa) as providing the Space which things manifest. Dik (Space) has reference to that power or force that holds all discrete things in their respective positions in relation to each other as they appear in Space (Ākāśa). The difference between Ākāśa, as space, and Dik, as position, is the same as a chandelier and the room in which it hangs. The room provides the space (Ākāśa), and the chain which holds the chandelier suspended in the room is the positional force (Dik). In this manner Dik (Space) holds all things that manifest themselves in the all-pervading continuum, Ākāśa.

Ātman

The eighth Eternal Reality (Dravya) is called Ātman in Sanskrit and is translated as "Soul, Self, Principle of Life and Sensation, or Abstract Individual." Its characteristics given in the *Sūtras* are:

"The ascending life-breath [Prāṇa], the descending life-breath [Apāna], the closing of the eye-lids [Nimeṣa], the opening of the eye-lids [Unmeṣa], life [Jīvana], the movement of the mind [Manogati], and the affections of the other senses [Indriya-antara-vikārah], and also Pleasure [Sukha], Pain [Duḥkha], Desire [Icchā], and Volition [Prayatnā] are marks [Liṅgāni] (of the existence) of the Soul [Ātman]." [8]

The necessity for postulating another reality arises from the universal experience of consciousness which is the property of awareness attributed to all animate things. As a property it can have no independent existence of its own; therefore, it must inhere in something.

Consciousness cannot be said to be a quality of any one of the

[8] *Ibid.*, iii, II, 4.

seven realities already named. Paramāṇus cannot be its substance, because it does not manifest in the various productions of Paramāṇus, Earth, Water, Fire, and Air. Ether (Ākāśa) is ruled out by definition, because sound is the only property of Ether (Ākāśa). There is no manifestation of consciousness in the operations of Space (Dik) or Time (Kāla); therefore, they cannot be its substance.

As a general rule, consciousness is thought of in connection with the body, but the body cannot be its substance because the body is composed of the four Bhūtas: Earth, Water, Fire, and Air, which we have already shown not to be the substance of consciousness. Some thinkers agree to the fact that consciousness is not a property of the Paramāṇus, Odour, Flavour, Colour, and Touch, or the Bhūtas, Earth, Water, Fire, and Air; but they maintain that when these basic elements of Nature combine and form a new thing, this new thing has special properties of its own. This is true, but it does not apply to the body, because the special property of the new thing is contained in every part of the new thing as well as in the whole. For example, alcohol is not found in the grain from which it is produced; but once it is produced, the property of intoxication is as much in a drop of alcohol as in an entire bottle. But this is not the case with the body, for it is seen that consciousness is not in the parts separated from the body. Then, too, the property of intoxication endures as long as the alcohol endures; but this is not the case with the body, for consciousness is gone from the body during states of trance, swoon, and at death. Consciousness does not endure with the body as does colour, a property of the body. Even though colour may change, it is always present so long as the body exists. Some critics urge that consciousness changes to unconsciousness, but this clearly is wrong, because unconsciousness is not a positive quality as are the various shades of colour. Unconsciousness is the want of consciousness. So consciousness must inhere in something else which is intimately associated with the body.

The body cannot be the substance in which consciousness inheres for still another reason. The body is a created thing, and, therefore, must be made for the purpose of something other than itself, in the same way that an automobile is made for the use of man, for it is impossible for an automobile to use itself. It is as impossible for a thing to use itself as it is for fire to burn fire or water to wet water. Therefore, the mere existence of a body implies there must be something to use it.

To be conscious is to be aware, which necessitates two things, a subject and an object, or a perceiver and that which is perceived. There is no question about the fact that consciousness exists in the subject and never in the object; therefore, anything that is an object cannot be the abode of consciousness. It is this very inner feeling that enables us to divide the world into the two large categories of object and subject. Another attribute that is always associated with the subject is volition, which enables it to function; so anything that serves as an instrument means that it has an agent, and that agent is the subject or perceiver. This perceiver or subject gives us the feeling of being a possessor; for instance when we say, "this is My body"; and it is postulated as the Reality to reconcile these conditions in which consciousness dwells. It is called Ātman.

Since the body can be an object, it cannot be the seat of consciousness which is associated with the subject. For the same reason the senses are ruled out, for they, too, serve as objects as well as instruments of the perceiver. Then, too, the senses are capable of perceiving only a single class of objects, but we have the experience of seeing and tasting an apple; therefore, there must be something which has this manifold perception. The mind is in a similar position, for its ideas and fantasies are objects of consciousness, and it can be directed according to our will. The vital processes of respiration, digestion and assimilation likewise cannot be the seat of consciousness, for through the practice of Yoga we can become aware of them and temporarily suspend them, still remaining conscious.

Still other facts prove the existence of Ātman as the perceiver within us. If there were no permanent substratum in us, memory would not be possible, and we could not have the feeling of self-identity throughout the span of a life-time. From infancy to old age, we pass through many physical and mental transitions, yet we always feel we are the same individual. Physiologists tell us that the cellular structure of the body is completely renewed every few years. If this is the case, there must be something which remains the same and is apart from that which is changing in the same way that a thread strung through rose-petals remains the same, even though the petals wilt and fall away.

The existence of the Ātman offers the simplest explanation of the most mysterious phenomena of human existence. Other explanations which are merely dogmatic assertions or which are thinly veiled with vague and obscure arguments cannot be accepted by a reasonable person in the presence of such a simple principle. Then, too, no one to date has positively proved the non-existence of Ātman; therefore, it cannot arbitrarily be set aside.

We cannot disregard the universally accepted teaching of Moral Justice which has been the cornerstone of the most far reaching and far influencing creeds followed by man. The principle of Ātman reconciles the dogma that every man will reap according to what he sows, even beyond the grave. The feeling that we have a soul is inborn in every human being, and the doctrine of Ātman affords the simplest and most tenable explanation; so for the same reason that a man is innocent until he is proved guilty, every man must have a Soul until it is proved to the contrary.

The plurality of Ātmānas (souls) is established by the variety of status which exist amongst human beings, from rich to poor, happy to miserable, and ignorant to wise. That the ultimate source of Ātman must be one, in the same way as is the universal continuum, Ākāśa, is demonstrated by the fact that all pleasure and pain experienced by man throughout the history of time is the same, just as all sound is the same, no matter where or when it is experienced.

That Ātman is a universal, all-pervading reality is seen from the fact that it pervades the body as a whole; therefore, it is infinite in scope, without parts, unproduced, incapable of destruction and, therefore, eternal.

Consciousness inheres in Ātman as Sound inheres in Ākāśa, that is, it is not essential to it, for Ātman can exist without the manifestation of consciousness, as Ākāśa can exist without the manifestation of sound. Consciousness appears only when Ātman is in special relationship with something.

Manas

The ninth and final Eternal Reality (Dravya) is called Manas in Sanskrit. This term is derived from *man,* "to think, believe, imagine, suppose, or conjecture." It is translated as "Mind," and is used in the widest sense of the word, for it is applied to all the mental powers, that is, the intellect, understanding, perception, sense, conscience, and will. It refers to the entire internal organ of perception, the faculty or instrument through which thoughts enter or by which objects affect the Soul (Ātman). In the *Sūtras* it is described as follows:

"The appearance and non-appearance of knowledge [Jñāna], on account of the Soul [Ātman] with the senses [Indriyas] and the objects [Arthas] are the marks (of the existence) of the Mind [Manas]." [9]

The necessity for postulating this Reality arises from the fact that we observe on occasions that the Ātman, which is all-pervading, does not perceive an object even though the object is in contact with the sense-organ which is the instrument of perception by which the Ātman perceives. Since the Ātman is all-pervading, it can be in contact with all senses at all times; therefore, if the sense-organ is in contact with an object, there can be no reason for its lack of perception, unless the Ātman needs another instrument with which it can come in contact with the respective senses. This phenomenon of non-perception is a common occurrence, especially when we are deeply absorbed; therefore, the Reality of Manas (mind) is postulated to explain this everyday experience.

The existence of Manas (Mind) is clearly shown from the fact that we can perceive only one thing at a time, and can never have a simultaneous perception of several objects, nor can we taste and

[9] *Ibid.,* iii, II, 1.

smell an object at the same time. Such a phenomenon should be possible if there were a direct contact between the all-pervading Ātman and the sense-organs, for, being all-pervading, there is no reason why it should not receive impressions from all the senses at once. Since the Ātman does not and since we know that all perceptions are in succession, there must be an intermediate instrument, the Manas (Mind).

That the Ātman can perceive objects only by means of some instrument of perception is seen from the need of the five sense-organs, which reveal the objects of the external world to the Ātman. We know that the Ātman perceives objects of the subjective or internal world in the nature of ideas, thoughts, and feelings; therefore, since its nature is to use an instrument for perceiving objects, and since each sense-organ is capable of perceiving only its own class of objects, there must be a sense-organ different from the sense-organs of smell, taste, sight, feeling, and hearing in order for the Ātman to perceive this new class of objects, ideas, thoughts, and feelings; for it would not be reasonable for this to be the single exception; therefore, the Manas (Mind) is this instrument.

There is yet another need for some kind of an instrument. The phenomenon of forgetting is a common experience, and so is the phenomenon of remembering. This means that an object which was previously in the presence of the Ātman has passed out of the realm of consciousness; and at another time, the Ātman has recalled this object or impression that is brought back into the field of consciousness. In other words, the Ātman has had to make use of an instrument which must be postulated to be the Manas (Mind).

The existence of only one Manas (Mind) is proved by the fact that there can be no simultaneous perceptions which would be possible if there were several Manāṅsi (Minds) to associate the all-pervading Ātman with the respective senses all at the same time.

The fact that there can be no simultaneous perceptions reveals to us two qualities of Manas (Mind). The first is that it cannot be of infinite magnitude, that is all-pervading, for if this were true, there could be simultaneous perception. If it is not of infinite magnitude, the only alternative is the opposite, which means that it has no magnitude, like the Paramāṇus. The fact that we sometimes feel that simultaneous perception has occurred brings to light the second quality, that it must be of instant motion, which is possible of all things without magnitude.

Since Manas (Mind) is without magnitude, it can have no parts, which means that it is unproduced, indestructible, and, therefore, eternal. It has no special qualities, such as odour, flavour, colour, touch, sound, and consciousness; therefore, it does not enter into special relationship with anything, that is, create a new thing by combining with other elements, as do the Paramāṇus when they combine to form Earth or one of the other Bhūtas. Manas (Mind) has only a general relationship, that is, it comes in contact with the senses only to carry out its function as an instrument of perception.

Ātman (Soul) is the basis of all experience, while Manas (Mind) is only an instrument for experience; but there must be as many Manāṅsi (Minds) as there are Ātmānas (Souls); therefore, they are infinite in number.

Literature

The *Vaiśeṣikasūtra* proceeds by the method of "enunciation," "definition," and "examination," and is divided into ten books, as follows:

Book one discusses the characteristics by which things must be known.
Book two discusses substance.
Book three discusses the soul and the inner senses.
Book four discusses the body and its constituents.
Book five discusses the various kinds of action.
Book six discusses the laws of conduct.
Book seven discusses attribute and combination.
Book eight discusses the source and manifestation of knowledge.
Book nine discusses species.
Book ten discusses the different attributes of the soul.

Each book is divided into two chapters, and the sūtras are followed by remarks by some of the most outstanding commentators; but the subject matter is not presented as clear cut as this outline indicates. The discussion to follow attempts to give only an outline of the system and a few of the key arguments offered for its support.

From time to time the original treatise has received several additions, which will not be considered here. The greatest contribution has been made by the famed scholar Praśastapāda in his *Padārthadharmasaṁgraha* (4th cent. A.D.) which is an independent work, developing suggestions hinted at in Kaṇāda's work, rather than a commentary. An outstanding Vaiśeṣika treatise based on Praśastapāda's work is Candra's *Daśapadārthaśāstra,* preserved for us in a Chinese version (648 A.D.). The four standard commentaries are Vyomaśiva's *Vyomavatī,* Srīdhara's *Nyāyakandalī* (991 A.D.), Udayana's *Kiraṇāvali* (10th cent.), and Śrīvatesa's *Līlāvatī* (11th cent.). Two works which belong to this period, but present Nyāya and Vaiśeṣika principles as parts of one whole, are Śivāditya's *Saptapadārthī* and Laugākṣi Bhāskara's *Tarkakaumudī.* Other works on the *Vaiśeṣikasūtras* worth considering are Śaṁkaramiśra's *Upaskāra* (about 1600), Viśvanātha's *Bhāṣāpariccheda* (17th cent.) and the commentary on it called *Siddhāntamuktāvali.* Other useful compendiums of the *Sūtras* are Annaṁ Bhaṭṭa's works, Jagadīśa's *Tarkāmṛta* (1635 A.D.) and Jayanārāyaṇa's *Vivṛti* (17th cent.). This last work, though based on the *Upaskāra,* differs from it on certain points.

SĀṀKHYA

The Sāṁkhya is the oldest school of Hindū Philosophy, for it is the first attempt to harmonize the philosophy of the Vedas through reason. The unique position of the Sāṁkhya in the history of thought is the fact that it expounds by careful reflection the first systematic account of the process of cosmic evolution which attempts to comprehend the universe as a sum total of twenty-five categories. This exposition is no mere metaphysical speculation, but is a purely logical account based on the scientific principles of conservation, transformation and dissipation of energy. The Sāṁkhya is held to be the most notable attempt in the realm of pure philosophy.

The term Sāṁkhya is derived from the word *sāṁkhyā*, "number." This name is used because the Sāṁkhya enumerates the principles of cosmic evolution by rational analysis; and in the philosophical sense, the term is used because this system teaches discriminative knowledge which enables us to distinguish between Spirit and Matter.

The founder of the Sāṁkhya was Kapila. Very little is known of this renowned sage and there is much controversy as to his actual date; however, the weight of authority places him in the sixth century B.C. According to tradition his father's name was Kardama, and his mother's name was Devahūti. His father was an Ṛṣi (inspired sage), but Kapila is believed to have learned the rudiments of philosophy and the nature of the soul from his mother. A likeness of Kapila is carved in the cave temple of Anuradhapura in Ceylon. The latter part of his life was passed on an island called Sāgara, situated in the mouth of the Ganges River ninety miles from Calcutta. Each year on the last day of the Hindū month Māgha (January-February) thousands of devotees visit the place where Kapila meditated and gave the fruits of his meditations to his disciples. In this manner the tradition of his life is still kept. Throughout India the memory of Kapila is worshipped as a Great Sage and Philosopher.

Purpose

The purpose of the Sāmkhya is to provide that knowledge which will forever remove the cause of misery and thereby release the soul from its bondage. According to this system misery is threefold: (1) ādhyātmika, i.e., proceeding from intrinsic causes, such as disorders of the body and mind; (2) ādhibhautika, i.e., proceeding from extrinsic causes, such as other men, beasts, birds, or inanimate objects; (3) ādhidaivika, i.e., proceeding from supernatural causes, such as the influence of the atmosphere or planets. It is undisputed that misery constitutes the real torment of the soul. The problem arises, how to terminate misery? If known means were sufficient, there would be no need to seek further, but all known means fail to be absolute. Medicine cannot cure forever, no more than a banquet can banish hunger for all time; therefore, it is necessary to search for that knowledge which will forever terminate misery.

The Sāṁkhya argues that if misery is an attribute of the soul, there is no need to seek further, but it is universally agreed that the soul is free and devoid of all suffering; therefore, misery must belong to the body. The misery of the soul is said to be caused by its intimate association with the body. When the true nature of the soul is understood, bondage will no longer exist, and the soul will be forever free from all suffering. Bondage is claimed to be purely an illusion caused by incorrect knowledge of the true nature of things. The release and bondage of the soul depend solely upon knowledge and ignorance; therefore, it is believed that discriminative knowledge will forever release the soul from all misery.

Scope

The Sāṁkhya deals exclusively with the empirical world which is governed by the rules of reason and can be known. It leaves the more transcendental speculations to other systems, maintaining that questions pertaining to the beginning of things are not conducive to enlightenment, concerning itself solely with the evolution of the existent universe.

The Sāṁkhya teaches that the world-order is reason and is an expansion of the highest kind of intelligence; that there is no part without an assignable function, a value, a purpose; that there is always an exact selection of means for the production of definite ends; that there is never a random combination of events; that there is order, regulation, system, and division of function.

The phenomenal universe is considered as a dynamic order, an eternal process of unfolding, without beginning or end. All has evolved out of an Uncaused Cause which is postulated in order to evade the fallacy of *regressus ad infinitum,* which is not consistent with a rational solution. The Sāṁkhya leaves the Uncaused Cause undefined as being impossible to be conceived by the intellect. This absolute is beyond time, beyond space, beyond thought; it is without difference, without attribute, and without form. It is forever removed from empirical knowledge, which concerns itself with the phenomenal world.

True evolution, according to the Sāṁkhya system, does not exist in the phenomenal world, but only in the chain of causation from the cosmic substance (prakṛti) to the gross elements (mahābhūtas). The manifestations of the physical and biological world, such as insentient objects and animal bodies, are only modifications of five gross elements (mahābhūtas) and are not new modes of being. The gross elements (mahābhūtas) are classified as evolutes, which means that they are incapable, by definition, of producing a new mode of being. All their effects, from a ball of clay to a cow, are not new modes of being; they are only modifications of these gross elements (mahābhūtas). All such manifestations are just as gross as the matter from which they come; they are perceptible by the same organs of cognition; they have the common properties of grossness and perceptibility. This is not evolution; it is only modification.

For the investigation of the causal process, the Sāṁkhya recognizes three means of correct knowledge; perception, inference, and valid testimony. According to the Sāṁkhya, all known means of correct knowledge are comprehended in these three. As to which of these means of knowledge is to be used in a particular instance depends solely upon what is to be known. Perception is used for objects which are in contact with sense-organs; inference is used when only the characteristic marks are known; valid testimony is used for knowledge of those things that are beyond the perception of the senses and beyond the logical analysis of the mind.

The Sāṁkhya is said to be the philosophical foundation of all Oriental culture, the measuring rod of the entire mass of Hindū literature, the basis for all knowledge of the ancient sages (ṛṣis) and the key to all Oriental symbolism.

Philosophy

For the purpose of study, the Sāṁkhya postulates two ultimate realities, Spirit (Puruṣa) and Matter (Prakṛti), to account for all experience. They exist as logical principles and serve as the source out of which all things evolve. The Sāṁkhya views the evolution of matter from its cosmic cause as a process of unfolding, a projection of potentialities into realities according to fixed laws that can be understood and controlled by man. This chain of causation is based on the fundamental tenet of the Sāṁkhya that creation is impossible, for something cannot come out of nothing; change implies something to change; whatever is, always is, and whatever is not, never is.

For the sake of analysis, the Sāṁkhya divides the process of cosmic evolution into twenty-five categories which are classified under four headings:

(1) That which is neither produced nor produces.
(2) That which is not produced but produces.
(3) Those which are produced and do produce.
(4) Those which are produced and do not produce.

The first is called Puruṣa (Cosmic Spirit). It is the unevolved which does not evolve, the uncaused which is not the cause of any new mode of being.

The second is called Prakṛti (Cosmic Substance). It is the unevolved which does evolve, the uncaused cause of phenomenal existence.

The third group consists of seven categories called evolvents which are caused and serve as causes for new modes of being. They are Mahat (Cosmic Intelligence), Ahaṁkāra (Individuating Principle) and five Tanmātras (Subtle Elements).

The fourth group consists of sixteen categories called evolutes which are caused, but do not serve as causes for new modes of being. They are Manas (Cosmic Mind), five Jñānendriyas (Abstract Knowing-Senses), five Karmendriyas (Abstract Working-Senses), and five Mahābhūtas (Sense Particulars).

Puruṣa

The first principle postulated by the Sāṁkhya system is called Puruṣa and is used to mean the soul of the universe, the animating principle of nature, the universal spirit. It is that which breathes life into matter; it is the source of consciousness. It is frequently identified with the deities Brahmā, Viṣṇu, Śiva, and Durgā.

By logical implication, Puruṣa is postulated to account for the subjective aspect of nature. It is the universal spirit, eternal, indestructible, and all-pervasive; it is pure spirit, without activity and attribute, without parts and form, uncaused, unqualified, and changeless. It is the ultimate principle of intelligence that regulates, guides, and directs the process of cosmic evolution; it accounts for the intelligent order of things, why the universe operates with such precision, why there is cosmos and not chaos. It is the efficient cause of the universe that gives the appearance of consciousness to all manifestations of matter; it is the background that gives us the feeling of persistence; it is the static background of all manifest existence, the silent witness of nature.

The existence of Puruṣa is supported in the text by the following grounds:

"Spirit exists (as distinct from matter), since collocations serve a purpose of some (being) other than themselves, since this other must be the reverse of (what is composed of) the three constituents, and so on, since there must be control (of the collocations), since there must be an enjoyer, and since there is activity for the purpose of release (from three-fold misery)." [1]

These arguments can be further explained in the following manner:

1. Since everything that is produced is for the use of something other than itself (e.g., a chair is for another not itself), there must be a universal spirit to use the products of the Cosmic Substance (Prakṛti).
2. Since all manifestations of the Cosmic Substance (Prakṛti) are objects composed of the constituents (guṇas), there must be, by definition, a knower of these objects, devoid of the constituents (guṇas).
3. Since everything of the objective world is composed of the three constituents (guṇas) there must be something that controls them for the same reason that a car needs a driver.
4. Since the Cosmic Substance (Prakṛti) is incapable of experience, there must be something else to account for universal experience.
5. Since all scriptures promise release, there must be something that transcends the Cosmic Substance (Prakṛti) out of which all things come.

The characteristics of Puruṣa described in the text are given as follows:

"And from the contrast with that (which is composed of the three constituents, etc.), there follows, for the Spirit, the character of being a witness, freedom (from misery), neutrality, percipience, and non-agency." [2]

[1] The *Sāmkhyakārikā,* XVII.
[2] *Ibid.,* XIX.

Prakṛti

The second principle postulated by the Sāṁkhya system is called Prakṛti. This is a Sanskrit word composed of the prefix *pra*, "before or first," and the root *kṛ*, "to make or produce." Here the term means that which existed before anything was produced, the primary source of all things, the original substance out of which all things have come and into which all things will eventually return. It is also called *pradhāna*, "primary matter," and *avyakta*, "non-manifest matter." In English Prakṛti is called Primal Nature or Cosmic Substance.

Prakṛti is established on purely logical grounds. The central argument used by the Sāṁkhya system is that something cannot come out of nothing. This view is technically called satkāryavāda and is the distinguishing feature of this system. Upon this principle the material universe is traced back to a first cause. This first cause is Prakṛti (Cosmic Substance). To avoid infinite regress, Prakṛti is postulated to be an uncaused cause. It is paramount to keep in mind that Prakṛti is merely a logical assumption for the sake of analysis. It is only a condition in nature. It is beyond the mind and can never be perceived by the mind, no more than a surgeon can see the soul. It can be understood through reason, but it can be known only through the practice of Yoga.

The existence of Prakṛti (Cosmic Substance) is supported in the text by the following arguments:

"The effect subsists (even prior to the operation of the cause) since what is non-existent cannot be brought into existence by the operation of a cause, since there is recourse to the (appropriate) material cause, since there is not production of all (by all), since the potent (cause) affects (only) that of which it is capable, and since (the effect) is non-different from the cause." [3]

The arguments can be further explained, thus:

1. The effect must have existed in the cause, because whatever does not exist can never be brought into existence; e.g., milk cannot be extracted from sand.

[3] *Ibid.*, IX.

2. The effect must have existed in the cause, because every effect has its appropriate material cause, e.g., when butter is wanted, milk is sought, and not water.
3. The effect must have existed in the cause, because there must be a causal relationship between things that exist; otherwise, any cause could produce any effect, which is contrary to the cause.
4. The effect must be potentially contained in the cause, because only a particular cause can produce a particular effect; otherwise, any cause could produce any effect.
5. The effect must have existed in the cause, because the effect is never different from the cause, e.g., a cloth is of the same quality as the thread from which it is woven.

Cause and effect are only different states of the same thing, there is only a change of form, never of substance; therefore, the distinction is only the marking of two events in time. The cause is unevolved, and the effect is evolved. Both are real. The manifestation of the phenomenal world is only an evolution of the Cosmic Substance (Prakṛti), and the dissolution of the phenomenal world is only an involution of the Cosmic Substance (Prakṛti). Nothing new is created; all is but a manifestation of what already existed. According to the Saṁkhya system, the eternal process of nature is without beginning or end.

The characteristics of Prakṛti are described in the text, thus:

"The evolved is caused, non-eternal, non-pervasive, mobile, manifold, dependent, mergent, conjunct, and heteronomous; the unevolved is the reverse (of all these)." [4]

By logical implication, Prakṛtí (Cosmic Substance) is the uncaused cause; therefore, it is eternal, indestructible, and all-pervasive. It is formless, limitless, immobile, and immanent. It has position but no magnitude; "its centre is everywhere, and its circumference is nowhere." It is inanimate and unintelligent. It is an ultimate and not a derivative principle; it is the root-principle, the seat of all manifestation, the normal cause of the phenomenal world, the potential power of becoming, the instrumental cause of the world, the sub-

[4] *Ibid.*, X.

stance in which all attributes and action inhere. It is not produced, yet it brings everything else into existence; it is the support of all things, yet it is unsupported; it absorbs all things, yet it is not absorbed by anything else.

The Guṇas

Prakṛti (Cosmic Substance) consists of three constituents, powers called Guṇas. These are postulated to account for the diversified objects of experience. The word guṇa is derived from the Indo-European base *gere,* "twirl, wind." Here the term is used to mean a single thread or strand of a cord, that is, a constituent of Prakṛti (Cosmic Substance). The Guṇas are as essential to Prakṛti as heat is to fire, for one cannot exist without the other. The three constituents are called sattva guṇa, rajas guṇa, and tamas guṇa and each has its characteristic function.

Sattva Guṇa is derived from *sat,* "that which is real or existent." Here it is used to connote that power of nature that illuminates and reveals all manifestations. It is responsible for the lightness of things, the upward movement of fire, and the blowing across of wind. It is devoid of excitement and is the cause of equilibrium. It has no motion of its own; therefore, it is incapable of action or reaction. It manifests itself as light.

Rajas Guna is according to one authority, derived from *rañj,* "to be coloured, affected or moved," and must be a homonym of *rajas,* "darkness." Here it is used to connote that power of nature which affects and moves the other two constituents. It is the activating and exciting potency without which the other constituents could not manifest their inherent qualities. Its function is to move things, overcome resistance, do work. It is responsible for all motion and change that goes on throughout nature. It gives matter its force and impetus and imparts motion to air and fire. It manifests itself as the force of the winds.

Tamas Guṇa means "darkness." Here it is used to connote the power of nature that restrains, obstructs, and envelops the other two constituents by counter-acting the tendency of rajas to do work and sattva to reveal. It is the restraining and binding potency of nature. Its function is to resist motion. It is responsible for the attraction and downward pull of the earth and the tendency of water to descend. It is the cause of mass, weight and inertia. It makes it possible for us to feel invisible air.

These three constituents are the sum and substance of Prakṛti (Cosmic Substance). They are the root of all change, the foundation of reality, the essence of all things. Before the manifestation of the objective world, they are in a state of perfect balance, equipoise. When this condition of equilibrium is disturbed, the phenomenal world begins to make its appearance. The predominance of one or the other of these three constituents accounts for the various stages in the process of cosmic evolution.

During the potential condition of Prakṛti (Cosmic Substance) the three Guṇas are in a state of constant motion within themselves without affecting one another. This inherent subtle movement is the nature of the Guṇas and exists without effecting any objective result. Because of this inherent movement, no external cause is necessary to upset this triune state of balance. The initial stress in nature is the result of past action (karma).

In the process of cosmic evolution, the three Guṇas are never separated; they co-exist in everything. Never do they function separately, but one or the other may predominate. They always support one another and intermingle with one another. They are as intimately conjoined as an electron and proton, the constituents of an atom. As the arrangement of atoms accounts for all the elements known to science, so does the arrangement of the Guṇas account for all the manifestations of nature.

When the balance of nature is first disturbed, Rajas Guṇa is activated and tries to make Sattva Guṇa manifest, but this is restrained by Tamas Guṇa. With the first manifestation, Sattva Guṇa predominates in varying degrees down to a point where it is equalized by Tamas Guṇa, which then remains in control down to the manifestation of gross matter. Sattva and Tamas Guṇas interact as expansion and contraction by the power of Rajas Guṇa. This gives rise to the motion and pause witnessed throughout nature. It is this interaction of the Guṇas that accounts for the diversified objects of the manifest world.

The three Guṇas lose their individual characteristics during the potential condition of Prakṛti (Cosmic Substance) when they are in a state of perfect balance; however, they never coalesce, but ever remain potentially ready to emerge as distinct aspects when the conditions for the next manifestation arise. Never are they non-existent, nor is their power diminished or altered in any way.

Puruṣa (Spirit) and Prakṛti (Cosmic Substance) with the three Guṇas (constituents) constitute the soul and substance of the universe. Actually, they are two aspects of a single thing which is a mere abstraction of thought that exists only in the mind. They coexist and are separated only for the purpose of formal demonstration, for they do not have any separate existence. All manifestation is the interaction of these two principles. Neither has independent function. The formless Spirit (Puruṣa) cannot act by itself because it has no vehicle; the Cosmic Substance (Prakṛti) can have no urge to action because it is inanimate; therefore, it is only by the union of Spirit (Puruṣa) and Matter (Prakṛti) that existence can manifest. They are dependent upon one another and come into existence by the inseparable attribute of one another. Both are eternal realities, unmanifest, without beginning or end, all-pervading and omnipotent. These features are the salient points of this doctrine and must be correctly understood.

The original polarity appears as consciousness and unconsciousness, subject and object, knower and known. Creation is the first logical operation by which consciousness becomes disposed to remain as such on the one hand, and appear to cease to be as such on the other; however, consciousness never ceases to be, no matter how heavily veiled by cosmic substance. The process of creation, maintenance and dissolution unceasingly recurs as an eternal rhythm of life and death, two phases of a single process.

As the result of past action (karma), the great Cosmic Substance

(Prakṛti) quickens under the influence of the Spirit (Puruṣa). When the karmic stress appears, the Cosmic Substance (Prakṛti) becomes massive as milk becomes massive when it condenses into curd. This is the first manifest condition of nature.

Mahat

The third principle postulated by the Sāṁkhya system is called Mahātattva, the "Great Principle," or simply Mahat. Here the term is used to mean Cosmic Intelligence. In this instance, intelligence is understood as the capacity to expand, reveal, and ascertain. Here there is no ideation, relationship, or identity.

Mahat (Cosmic Intelligence) is the first motion that arises in the supreme ideal universe, the first stage away from the original condition, the first product of the Cosmic Substance (Prakṛti). It is the first appearance in the universe, the order that fulfills the ultimate destiny of nature, the first birth of intelligence. It pervades all space and permeates all manifestations. It is the stage when the previously undifferentiated energy determines upon a definite direction, toward a well-defined line of evolution. It is cosmic volution, will, or urge to satisfy a want that has been created by a disturbance of the perfect balance of nature. It is likened to the swollen state on the surface of the ocean just before the appearance of a wave. It is caused by a spiritual (karmic) stress that upsets the equilibrium of the Cosmic Substance (Prakṛti) and sets in motion Rajas Guṇa, the activating aspect of the causative constituents. This brings into being Sattva Guṇa which manifests itself as pure light. It is classified as an evolvent, because it is produced and it produces a new mode of being.

Ahaṁkāra

The fourth principle is Ahaṁkāra. This term is composed of the personal pronoun *aham,* "I," and the root *kṛ,* "to do, make or perform." Here it is used to mean the Individuating Principle. It is responsible for the limitations, separation, and variety that come out of harmony. It is the state of active consciousness in which the "I" or illuminating aspect of consciousness identifies itself with the total "this" and forms the dualistic state of the yet unmanifest universe. It is a state of Self-Realization where the universal will resolves to act, a necessary condition before any act can be undertaken. It is classified as an evolvent, because it is produced and it produces new modes of being.

Manas

The fifth principle is Manas, derived from the root *man,* "to think." Here the term is used to mean the Cosmic Mind, the principle of cognition. It is important to understand the distinction between Mahat (Cosmic Intelligence) and Manas (Cosmic Mind). Mahat (Cosmic Intelligence) is classified as an evolvent, that is, it is produced and produces new forms of being; while Manas (Cosmic Mind) is an evolute, that is, it is produced, but does not produce new forms of being.

Manas (Cosmic Mind) is that state when the ideal universe becomes the object, emerging into view and forming a clearly defined picture. Ahaṁkāra (Individuating Principle) was concerned with the "I"; Manas (Cosmic Mind) is concerned with the "this" aspect of the universal relationship, "I am this."

These three stages, Mahat (Cosmic Intelligence), Ahaṁkāra (Individuating Principle), and Manas (Cosmic Mind) are not marked out in time, but arise simultaneously. They are the outcome of the unbalance of the three causative constituents; they are universal, and unlimited by time and space, by name and form. Each step is discussed separately only for the purpose of understanding; but as to content of transcendental experience, they are identical.

Indriyas

The next ten principles are called Indriyas, meaning power, force or capacity. They are divided into two groups, five Abstract Knowing-Senses or powers of cognition called Jñānendriyas, and five Abstract

Working-Senses or capacities for action called Karmendriyas. These powers are evolved to construct the world as a system of purposes or objects of desire. Their function is to give position to the objects.

The Jñānendriyas (Abstract Knowing-Senses) are the power to Hear (Śrota), the power to Feel (Tvak) the power to See (Cakṣus), the power to Taste (Rasana), and the power to Smell (Ghrāṇa). The Karmendriyas (Abstract Working-Senses) are the power to express (Vāk), the power to procreate (Upastha), the power to excrete (Pāyu), the power to grasp (Pāṇi), and the power to move (Pāda).

It must be kept in mind that these Abstract Sense-Powers (Indriyas) are only inherent capacities on the part of the Cosmic Mind (Manas) to cognize and act in one of five ways. They are powers which need instruments through which to function. All the Indriyas (Sense-Powers) arise simultaneously with Mind (Manas), and are classified as evolutes since they are produced, and do not produce new modes of being.

These ten-fold Abstract Sense-Powers (Indriyas) could have no real existence without objects. For example, the power to hear could have no meaning without something to hear, that is, sound. Similarly, with the other sense powers of feeling, seeing, tasting, and smelling. They must have something upon which to operate. So the moment these ten-fold Abstract Sense-Powers (Indriyas) manifest themselves, their correlated Subtle Elements (Tanmātras) come into being.

Tanmātras

The next five principles are called Tanmātras. This term is composed of the pronoun *tad,* "that," and the root *ma,* "to measure," used here in the word *mātra,* meaning "an element or elementary matter." Here it is translated as "merely that" or "thatness." They are the Subtle Elements of the Indriyas (Sense-powers). They are: the essence of Sound (Śabda), Touch (Sparśa),[5] Form (Rūpa), Flavour (Rasa), and Odour (Gandha).

[5] See definition, p. 195.

These Subtle Elements (Tanmātras) are the fivefold extensions of the formless manifestation of energy, the first conceivable division of matter, the subtlest form of actual matter, without magnitude, supersensible, and perceived mediately only through particular objects. They are classified as evolvents, for they are produced and produce new modes of being. From these the universe comes forth, continues, and finally disappears.

Through a further increase of the restraining aspect of the Tamas Guṇa, there is produced in the five Subtle Elements (Tanmātras) an accretion of mass which forms the five Sense-Particulars (Mahābhūtas).

Mahābhūtas

The last five principles of the Sāṁkhya system are called Mahābhūtas, derived from the root *bhu,* "to be, to come into being, to exist." They are the five forms into which Cosmic Substance (Prakṛti) differentiates itself, namely: Ether (Ākāśa), Air (Vāyu), Fire (Tejas), Water (Āpas), and Earth (Pṛthivī).

The five Sense-Particulars (Mahābhūtas) are postulated in order to account for the vehicles through which the Subtle Elements (Tanmātras) manifest themselves, for example the Tanmātra of Sound (Śabda) cannot be heard if it does not have the Mahābhūta of Ether (Ākāśa) to serve as its vehicle. Each Sense-Particular (Mahābhūta) is conditioned and evolved from the one immediately preceding it, and has a special property in addition to the general qualities of the others from which it was evolved. For the sake of discussion, each can best be considered separately.

The first Sense-Particular (Mahābhūta) is Ākāśa (Ether), derived from the prefix *a* and the root *kas,* "to appear." Here it is used to mean the principle of vacuity. It has the special property of sound, therefore, it can be heard, but it cannot be felt, seen, tasted, or smelled: i.e., a clear sound has no touch, no form, no flavour, no odour. It is only a sound beyond the range of the four senses.

The second Sense-Particular (Mahābhūta) is Vāyu (Air), derived from the root *va,* "to blow." Here it is used to mean the principle of motion. Its function is pressure or impact. It has the special property of touch and the general quality of sound; therefore, it can be felt and heard: i.e., a gust of pure air has a touch and a sound, but no form, no flavour, no odour; therefore, it cannot be seen, tasted, or smelled.

The third Sense-Particular (Mahābhūta) is Tejas (Fire), derived from the root *tij,* "to be sharp." Here it is used to mean the principle of luminosity. Its function is expansion. It has the special property of form and the general quality of touch and sound; therefore, it can be seen, felt, and heard: i.e., a pure blue flame has a form, a touch, and a sound, but no flavour or odour; therefore, it cannot be tasted or smelled.

The fourth Sense-Particular (Mahābhūta) is Āpas (Water), derived from the root word *ap,* "water." Here the term is used to mean the principle of liquidity. Its function is contraction. It has the special property of flavour and the general quality of form, touch, and sound; therefore, it can be tasted, seen, felt, and heard: i.e., a glass of pure water has a flavour, a form, a touch, and a sound, but no odour; therefore, it cannot be smelled.

The fifth Sense-Particular (Mahābhūta) is Pṛthivī (Earth), derived from the Indo-European base * *plet(h)e,* "broad, flat, extended." Here it is used to mean the principle of solidarity. Its function is cohesion. It has the special property of odour and the general qualities of flavour, form, touch, and sound; therefore, it can be smelled, tasted, seen, felt, and heard; i.e., an apple has an odour, a flavour, a form, a touch, and a sound; therefore, it can be known by the five senses.

The following outline shows the relation of the five Sense-Particulars (Mahābhūtas) to one another:

Ether	has	sound						
Air	"	sound	and	touch				
Fire	"	sound	"	touch	and	form		
Water	"	sound	"	touch	"	form	and	flavour
Earth	"	sound	"	touch	"	form	"	flavour and odour.

With the manifestation of the Sense-Particular (Mahābhūta) the process of cosmic evolution comes to rest; therefore, these principles or tattvas are classified as evolutes, that is, they are produced and do not produce any new mode of being. All manifestations in the phenomenal world are said to be modifications of these principles and not the creation of anything new.

Literature

The oldest account of the Sāṁkhya system, according to some authorities, is given in the *Sāṁkhyapravacanasūtra* and the *Tattvasamāsa.* These works are generally attributed to Kapila, but there is no tangible evidence to support this claim. According to tradition, Kapila left no written works, but passed his knowledge on to Āsuri, who, in turn, taught Pañcaśikha, the reputed author of the works just mentioned. The *Sāṁkhyapravacanasūtra* consists of six chapters, of which the first three are devoted to an exposition of the Sāṁkhya principles; the fourth gives some illustrative stories; the fifth refutes rival views; and the sixth gives a recapitulation.

The classic textbook on the Sāṁkhya system is the *Sāṁkhyakārikā* by Īśvarakṛṣṇa. This is the oldest extant systematic exposition of the Sāṁkhya system and is the most popular manual used today; and it is the basis for this present account. The *Sāṁkhyakārikā* claims to be merely a condensation of an earlier text called the *Ṣaṣṭitantra,* leaving out only the parables and the refutation of rival systems. There is considerable controversy over the *Ṣaṣṭitantra,* and the available data are not sufficient to allow for any definite statement. The two best known commentaries on the *Sāṁkhyakārikā* are Gauḍapāda's *Bhāṣya* (8th cent. A.D.) and Vācaspati Miśra's *Sāṁkhyatattvakaumudī* (9th cent. A.D.). The commentary of Gauḍapāda is held to be based on the *Māṭharavṛtti,* but there is able argument to the contrary. Vācaspati is supposed to have based his account of the sixty topics on the *Rājavārttika.* A commentary based chiefly on the work of Vācaspati Miśra is the *Sāṁkhyacandrikā* by Nārāyaṇatīrtha. Some authorities say that it is a treatise on

Gauḍapāda's work. The *Sāṁkhyakārikā* was translated into Chinese by Paramārtha, a Buddhist monk of the sixth century A.D. The latest commentary is the *Sāṁkhyataruvasantaḥ* by Muḍumba Narasiṁhasvāmin, who tries to relate the Vedānta and the Sāṁkhya. The actual date of the *Sāṁkhyakārikā* is not known. Some authorities assign it to the first or the first half of the second century A.D., while others contend that it belonged to the third century A.D., and some place it in the fifth century A.D.

Other works of interest are: Aniruddha's *Sāṁkhyavṛtti* (15th cent. A.D.); Mahādeva's *Sāṁkhyavṛttisāra* (17th cent. A.D.); Nāgeśa's *Laghusāṁkhyasūtravṛtti*, of minor importance; and Vijñānabhikṣu's *Sāṁkhyapravacanabhāṣya* (16th cent. A.D.) which is the most important work on the *Sāṁkhyapravacanasūtra*. Vijñānabhikṣu tries to minimise the differences between the Vedānta and the Sāṁkhya. Other important works by Vijñānabhikṣu are *Sāṁkhyasāra, Yogavārttika, Yogasārasaṁgraha,* and *Vijñānāmṛta,* a commentary on the *Vedāntasūtra.* Two later works of philosophical value are Sīmānada's *Sāṁkhyatattvavivecana* and Bhāvāgaṇesa's *Sāṁkhyatattvayathārthyadīpana.*

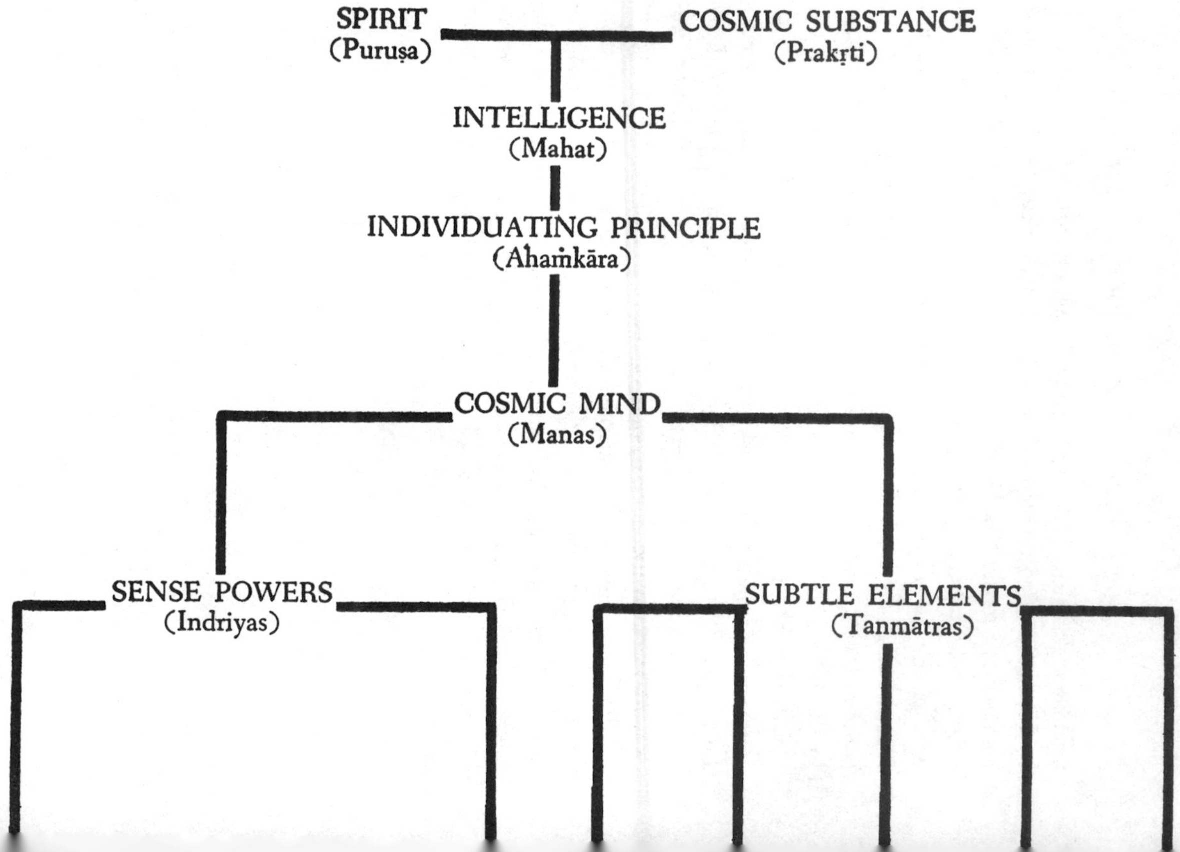
SPIRIT
(Puruṣa)
COSMIC SUBSTANCE
(Prakṛti)
INTELLIGENCE
(Mahat)
INDIVIDUATING PRINCIPLE
(Ahaṁkāra)
COSMIC MIND
(Manas)
SENSE POWERS
(Indriyas)
SUBTLE ELEMENTS
(Tanmātras)

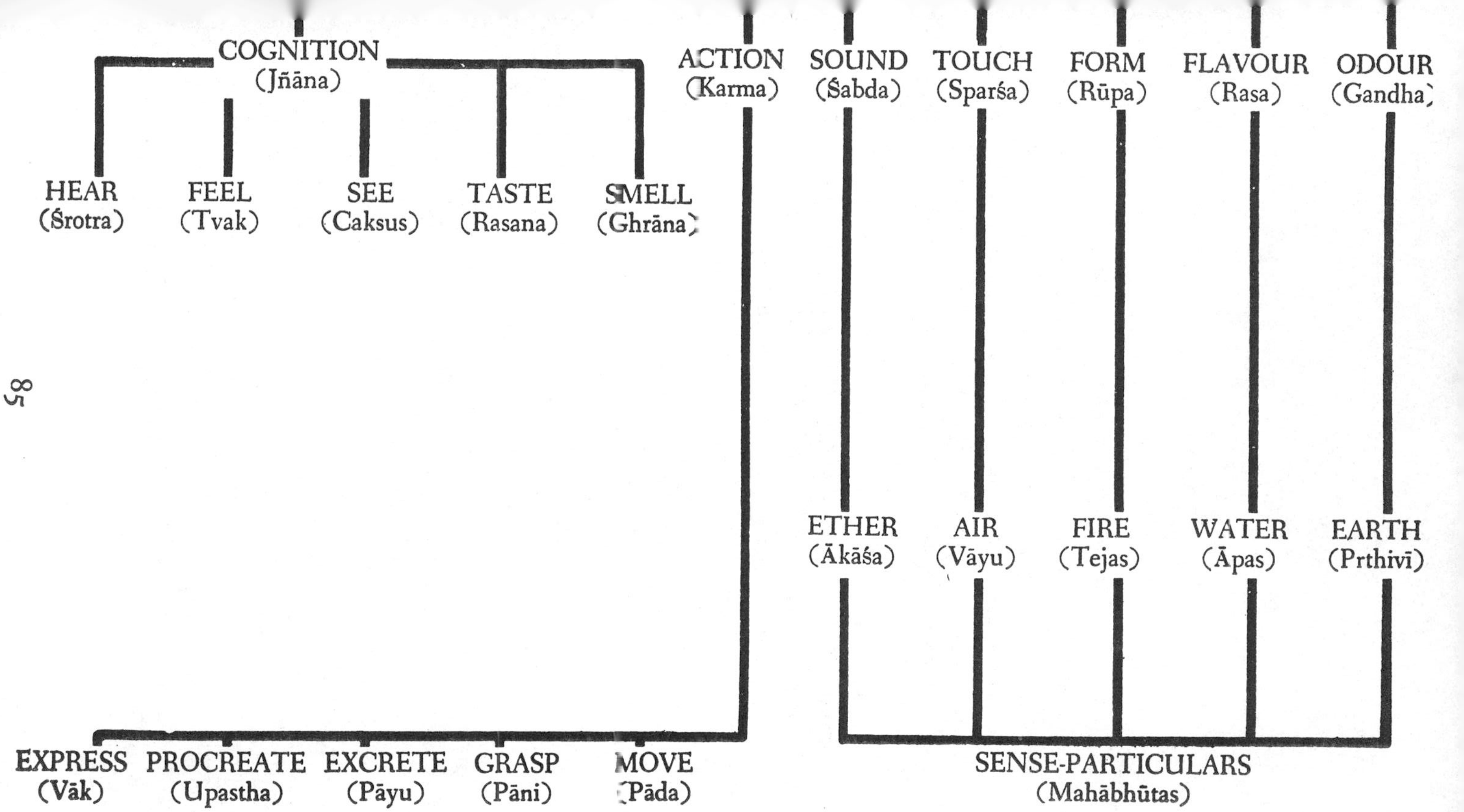
COGNITION
(Jñāna)
ACTION
(Karma)
SOUND
(Śabda)
TOUCH
(Sparśa)
FORM
(Rūpa)
FLAVOUR
(Rasa)
ODOUR
(Gandha)
HEAR
(Śrotra)
FEEL
(Tvak)
SEE
(Caksus)
TASTE
(Rasana)
SMELL
(Ghrāna)
ETHER
(Ākāśa)
AIR
(Vāyu)
FIRE
(Tejas)
WATER
(Āpas)
EARTH
(Prthivī)
EXPRESS
(Vāk)
PROCREATE
(Upastha)
EXCRETE
(Pāyu)
GRASP
(Pāni)
MOVE
(Pāda)
SENSE-PARTICULARS
(Mahābhūtas)

YOGA

The term Yoga comes from the root *yuj*, "to yoke or join." Here it is used to mean the union of the individual spirit (jīvātman) with the Universal Spirit (Paramātman). The art of Yoga is defined as a system of culture for perfecting human efficiency. It claims to destroy the defects and diseases of the body and mind, to establish health and bestow happiness, to develop intelligence and reveal true knowledge of Self, and to extract the nectar of all things.

The philosophical basis of Yoga is the Sāṁkhya. The ancient teachers (ṛṣis) have extended the laws that govern the evolution of the universe to cover the evolution of the individual, showing that the individual is but the microcosm of the macrocosm. The system as it applies to the individual is called the Yoga Philosophy. It is said that there is no knowledge equal to the Sāṁkhya and no power equal to Yoga.

The founder of the Yoga was Patañjali. He did not discover the science of the Yoga, for it is an art that has been used since the beginning of time. Its techniques and teachings have been accumulated through a ceaseless stream of adepts, self-fulfilled personalities, who have handed it down from generation to generation through a group of devoted followers. Patañjali is credited with having given us the present literary form of the Yoga doctrine in his famous treatise, the *Yogasūtra*. However, he indicates that there must have been a previous account by the opening sūtra which says, "Now a revised text of Yoga." According to the *Yājñavalkya Smṛti*, Hiraṇyagarbha was the original teacher of the Yoga; however, Patañjali is traditionally accepted as the founder of the Yoga. Very little is known of the life of Patañjali, and the few fragments that are available are so full of legend, that they cannot be relied upon. There is considerable controversy over the identity of Patañjali. Some authorities claim that he is the same Patañjali who wrote the famous commentary called the *Mahābhāṣya* on the grammar of Pāṇini, but the available evidence is too conflicting to warrant a settled opinion. There is no reliable source to determine the time when Patañjali flourished; so he is assigned to various periods ranging from the third century B.C. to the fourth century A.D.

Purpose

The paramount aim of the Yoga is to free man forever from the three sorts of pain:

1. Those arising from his own infirmities and wrong conduct, such as disease.
2. Those arising from his relations with other living things, such as a tiger, thief, and the like.
3. Those arising from his relations with external nature, such as the elements and other abstract and subtle powers.

This is accomplished, first, by achieving non-attachment to the world, but not necessarily isolation from it; secondly, by gaining restraint over the mind and its creations, thereby purifying the manifest consciousness; and, finally, by attaining positive and absolute union of the individual soul and universal soul. This condition is known as samādhi, and is the true purpose of Yoga.

The Yogi strives to become entirely and completely free from the eternal cycle of life and death. He views nature as a single force working in two directions. From the outside, it struggles to separate; from the inside, it struggles to reunite. The inner force is called Life; the outer force is called Death. The purpose of Yoga is to unite these two. It lays down the laws by which they operate and the means by which the individual consciousness gains control and ultimately becomes one with the Universal Spirit. When the individual soul reaches the source of its own substance, it is said to become free from all circumstances of storm and calm, joy and pain, and is thereby eternally released from all misery.

The Yoga assumes that the individual is part and parcel of the universal substance, but so involved in the matter of Time and

Space as to have lost all recognition of his or her true reality; therefore, this school sets forth a means and way of life to bring the individual back to his true and original position, to absolve him from the clutches of matter, to return him to the essence from which he came, to abstract him from every aspect of Time and Space.

Yogis hold that all in the manifest and unmanifest world comes from one source, the divine and primordial intelligence; that man is but a spark of this intelligence and, by the process of Yoga, is able to get a glimpse of this great intelligence which bestows all knowledge, all wisdom, all power, and all there is in the seen and unseen universe.

Scope

The best proof of the practical nature of Yoga and the extent of its influence is the fact that every system of religion in India and every school of philosophy has recognized Yoga as the most scientific means of realizing philosophical truths. Men of marvelous mental powers and intense heroism in ancient India, Tibet, and China were the outcome of the teachings and practice of Yoga. It is said that all methods of human culture other than Yoga are like beating about a hole to kill a snake. What would require many lives by methods known to the world at large, is done in a remarkably short time by the art of Yoga.

Yoga gives its devotees a tangible knowledge of the future and unseen world; it enables man to appreciate the life around him and gives him the power to make that life worth appreciating. What the intellectual, moral, and spiritual man hopes for, whatever he loves, wishes, or wills is to be found in the teachings of the Yoga. The practice of Yoga enhances the sensibilities and powers of man; therefore, Yogis claim a far-reaching knowledge of the secrets of nature and an extensive control over natural phenomena.

The systematic study of the Yoga has now been stopped for hundreds of years, having gone into a state of decay on account of idleness, ignorance, and the unscrupulousness of the generality of its latter-day followers. The cancer of laziness, selfishness, vanity, and delusion commenced to work its destruction at the beginning of this age (Kali Yuga). Corrupted rites, false ideas, dogmatic tenets, which human selfishness begot in the course of ages, led man to practice social abuses and crimes, evils so common and rampant that Yoga was perforce compelled to retire to secret abodes, until in this day only mere remnants of it are available to the average seeker. Even in India, the home of Yoga, supreme ignorance prevails about Yoga in general, and especially is this so in educated circles. Yet it is not thought to be lost by those who are well practiced in some of its arts, and who may be presumed to know. However, very few persons are really competent for Yoga in its higher forms, since they have not the determination to devote the time to Yoga necessary for this accomplishment; but it is there, none the less, for him who has the capacity.

Philosophy

The Yoga system assumes the same cosmological doctrines as set forth in the Sāṁkhya system. The only difference between the two is that the Sāṁkhya system pertains to the universal condition of nature, and the Yoga system pertains to the individual condition of nature. The process of evolution and involution of both is the same. Both are based on the fundamental logical premise that something cannot come out of nothing, that every shadow must have its substance. Therefore, the Yoga system maintains that the gross individual must have a subtle aspect from which it manifests itself and to which it will return. This subtle aspect is but a spark of the divine, and is the sole concern of Yoga.

Before it is possible to understand man fully, it is necessary to examine first the forces which sustain him and cause him to be what he is. The energies of nature operate in him according to the necessities of survival, yet man has the inherent quality of dissolution, for he is a compound being. He is constituted of both the gross and the subtle. The gross can be known by perception, but the subtle can be known only by the power of spiritual perception. The subtle aspect consists of the abstract energies of his nature; they are always invisible, for they are beyond the mind, beyond the senses, never to be seen, but to be known only through the practice of Yoga.

The Yoga system is based upon the principle that there is but one law that governs a single force which operates in all conditions of nature, manifest and unmanifest. That force is called life. It is the invisible force that unites spirit and matter and brings all things into being. It is not the result of the chemical stimulation of protoplasm, yet protoplasm is a carrier of life. Death does take an inexorable grasp of the manifest individual, but the continuance of life is not affected. Life is actually the sensibility that precedes the senses.

Life is not the creation of something new; it is only an expansion of what is; therefore, it is linked to the unseen realities which constitute the essence of man before he becomes manifest in the gross form. We see only the middle link in the chain of existence and call it life; we utterly fail to take notice of the preceding and succeeding invisible stages. Inasmuch as nothing can exist without being attached to its antecedents, the material manifestation called life must be linked to a finer and immaterial form; therefore, man is said to be the offspring of the invisible aspect of nature, appearing only when a condition for his manifestation has been created. Since the effect must always be uniform with the cause, life must proceed from life as light proceeds from light, and not from darkness.

Each conception is the influx of a new self, for the lifeless constituents of a human body cannot create a man, no matter how many chemicals or physiological actions are postulated. The manifestation in the visible world is not the creation of something new. The phenomenon of birth is merely the manifestation of an individual aspect of universal consciousness. Therefore, the soul can operate in both the visible and invisible world.

Those individuals who observe only the superficial appearances of nature confound the eternal order of things, and fail to perceive the true nature of man. Man is a combination of a self-conscious self and five kinds of matter formed into an organic body. He possesses infinite consciousness and is ever subject to the process of being evolved into a finite organic individual through the dynamics of the combined sperm and ovum. The soul is not corporeally and dimensionally present, but is spiritually present as one's voice is present throughout the room. It has no inside or outside, but is only a mass of intelligence, just as a mass of sweetness has no inside or outside, but is simply a mass of taste.

The manifestation of an individual is the reduction of the universal force to an individual principle caused by a stress raised in the universal consciousness. Man as a genus is the result of the differentiation of the whole into an infinite multiplicity of correlated centers called individuals, effects of nature. In order to produce the differentiation, energy must become concentrated so as to create a field in which a stress can take place. This is caused by the dynamic energy of the individual's past action (karma). As a section becomes enveloped, it operates as a limited and determining principle called man. This center of individual consciousness is cast into a mould and likened to a tightly wound spring. As the individual consciousness begins to manifest, it takes on forms and becomes a thinking, speaking and experiencing entity. Its experiences become logical only when circumscribed in review. The more compact and condensed this conscious energy becomes, the more power it manifests.

Jīva

The individual spirit is called Jīva in Sanskrit, from the root *jiv,* "to live." Here it is used to mean the principle of life. It is the individual soul as distinguished from the Universal Soul, called Puruṣa in the Sāṁkhya system. The Universal Spirit (Puruṣa) is postulated to account for the subjective aspect of nature; the individual spirit (Jīva) is postulated to account for the subjective aspect of the individual in the phenomenal world. It is the spark of life, the animating principle, the feeling of persistency experienced by every individual. It is that which produces the feeling of Being. It is postulated to account for a condition; therefore, it can never be seen, no more than the center of gravity can be seen.

Guṇas

In the universal condition of nature, the Cosmic Substance (Prakṛti) is postulated to account for the objective side of existence; it is the potential phase of nature out of which all things come. The Cosmic Substance (Prakṛti) consists of three constituents called Guṇas. They are Sattva, Rajas, and Tamas. The function of the Guṇas in the universal condition of nature is to reveal, move, and restrain; they function through suppression, cooperation, and transformation as the result of their intimate intercourse with one another. In the phenomenal world they signify adhesion, cohesion, and disintegration. While the modes of the Guṇas come and go throughout eternity, they forever remain the same; therefore, since the effect must partake of the substance out of which it is made, the individual who is an effect of nature must necessarily consist of these three aspects of nature. In the universal condition of nature, they are the substance of all things; in the individual manifestation of nature, they are the psychological basis of all things.

In the psychological world the three Guṇas serve to illuminate, activate and obscure. They manifest as the nature of pleasure, pain, and indifference; Sattva Guṇa attaches to happiness; Rajas to action; and Tamas to heedlessness. On the moral plane they represent affection, love, and hate; in the psychic field they represent emancipation, affinity, and sin.

Sattva Guṇa means real or truth. It is the abstract principle of illumination. In the mental world, it accounts for such qualities as joy, pleasure, enlightenment, faith, forbearance, forgiveness, courage, valour, concentration, humility, modesty, indifference, detachment, compassion, and pure action.

Rajas Guṇa is energy, the abstract principle of activity which moves Sattva Guṇa to suppress Tamas Guṇa or works on Tamas Guṇa to suppress Sattva Guṇa. In the mental world, it accounts for such qualities as argumentation, opinion, remorse, frenzy, wrath, attachment, jealousy, backbiting, egoism, selfishness, desire to afflict and kill, desire to buy and sell, the habit of evil thoughts, suspicion, insulting criticism, abusiveness, falsehood, deception, doubt, skepticism, animosity, envy, braggadocio, heedlessness, irregularity in conduct, treachery, disrespect, thievery, ostentation, lack of shame, gambling, scandalmongering, quarreling, drudgery, and all cravings of the senses. From the predominance of Rajas Guṇa, all temptations and fancies arise.

Tamas Guṇa is the abstract principle of restraint. It is that which veils consciousness and obstructs action. In the mental world it accounts for such qualities as indolence, carelessness, delusion, ignorance, indecision, sleepiness, laziness, fear, avarice, grief, lewdness, want of faith, pride, stolidity, lassitude, and deluded conviction. It is the cause of want of discrimination, faith, knowledge, memory, and liberality. It is the cause of immorality. It is the power by which other things are measured.

The individual proceeds from the universal condition of Spirit (Puruṣa) and Matter (Prakṛti) manifesting as an individual soul or jīva. So it is that man consists of a subtle aspect and a gross aspect. All things must have a vehicle in which to manifest themselves; these spiritual forces have their vehicle in what is called the *liṅga śarīra*. *Liṅga* means that invariable mark which proves the existence of anything; śarīra means "body." Here the two terms mean the subtle body which accompanies the individual spirit or soul (jīva) and survives the destruction of the physical body. This subtle body (*liṅga śarīra*) is the invisible vehicle of the soul (jīva); it is constant and does not change throughout the cycles of life and death; however, it is not eternal, for it is eventually re-absorbed into the elements of which it is composed. The subtle body (*liṅga śarīra*) consists of eighteen elements: intelligence (buddhi), ego (ahaṁkāra), mind (manas), five knowing-senses (jñānendriyas), five working-senses (karmendriyas) and five subtle elements (tanmātras). The gross aspect is called the sthūla śarīra or "gross body," that is, the material and perishable body. This perishable body is, of course, destroyed at death, and another is formed at birth. It consists of the five gross aspects of the five tanmātras, technically called bhūtas or the five gross elements. All this is the sum and substance of man. All proceed from the Cosmic Substance (Prakṛti), and represent the true essence of each individual of the manifest world. The philosophy of the Yoga interprets these principles as they apply to the individual, and the art of the Yoga teaches one how to control these forces.

Citta

Patañjali says, "Yoga is the restraint of mental modifications." Here the term *citta* is used for the word Mind. It is derived from the root *cit,* "to perceive, comprehend, know," and is here employed to mean the entire knowing faculty, Mind in the collective sense. Another term frequently used for Mind as a whole is *antaḥkaraṇa,* derived from the prefix *antar,* meaning "internal," and the root *kṛi,* "to do"; therefore, "the internal doer" or "Mind" as a whole, the internal organ, the seat of thought and feeling, the thinking faculty. It is the restraint of this function that Patañjali refers to in the aphorism just quoted.

The Mind (Citta), in this instance, is the first manifestation in the world of name and form. It is defined as the organized totality of conscious experience; it consists of all the activities of an organism by means of which it responds as an integrated, dynamic system to external forces, usually in some relation to its own past and future. It is the first birth of consciousness and manifests itself with the first breath of life. Its distinguishing feature is awareness. It has the capacity to know and influence its environment. Its processes are divided into two general divisions, conscious and unconscious. Conscious behavior includes all those processes of sensation and feeling of which the individual is aware. Consciousness is characteristic of an organic creature who is receiving impressions or having experiences.

Unconscious activity consists of all those processes which occur with no awareness on the part of the individual. They are dynamic processes which do not reach the threshold of consciousness in spite of their effective intensity; and they cannot always be brought into conscious experience by an effort of the will or act of the memory. They are frequently referred to as the subliminal or sub-conscious experiences of the individual.

For the purpose of our understanding the Mind (Citta) is divided into three categories in accordance with its respective functions. They are intelligence (buddhi), ego (ahaṁkāra), and mind (manas). Each has its distinguishing characteristics and individual function; however, they are actually a single functioning unit, and do not form separate and individual parts.

Buddhi

The first stage of this synthetic unit called Mind (Citta) is buddhi, derived from *budh,* "to wake up, recover consciousness, observe." Here the term is used to mean the seat of intelligence, the intuitive capacity of the individual, his means of direct perception. It accounts for the capacity of illumination, abstraction, determination, certainty. It is the seat of virtue, non-attachment and wisdom. It manifests itself through determination, resolution in thought and action, formation and retention of concepts and generalizations. It is the last to act in all cognitional, affectional, and volitional processes of the ego (ahaṁkāra), mind (manas), and senses (indriyas). It is the sole basis for knowing, willing, feeling and resolving. It is the background or mere awareness, without thought of "I." When the mind (manas) is registering the objects of thought, it is the intelligence (buddhi) that discriminates, determines, and recognizes. In contemplation, the mind (manas) raises the objects of thought, and the intelligence (buddhi) dwells upon them.

Ahaṁkāra

The second stage of this synthetic unit called Mind (Citta) is the ego (ahaṁkāra). It is the vast reservoir of instinctive impulses, dominated by pleasure and pain and blind impulsive wishing. It is the individuating and arrogating principle, the storehouse of all experiences. It is the first manifestation of individual consciousness, personal position, individual identity. It is the "I-making principle" and gives one the feeling of "I am here." It is the individuality, apperception, or focused perception, that mental function or operation which brings about the focusing of attention, conscious realization, and persistent identity. It accounts for the mental attitude of "I know," "I exist," "I have." It is the condition wherein the personal consciousness realizes itself as a particular "I-experiencer." It is the basis of ideation and self-identity, however much subdued or indistinct. Here there is no decision, no reflection, no conception. It rationalizes nothing, but is satisfied with things as they are. It is a self-conscious principle where all that constitutes man is welded into an ego; where the soul thinks of itself as a particular entity in relation to objects of experience. Its function is the testing of reality, accepting or rejecting the demands or wishes made by impulses emanating from the individual organism as a single vital unit for its benefit as a whole. It arrogates to itself the experience had by the mind (manas) and passes it on to the intelligence (buddhi) to be determined. It is the conscious subject of all psychological experiences; it is the individualized Self.

Manas

The third stage of this synthetic unit called Mind (Citta), technically termed *manas* in Sanskrit, is best translated as "mind," in small letters. It constitutes that group of cognitive processes that have the capacity of discovering relationships and performing mental processes. It is the seat of responsible conscious activity. It accounts for the process of rationalization. It is a material force that envelops or obscures consciousness. It is the directing power behind all action. It is of limited extension, finite, radiant, and transparent. It is the seat of desire and functions in association with the knowing-senses (jñānendriyas) and the working-senses (karmendriyas). It has the capacity of attention, selection, and rejection; yet it is unable to reveal itself to the experiencer. It merely synthesizes the discrete manifold. It can perceive but cannot conceive, as does intelligence (buddhi). It is continually vacillating between objects. It has the capacity of mere apprehension without the assimilation of knowledge. It is the collective organ of sensation between the knowing (jñānendriyas) and the working senses (karmendriyas). It is sometimes called the Sixth Sense, the internal organ of perception and recognition that automatically registers the facts which the senses perceive. It is the instrument through which thoughts enter from the subjective side or by which the objects of the senses affect the inner self. It is the sensorium. It is the seat of all such conditions as thought, rationalization, ideation, imagination, dreaming, cognition, affection, desire, moods, and temper. The capacity of thinking is an internal quality of its nature and never ceases.

In relation to the external world, the mind (manas) perceives and presents; the ego (ahaṁkāra) arrogates; and the intelligence (buddhi) discriminates, decides, and resolves, after which action arises. These three aspects constitute the Mind (Citta) as a whole.

Indriyas

The next stage in the structure of a conscious being is the knowing (jñānendriyas) and the working senses (karmendriyas). The indriyas (sense powers) mean the sense-consciousness through which the mind (manas) receives all of its impressions from the objective world, and not the organs themselves, which are only the physical instruments. Both the knowing (jñānendriyas) and the working senses (karmendriyas) arise simultaneously, but they are discussed separately for the purpose of understanding.

The knowing senses (jñānendriyas) are: the power to hear (śrota), the power to feel (tvak), the power to see (cakṣus), the power to taste (rasana), and the power to smell (ghrāṇa). They function respectively through the organs of ears, skin, eyes, tongue and nose. The working senses (karmendriyas) are the powers or capacities to express (vāk), to procreate (upastha), to excrete (pāyu), to grasp (pāṇi), and to move (pāda). Their physical organs are the voice, sex organs, anus, hands, and feet. (1) The power of expression means the working of ideas, and not the mere production of vocal sound; (2) the power of procreation means the capacity of the entire being for recreation and passive enjoyment and not the mere physical act; (3) the power of excretion means the process of rejection throughout the entire organism, and not the single capacity of elimination; (4) the power of grasping means the capacity of permeating things, and not necessarily the physical act of handling objects; (5) the power of locomotion means the mental life behind all function, and not the aimless walking about.

The physical instruments are not positively necessary for the function of these respective powers; the deaf have lost the use of the ear, but science has made it possible for them to hear through the medium of certain bones. The mute can no longer speak, but they can express ideas by the use of their fingers. The paralyzed can no longer feel physical pain, but they are sensitive to kindness, consideration, and thoughtfulness. The blind have lost the use of the physical organ, the eye, but they can still perceive ideas by using their fingertips in reading Braille. The lame are unable to walk, but they can move about on crutches. So it is seen that these powers are not identical with the instruments, nor are they absolutely dependent upon them.

All these senses (indriyas) constitute the awareness and reactive responses which the Self makes to the objects that follow, the means whereby enjoyment is had, which is the will to life. Existence is the tying of these experiences together into an endless chain; life is the force that holds them.

Tanmātras

The next stage in the integration of a Being is the manifestation of the five subtle elements (tanmātras) or rudiments of matter. They are the ethereal essence of sound (śabda), touch (sparśa), form (rūpa), flavour (rasa), and odour (gandha). They are elements which cannot be apprehended by the gross senses, but can be perceived only by superior beings through direct intuition.

These subtle elements (tanmātras) are the subtle forms of matter and are referred to as mere dream stuff. It is said that they manifest themselves to the mind as lights which may be seen in kind, when the eyes are closed and pressure is exerted upon the lids. They are not independent entities outside one another, but are aspects of a whole. They are the subtle body not yet massive.

Bhūtas

The last stage in the manifestation of a Being is the appearance of the gross elements (bhūtas) as perceived by the senses. They are ether (ākāśa), air (vāyu), fire (tejas), water (āpas), and earth (pṛthivī). They are the result of the aggregation of the subtle elements (tanmātras) with the accretion of a material force and come to pass as the result of the slowing down of nature. Their existence is dependent upon the subtle elements (tanmātras) which act as their support and without which they could not exist. They are the gross elements of sensation experienced in the physical world.

Each of the gross elements (bhūtas) evolves out of the one immediately preceding it. The original homogeneous unit is ether (ākāśa), the vehicle of sound (śabda). The first division brings into existence the element called air (vāyu), the vehicle of touch (sparśa). As further variety arises, the element of fire (tejas) manifests, which is the vehicle of form (rūpa). The next evolute is water (āpas), the vehicle of flavour (rasa), the last division or evolute to manifest itself in nature is earth (pṛthivī), the vehicle of odour (gandha). This is the lowest vibration of nature. Each element has one more property than the preceding element out of which it is evolved, caused by the addition of another subtle element (tanmātra). These five forms of gross matter (bhūtas) are transformed states of original nature characterized by the three qualities of sattva guṇa, rajas guṇa, and tamas guṇa, as are all things mobile and immobile.

Literature

The oldest text book on Yoga is the *Yogasūtra* of Patañjali. It is divided into four books; the first consists of fifty-one aphorisms and discusses the nature and aim of samādhi (samādhipāda), that is, the theory or science of Yoga. It is hardly detailed enough for the average individual to make progress by independent study. The second consists of fifty-five aphorisms and discusses the art of Yoga, explaining the means of attaining this end (sādhanapāda). The third consists of fifty-four aphorisms and discusses the supernormal powers that can be attained through Yoga practices (vibhūtipāda). The fourth consists of thirty-four aphorisms and discusses final emancipation (kaivalyapāda), man's realization that he is separated from mind-matter. This last chapter, according to some authorities, is a later addition since the word *iti,* denoting the conclusion of a work, appears at the end of the third book.

Other works of outstanding interest are: Vyāsa's *Bhaṣya* (commentary; fourth century, A.D.) on the *Yogasūtra,* the standard exposition on Yoga principles; Vācaspati's glossary on Vyāsa's *Bhāṣya,* called *Tattvavaiśāradī* (ninth century); Bhoja's *Rājamārtāṇḍa*; Vijñānabhikṣu's *Yogavārttika* and *Yogasārasaṁgraha,* important manuals criticizing some of Vācaspati's views and attempting to bring the Yoga system nearer to the philosophy of the Upaniṣads. A few important writers on the Yoga system who modify the views of Patañjali to suit their own preconceptions are: Nāgoji Bhaṭṭa (also called Nāgeśa Bhaṭṭa), Nārāyaṇabhikṣu and Mahādeva. Some of the later Upaniṣads that attach great importance to the principles of the Yoga are: *Maitrāyana, Śāṇḍilya, Yogatattva, Dhyānabindu, Haṁsa,* and *Nādabindu.*

MĪMĀṀSĀ

Mīmāṁsā is classified under the third division of Hindū Philosophy. The term is derived from the Sanskrit root *man,* "to think, consider, examine, or investigate." Here the term, etymologically meaning "desire to think," is used to signify a consideration, examination, or investigation of the Vedic Texts. Because it provides an insight into the Veda, the Eternal Truth, it is classified as a Darśana, the Indian term for philosophy, meaning a view of the Truth.

Mīmāṁsā is divided into two systems, viz., the Pūrvamīmāṁsā and the Uttaramīmāṁsā. The adjective *pūrva* means "earlier"; therefore, that which deals with the earlier part of the Vedas. The adjective *uttara* means "latter"; therefore, that which deals with the latter part of the Vedas. Both are based on the Vedas; both use the same logical method of handling their problems; both use the same literary form; but each has its own limited sphere of interpretation. Pūrvamīmāṁsā interprets the actions enjoined in the Vedas, leading to freedom of the soul; Uttaramīmāṁsā interprets the knowledge revealed in the Vedas, leading to freedom of the soul. When these two systems are referred to in this light, they are respectively called Karma Mīmāṁsā and Jñāna Mīmāṁsā, but their popular names are simply Mīmāṁsā and Vedānta. Other terms used for Vedānta are given in the next chapter where this system is discussed.

The founder of Mīmāṁsā was Jaimini. He did not originate the teachings, but for the first time reduced to writing the traditional interpretations that had long been in the memory of man. Very little is known of his life aside from the tradition that he was a pupil of Bādarāyaṇa, founder of the Vedānta System. His actual date is quite unknown; however, the style of his writings assigns him to the Sūtra period which extended from 600–200 B.C. The word sūtra, "thread," is derived from the root *siv,* "to sew." Here the term is used to mean that which like a thread runs through and holds everything together. A sūtra is a short, pithy, mnemonic sentence used to facilitate learning. It is the style used for all philosophical literature.

Purpose

The purpose of Mīmāṁsā is to inquire into the nature of Right Action (Dharma). The basic premise of Mīmāṁsā is that action is the very essence of human existence. Without action, knowledge is fruitless; without action, happiness is impossible; without action, human destiny cannot be fulfilled; therefore, Right Action (Dharma) is the spiritual pre-requisite of life.

All actions are said to have two effects, one external and the other internal, one manifest and the other potential, one gross and the other subtle. The internal effect is eternal, regarded as being, while the external effect is transitory. Actions are, therefore, the vehicles for planting the seeds of life to come.

On this basic premise, Mīmāṁsā examines all actions enjoined in the Veda. For this purpose, it divides the Veda into two broad divisions, Mantra and Brahmanas, and classifies its contents under five different headings: (1) injunctions (vidhi), (2) hymns (mantra), (3) names (nāmadheya), prohibitions (niṣedha), and (5) explanatory passages (arthavāda). It then explains the method of interpreting every grammatical rule and literary device employed and of analyzing all Vedic ritual and ceremonies into their two fundamental sorts, principle and subordinate. Mīmāṁsā is, therefore, a general summary of the rules for the interpretation of Vedic texts.

Scope

Mīmāṁsā accepts the philosophical concepts of the other systems; it does not enter upon any philosophical analysis of the Ultimate Reality, Soul, and Matter, or the interrelation of one to the other, but its entire interpretation is dependent upon their existence. Its basic premise of right action is proved and defended by the means of knowledge taught by the Nyāya-Vaiśeṣika division; all the effects of right action would be meaningless without the analysis of the evolution of consciousness taught by the Sāṁkhya-Yoga division; however, it makes specific use only of those factors that are needed for its special problems. For example, it shows that Verbal Testimony (Śabda) is the only means of right knowledge that can be used to discover the nature of the invisible effects of action, and that all other means of right knowledge are necessary only to refute opponents. Although Mīmāṁsā does not enter into any philosophical analysis of the universe, it welcomes all philosophical discussion that will further an understanding of right action as enjoined in the Veda.

The sole concern of Mīmāṁsā is salvation, not liberation. It argues that salvation cannot be achieved by knowledge alone, for the soul must first exhaust its potentialities through action, as a seed fulfills itself through growth. No amount of contemplation will enable man to arrive at the ultimate goal of human destiny; therefore, the emphasis is on the ethical side of life rather than on the philosophical. All arguments are based on the premises that the soul by definition must survive this earthly manifestation. The actions to pursue and the rewards to follow are enjoined in the Veda and interpreted by Mīmāṁsā.

The importance of Mīmāṁsā is testified by its present-day effect, for no part of the daily life of the Hindū is without the influence of the teachings of Mīmāṁsā. All rituals and ceremonies depend upon it; all moral conduct is guided by it; all Hindū law is founded upon it. Mīmāṁsā breathes life into the very super-structure of Indian culture.

Philosophy

The central theme of Mīmāṁsā is stated in the opening verse: "Now is the enquiry of duty [dharma]." [1] This is the basis for

[1] The *Mīmāṁsāsūtra* of Jaimini, i, I, 1.

the interpretation of the entire Veda. Dharma is defined in the text:

"Duty [dharma] is an object distinguished by a command." [2] The term dharma is derived from the root *dhar*, "to hold, maintain, preserve." It has reference, therefore, to anything that holds, supports, or preserves. When used in the metaphysical sense, it means those universal laws of Nature that sustain the operation of the universe and the manifestation of all things, that without which nothing could be. When applied to the individual, it has reference to that code of conduct that sustains the soul, and enables man to fulfill his divine destiny. Here it has reference to the actions, practices, and duties that will benefit man in the world to come; therefore, it is that which produces virtue, morality, or religious merit leading toward the development of man.

All rituals and ceremonies enjoined in the Veda are said to lead to the enlightenment of the mind and the spiritual evolution of the soul. Therefore, it is necessary clearly to understand their import. On the surface they appear to be fruitless injunctions; therefore, Mīmāṁsā endeavours to show how they are all based on dharma and lead to the spiritual welfare of man. Mīmāṁsā interprets the Veda on the basis that eternal happiness is attained by the correct performance of rituals founded on dharma, thereby storing up seeds of virtue to fructify in the next life.

Knowledge of dharma, according to Jaimini, can be obtained only by Verbal Testimony (Śabda). The six means of knowledge employed by the other systems are not infallible when dealing with the invisible effects of ritual; therefore, Jaimini accepts only Śabda, or The Word. To support his position, he lays down five propositions:

1. Every Word (Śabda) has an inherent power to convey its meaning which is eternal.
2. The knowledge derived from the Word (Śabda) is called Upadeśa (teachings).
3. In the invisible realm, the Word (Śabda) is the infallible guide.

[2] *Ibid.*, i, I, 2.

4. In the opinion of Bādarāyaṇa, the Word (Śabda) is authoritative.
5. The Word is self-sufficient and does not depend upon any other for its meaning; otherwise, it would become involved in the fallacy of *regressus ad infinitum.*

Jaimini refutes several objections raised against the eternal character of the Word (Śabda): (1) The objector contends that the Word (Śabda) is a product of verbal utterance; therefore, it cannot be eternal. Jaimini asserts that only the pronunciation is the product of effort; the Word (Śabda) must have existed previously, otherwise it could not have been pronounced. (2) The Word (Śabda) vanishes after it is pronounced; therefore, it is not eternal. Jaimini points out that only the sound disappears; the Word (Śabda) still remains as does the drum after the sound is produced, (3) The verb "make" is used in connection with the Word (Śabda); therefore, it cannot be eternal. Jaimini explains that the verb "make" has reference only to sound which manifests the Word (Śabda); the word (Śabda) existed previously and the pronunciation only made it audible. (4) Since the Word (Śabda) is heard simultaneously by several people standing at an equal distance, there must be many sounds and not one; therefore, it is not eternal. Jaimini contends there is only one sound as there is only one sun, even though seen by many people; therefore it is eternal. (5) The Word (Śabda) undergoes modifications; therefore, it cannot be eternal. Jaimini answers that changes of letters are not modifications of the Word (Śabda); they are new words, and the original Word (Śabda) still exists. (6) When several people utter a sound, there is an increase in volume; therefore, it is not eternal. Jaimini argues that the Word (Śabda) never increases; only the sound which manifests the Word (Śabda) increases; therefore, the Word (Śabda) is eternal.

After establishing the eternal character of the Word (Śabda), Jaimini proceeds to show that the use of words in the sentences of the Veda have a meaning just as they have in ordinary language. Then he defends the divine origin of the Veda. It is beyond the scope of this chapter to present all these details, for they would obscure the purpose of this volume which is to provide a working basis for further study.

The method of interpretation of the Vedic texts used by Jaimini is best shown by an outline of the terms used at random throughout the text. For this purpose, the contents of the Vedas are classified under five heads: (1) Vidhi (Injunctions), (2) Mantra (Hymns), (3) Nāmadheya (Names), (4) Niṣedha (Prohibitions), and (5) Arthavāda (Explanatory Passages). These are further subdivided:

I. VIDHI–a command, precept or order.
  A. Utpattividhi–lays down a command with a certain object, thereby creating a desire.
  B. Viniyogavidhi–lays down the details of a sacrifice.
    1. Six accompaniments for the interpretation of procedure enjoined by the texts.
      (*a*) Śruti–primary sense of a word or collection of words, not depending upon any other word for its meaning.
        (1) Vidhātri–indicated by the verb from–*liṅ*.
        (2) Viniyoktrī–on hearing which one immediately sees the connection of the subsidiary and the principal.
          (a) Vibhatrirūpa–indicated by an affix of a declension.
          (b) Ekābhidhānarūpa–denoted by one word.
          (c) Ekapādarūpa–indicated by one pāda or sentence.
        (3) Abhidhātrī–indicates the material used in the sacrifice.
      (*b*) Liṅga–the secondary sense of a word inferred from another word or collection of words.
      (*c*) Vākya–when the meaning of a word or collection of words is indicated by the sentence in which it is used.
      (*d*) Prakaraṇa–when the meaning of a sentence or a clause depends upon the context in which it is used.
        (1) Mahāprakaraṇa–when the context relates to the rewards of the principal part of the sacrifice.
        (2) Avāntaraprakaraṇa–when the context relates

to the rewards of the subordinate part of the sacrifice.

(*e*) Sthāna—when the meaning depends upon the location or word order.

(1) Pāṭhasādeśya—equality of place in the text.

(a) Yathāsāṁkhyapāṭha—"relative enumeration," arranging verbs with verbs and subjects with subjects.

(b) Sannidhipāṭha—regulated by the text which is near it.

(2) Anuṣṭhānasādeśya—the quality of place according to the performance.

(*f*) Samākhyā—when it is necessary to break compound words up into their component parts in order to ascertain their meaning.

2. Two kinds of actions enjoined by Viniyogavidhi.

(*a*) Principal—that which produces the transcendental fruit (Apūrva), the invisible result to mature in another life.

(*b*) Subordinate—that which leads up to the completion of the principal action. These are called Aṅga and are of two kinds:

(1) Siddharūpa—an accomplished thing which consists of class, material number, and the like, and has a visible effect.

(2) Kriyārūpa—this is action.

(a) Pradhānakarma—the primary action.

(1) Sannipatyopakāraka—actions enjoined with respect to the substance. They produce visible and invisible results.

(2) Ārādupakāraka—actions which are enjoined without any reference to any substance or divinity. It leads directly to the ultimate result. It is the essence of the sacrifice.

(b) Guṇakarma—the secondary action.

(1) Sannipatyopakāraka

(2) Ārādupakāraka

C. Prayogavidhi—the injunction that lays down the order of performance of the subsidiary or minor parts. The succession or order (Karma) is of six kinds:

1. Śrutikrama–the order determined by a direct text.
   (*a*) Kevalakramapara—a text indicating an order or sequence only.
   (*b*) Tadviśiṣṭa padārthapara–indicating the order or sequence in the course of laying down certain other things.
2. Arthakrama–the order determined by the object.
3. Pāṭhakrama–when the order of the execution of things is governed by their order in the text. It is of two kinds:
   (*a*) Mantra–text–to be explained later.
   (*b*) Brāhmaṇa–text–to be explained later.
4. Sthānakrama–the transportation of a thing from its proper place by reason of being preceded by another thing which is followed by another.
5. Mukhyakrama–the sequence of the subsidiaries or the subordinate parts according to the order in the principal.
6. Pravṛttikrama–the order of a procedure which, once begun, will apply to others as well.

D. Adhikāravidhi–an injunction which creates a right in a person.

II. MANTRA–a text which helps one to remember the procedure of a sacrifice.

A. Apūrva–when a text lays down a new injunction for the attainment of an object which one cannot know by any other means.

B. Niyama—the restrictive rule–when the text lays down one mode of doing a thing that could be done in several ways.

C. Parisaṁkhyā–an implied prohibition.
1. Śrautī–directly stated by some text.
2. Lākṣaṇikī–inferred prohibition.

III. NĀMADHEYA–a proper noun used in defining the matter enjoined by it.

A. Matvarthalakṣaṇābhayāt–a figure of speech in which the *matup* affix is used.

B. Vākyabhedabhayāt–the splitting up of a sentence.

C. Tatprakhya–a conventional name given to a particular sacrifice, the description of which is given elsewhere in a separate treatise.

D. Tadvyapadeśa–the name given to a sacrifice by reason of its resemblance to another from which it derives its name.

IV. NIṢEDHA–the opposite of Vidhi. A negative precept which prevents a man from doing a thing which is injurious or disadvantageous to him.

A. Paryudāsa–a negative precept that applies to a person who is undertaking to perform a sacrifice.

B. Pratiṣedha–a negative precept of general applicability.

V. ARTHAVĀDA—passages in praise or blame of a Vidhi or Niṣedha.

A. Guṇavāda—a statement made by the text that is contradictory to the existing state of the affair and means of proof.

B. Anuvāda—a statement made by the text which is in keeping with the existing state of facts.

C. Bhutārthavāda–a statement made which is neither against the existing state of facts nor is it in conformity with it.

Jaimini's defense of the utility of the Veda will illustrate the way he interprets the Veda. Nine objections are raised against Vedic mantras. The objections are:

1. Vedic mantras do not convey any meaning because they stand in need of other passages to explain and support them.

   Jaimini contends that all Vedic words have a significance just as they do in ordinary language.

2. Vedic mantras are held useless because they depend upon a complicated system of orthoepy and grammar in order to understand them.

   Jaimini says that Vedic sentences have a subject, predicate and object which are governed by the same rules of grammar as ordinary language.

3. Vedic mantras are held useless because they teach what is already known.

   Jaimini says that the repetition of things already known is for the purpose of Guṇavāda (new qualities), Parisaṁkhyā (implied prohibition) or Arthavāda (explanation). It is also to produce an invisible effect (Apūrva).

4. Vedic mantras are held useless because they describe what does not exist. For example, "It has four horns, it has three feet, two heads, it has seven hands; the bull, being tied threefold, cries: the great god entered amongst the mortals."

Jaimini explains that such descriptions are figurative speech, technically called Catvāri Sṛṅga. For example: "The sacrifice is compared with a bull by reason of its producing the desired effect; it has four horns in the form of four kinds of priests; its three feet are the three libations (Savanas) (performed three times a day); the sacrificer and his wife are the two heads; the chhandas (desires) are the seven hands. Being tied up by the three Vedas, viz, the Rik, Yajus, and Sāma, it resounds with the roaring sound uttered by the priests: this great god in the form of the sacrifice is amidst the mortals." [3]

5. Vedic mantras are held to be useless because they are addressed to inanimate objects as if they possessed life.

   Jaimini says this is to extol the sacrifice and induce the adherent to practice it. The principal use is technically called Kaibhutikanyāya.

6. Vedic mantras are held to be useless because they have many self-contradictory passages.

   Jaimini explains that these passages are descriptive of subordinate qualities.

7. Vedic mantras are held to be useless because they are learned without understanding their meaning.

   Jaimini explains that this is no fault of the Veda which deals only with the performance of sacrifices. It is assumed that the meaning will be learned.

8. Vedic mantras are held to be useless because there are many mantras the meaning of which cannot be known.

   Jaimini says that every mantra has a meaning. Our ignorance is due to carelessness and indolence.

9. Vedic mantras are held to be useless because they mention transitory things.

   Jaimini explains that the common nouns used in the Veda were subsequently used by men for proper nouns.

For the interpretation of substantives, Jaimini mentions three principles:

1. Rūḍhi — a word, not compounded with any other word and with a conventional meaning which must be learned

[3] *Introduction to the Mīmāmsā Sūtra of Jaimini,* XXX.

from past authorities, such as Pāṇini, the most eminent of all Sanskrit grammarians. It has the inherent power to convey a sense.

2. Yaugika — a derivative word, made up of two or three words. It is a compound word and is used in the sense conveyed by the component parts of which it is made.
3. Yogarūḍhi — a compound word which has its own conventional sense.

Jaimini explains that substantives never convey the intention of the speaker. This requires the use of a verb, which always denotes action. He classifies action into two kinds:

1. Pradhāna or Principal—It is that action which produces an invisible effect called Apūrva, such as the attainment of heaven. The recitation of mantras in prose and poetry at the performance of a sacrifice is said to produce Apūrva, an invisible effect; therefore they are the principal action.
2. Guṇa or Subordinate—It is that action which produces visible effects, such as the use of materials in the sacrifice, e.g., kindling of fire, preparing of cakes or the pounding and threshing of rice.

For the application of these rules, the Veda is divided into two broad divisions, Mantra and Brāhmaṇa, which are further subdivided. For example:

I. Mantra or Saṁhitā—This is the mandatory portion of the Veda. It is a collection of hymns that regulate, define and create a right, impelling men to action. It has three parts.

   1. Ṛig-veda — a collection of verses which have a metrical arrangement to convey meaning.
   2. Sāma-veda — a collection of verses which are sung at the end of a sacrifice.
   3. Yajur-veda — is in prose and has no metre. It is of two kinds:
      a. Nigada—those which are pronounced aloud.
      b. Upāṁśu—those which are pronounced silently.

II. Brāhmaṇas:

   1. Hetu—reason

2. Nirvacanam–explanation
3. Nindā–censure
4. Praśaṅsā–praise
5. Saṁśaya–doubt
6. Vidhi–command
7. Parakriyā–the action of one individual.
8. Purakalpa–the action of many individuals or a nation. These are the historical descriptions of one individual or many individuals and are indicated by the particles *iti, āha* or *ha*.
9. Vyavadhāraṇakalpanā—interpretation of a sentence according to its context.
10. Upamāna–comparison.

The principles which are merely outlined here are used throughout the *Mīmāṁsāsūtra* in the interpretation of the many sacrifices that are enjoined for the benefit of man.

Literature

The *Mīmāṁsāsūtra* of Jaimini consists of twelve chapters (adhyāya), divided into four parts (pādas) each, with the exception of chapters three, six, and ten which have eight parts (pādas), making a total of sixty parts (pādas). Each part (pāda) is further subdivided into sections (adhikaraṇas), and each section (adhikaraṇa) is written in sūtras. There is a total of 890 sections (adhikaraṇas) and 2621 sūtras.

The entire work is bound by the same logical method used by Vedānta. Each section (adhikaraṇa) has five parts: (1) thesis (viṣaya), (2) doubt (saṁśaya), (3) antithesis (pūrvapakṣa), (4) synthesis or right conclusion (siddhānta), and (5) agreement or consistency (saṁgati) of the proposition with the other parts of the treatise (śāstra). This final step of consistency (saṁgati) is made to comply with three requirements: (1) consistency with the entire treatise (śāstrasaṁgati), (2) consistency with the whole chapter (adhyāyasaṁgati), and (3) consistency with the whole part (pādasaṁgati). There are also rules for the interrelation of each section (adhikaraṇa). They must be logically related according to six sorts: (1) objection (ākṣepa), (2) illustration (dṛṣṭānta), (3) counter-illustration (pratidṛṣṭānta), (4) harmony with context (prasaṅga-saṁgati), (5) citation (utpattisaṁgati), and (6) denial (apavāda-saṁgati). These rules are more strictly applied in the Uttara Mīmāṁsā or Vedānta.

Only the first chapter of the *Mīmāṁsāsūtra* is of any philosophical value. Here Jaimini states the purpose of the *Sūtra*: an inquiry into the nature of Right Action; he defines Right Action (Dharma) and examines the cause of Right Action, the means of right knowledge to be used, the authority of the Veda, and states the method for interpreting all the actions enjoined. The rest of the book is devoted to the interpretation of specific rituals and ceremonies.

Besides the twelve chapters in the *Mīmāṁsāsūtra* of Jaimini, there are four additional chapters which raise considerable controversy as to their rightful origin. They are called the *Saṁkarṣakāṇḍa*. In some instances they are referred to as the *Devatākāṇḍa*. They are classified by some as the apocryphal portion of the Mīmāṁsā, written either by Khaṇḍadeva or Bhāskara. It consists of four chapters, composed of four parts (pādas) each, but it does not contain any sections (adhikaraṇas) which are so characteristic of the work of Jaimini. The styles of the sūtras are quite different and meager in comparison with those of Jaimini, so that it can hardly be considered a supplement to the *Mīmāṁsāsūtra*.

The early commentators on the *Mīmāṁsāsūtra* were Bhartṛmitra, Bhavadāsa, Hari, and Upavarṣa. Unfortunately none of their works has come down to us. They are known only by reference to them in the later commentaries.

The most outstanding commentator on the *Sūtra* of Jaimini was Śabara. His exact date is unknown; tradition says he lived about the first century B.C., but the leading authorities say he belongs to the period between 200–500 A.D. His work is simply called the *Bhāṣya* (Commentary). The *Bhāṣya* is indispensable for the study of the *Mīmāṁsāsūtra*. He does not follow the pattern used by Jaimini, but arranges the sections (adhikaraṇas) to fit his own views, although he makes a very detailed analysis of every sūtra. His *Bhāṣya* is the basis for all later commentaries.

The first school of Mīmāṁsā was founded by Prabhākara. He wrote the first important commentary on the *Bhāṣya,* called *Bṛhatī.* There is considerable controversy as to his actual date, but due to his style and lack of mention of later commentaries, he is generally held to be the first. Important works of this school are Śālikanātha's *Ṛjuvimalā,* a commentary on *Bṛhatī, Prakaraṇapañcikā,* a popular manual on the views of Prabhākara, *Pariśiṣṭa,* a brief annotation on Śabara's work; and Bhavanātha's *Nayaviveka,* which deals at length with the views of Prabhākara.

The second important school of the Mīmāṁsā was founded by Kumārila (end of 7th cent. and first half of 8th cent. A.D.). Some authorities contend that he was the teacher of Prabhākara, but tradition disagrees. Kumārila was an early champion of Hindūism and argued vigorously for the support of the Vedas upon which all Brahmanical orthodoxy is based. He wrote his commentary (*Vārttika*) on the *Sūtra* of Jaimini and the *Bhāṣya.* His work is divided in three parts: (1) *Ślokavārttika,* which deals with the first part of the first chapter of Jaimini's *Sūtra;* (2) the *Tantravārttika,* which deals with the material up to the end of the third chapter; and (3) the *Ṭupṭīkā,* which covers the rest of the *Sūtra.* The important commentaries on the *Vārttika* of Kūmarila are Sucarita Miśra's *Kāśikā,* a commentary on the *Ślokavārttika;* Someśvara Bhaṭṭa's *Nyāyasudhā* (also known as Rāṇaka), a commentary on the *Tantravārttika;* and Veṅkaṭa Dīkṣita's *Vārttikābharaṇa,* a commentary on the *Ṭupṭīkā.* Pārthasārathi Miśra (14th cent.) wrote *Nyāyaratnākara,* a commentary on the *Ślokavārttika, Śāstradīpikā,* an independent manual on the Mīmāṁsā system, and *Tantraratna.* A follower of Kumārila who wrote two independent works was Maṇdana Miśra, the author of *Vidhiviveka* and *Mīmāṁsānukramaṇī.* Vācaspati's *Nyāyakaṇikā* (850 A.D.) interprets the views expressed in the *Vidhiviveka.*

A third school of the Mīmāṁsā is said to have been founded by Murāri, but no works have come down to us. Other important writers and their works are Madhava's *Jaiminīya Nyāyamālāvistara* (14th cent.) an exposition on the Mīmāṁsā system in verse with a commentary in prose; Appaya Dīksita's *Vidhirasāyana* (1552–1624), an attack on Kumārila; Āpadeva's *Mīmāṁsānyāyaprakāśā* (also known as *Āpadevī*) (17th cent.), a very popular elementary manual; Laugākṣi Bhāskara's *Arthasaṁgraha,* a popular work based on *Āpadeva's* work; Khaṇḍadeva's *Bhāṭṭadīpikā* (17th cent.) known for its logic, and *Mīmāṁsākaustubha,* dealing with the *Sūtra.* Minor works are Rāghavānanda's *Mīmāṁsāsūtradīdhiti;* Rāmeśvara Śivayogin's *Subodhinī;* the *Bhaṭṭacintāmaṇī* of Viśveśvara Bhaṭṭa (also called Gāgā Bhaṭṭa); and Vedānta Deśika's *Seśvaramīmāṁsā,* an attempt to combine the views of the Mīmāṁsā and Vedānta, contending that the two systems are parts of one whole.

VEDĀNTA

The Vedānta is technically classified as Uttaramīmāṁsā. *Uttara* means "last"; *mīmāṁsā* means "investigation, examination, discussion, or consideration"; therefore, the last consideration of the Vedas. This system of thought is commonly referred to as the Vedānta, composed of *Veda* and *anta*, "end"; literally, "the end of the Vedas." Because the central topic is the Universal Spirit, called Brahman in Sanskrit, the names *Brahmasūtra* and *Brahmamīmāṁsā* are frequently used. Another title is *Śārīrakamīmāṁsā*, an inquiry into the embodied spirit.

Tradition attributes the *Vedāntasūtra* to Bādarāyāṇa whose actual date is quite unknown. The dates given range from 500 B.C. to as late as 200 A.D. Some scholars contend that Bādarāyaṇa is an alias for Vyāsa, the celebrated mythical sage who is regarded as the one who originally arranged the Vedas, the *Mahābhārata*, the Purāṇas, and other portions of Hindū sacred literature as well as the *Vedāntasūtra;* but the name Vyāsa ("compiler") seems to have been given to any great compiler or author.

Purpose

The central theme of the *Vedāntasūtra* is the philosophical teachings of the Upaniṣads concerning the nature and relationship of the three principles, that is, God, the world, and the soul, this also including the relation between the Universal Soul and the individual soul. Several solutions are given for this highly abstract problem and a vigorous defense is offered against the attacks of all opponents; it is a philosophy that preserves the ancient writings of the seers of the past.

The Vedānta, in its effort to embrace all knowledge, makes a systematic study and comprehensive investigation of all that has gone before, ever striving to reconcile all differences of opinion and belief. It contends that we have no right to disregard the findings of any seer; we are morally bound to examine the teachings of all minds that have attained enlightenment; we are duty bound to see wherein they are all in accord, for this is likely to be the Ultimate Truth. Where they differ, we are privileged to have our own opinion. These differences are said to be due to various viewpoints, different stages of development and training, as well as to social and hereditary backgrounds; therefore, the same Truth will vary according to the capacity of each individual for insight.

The Vedānta endeavours to sum up all human knowledge, presenting as Truth all that is universal, and reconciling all that is different. It accepts every thought, idea, and concept as a step forward; it evades nothing, and encompasses everything; it discards nothing and collects everything that is within the realm of human experience. However, it does not accept anything as final, dogmatic, or as the last word; instead it investigates, analyzes, and criticises all alike, forcing every proposition to verify and substantiate itself according to the rules of logical inquiry. It is, therefore, considered to be the treasure-chest of the glittering gems of spiritual insight gathered by the truth-seekers of the past.

The teachings of the Vedānta are said to describe the highest goals of human aspiration, and show the way to all who strive to achieve these exalted heights. It enables all to realize these teachings during this lifetime, for it expressly says that we do not have to suffer now in order to enjoy heavenly bliss later; instead, it reveals that knowledge of the Supreme Ultimate brings enlightenment during this lifetime.

Scope

The scope of the Vedānta's influence is declared by the vast amount of literature and by the various schools of thought that have developed from the original teachings of Bādarāyaṇa. Its three principal interpretations have found many champions among the founders of great religious sects of modern Hindūism. The lives and writings of the three principal leaders have been briefly discussed in the introduction.

Bādarāyaṇa maintains that the human intellect can never fathom the nature of the Ultimate Principle (Brahman), the subject of the *Vedāntasūtra,* for it lies outside the ken of the mind in the same way that the stars are beyond the reach of man's hands. This Ultimate Principle (Brahman) can be known only by direct intuition, never by logical inquiry and analysis. He teaches that the laws of logical inquiry are to be used only to establish the truth of various scriptural passages by removing conflicts that seem to arise, and thus to reconcile apparent contradictions, but never to reveal the nature of the Ultimate (Brahman). Reasoning can be used with certainty only in secular matters, for with reasoning alone it is impossible to remove doubt. Regardless of what one mind lays down as final, another mind will eventually show that the opposite is just as true and logical. Never can there be certainty, doubt always remains. Reasoning is meant only for secular matters; never for transcendental matters, such as the existence of God, the existence of an after-life, the nature of final emancipation, salvation, or release. Here the human intellect is helpless; such truths can be known only by direct intuition, or accepted on faith from those who have gained spiritual insight into the eternal scheme of things and have recorded their experiences in the ancient body of literature called Śruti, that which has been "heard," that is, revealed. For this reason, the Vedas are the supreme authority for Bādarāyaṇa.

It is said that the mere study of the Vedas, Upaniṣads and the Darśanas, the other systems of philosophy, however profound, will never awaken spiritual conviction; at best, they will provide only a general knowledge which will help to refine the heart and to incline the mind toward knowledge of the Ultimate. Nevertheless, it is claimed that doubts will continue to rise in the mind, the mist of uncertainty will still remain, and our faith will falter; therefore, Bādarāyaṇa contends that it is necessary to study the Vedānta in order to have these doubts removed for all time, for only the Vedānta contains specific knowledge of the Ultimate Principle. Its teachings are said to fortify the mind with the necessary arguments and reasons to strengthen our position until we grow firm in our understanding. The illumination of the mind is a matter of growth, and, therefore, the pre-requisite is a certain trait of disposition and bent of character which can be obtained only from the performance of duties and from study and association with those who have achieved these exalted heights and are, therefore, capable of leading a searching mind. Toward this ultimate goal, we are required to pass through the four-fold discipline which consists of:

- I. Viveka — right discrimination between the eternal and non-eternal, the real and the unreal. This comes from proper study.
- II. Vairāgya — right dispassion and indifference to the unreal and transitory. This consists of renunciation of all desires to enjoy the fruit of action both here and hereafter.
- III. Satsaṁpat — right conduct, which consists of the six acquirements, namely:
    - A. Śama — tranquility or control of thought by withdrawing the mind from worldly affairs.
    - B. Dama — self-restraint or control of conduct, restraining the senses from external actions.
    - C. Uparati — tolerance and renunciation of all sectarian religious observances, with the object of acquiring wisdom.
    - D. Titikṣā — endurance, bearing heat and cold and other pairs of opposites.
    - E. Śraddhā — faith.
    - F. Samādhāna, balanced mental equipoise; freedom from much sleep, laziness, and carelessness.
- IV. Mumukṣutva — right desire, which consists of earnestness to know the Ultimate Principle and thereby to

attain liberation. This will come when one dedicates his life to this single goal.

There are three classes of students who will accomplish this ultimate goal. They are:

1. Those who perform all acts with zeal and faith,
2. Those who perform all works for the good of humanity.
3. Those who are continually immersed in meditation.

Philosophy

The principal question raised by the *Vedāntasūtra* in its analysis of all the other systems is, "What is the cause of the Primal Motion in Nature?" The Vedānta, after examining all the other systems, pushed the cosmological inquiry one step further. It makes the observation that the world around us is one of wonderful design and construction; therefore, there must be an intelligent agent, for such action is never seen to operate in the gross world without an agent, for instance a car needs a driver, a plane a pilot, and the coming into being of a house necessitates an architect. Because of these observations, the Vedānta postulates an Intelligent Agent that guides and directs the workings of the subtle forces of the universe. This new category is called Brahman, which is the Ultimate Principle beyond which the mind cannot go. Because it is conceived as an agent, it is translated in the West as God or the Supreme Lord, which is well enough for those who wish to deify philosophical principles for the sake of religious worship; but until the concept is firmly rooted in our minds, it is advisable to use the philosophical term Brahman or the Ultimate Principle.

In criticising Sāṁkhya, the *Sūtra* says: "And because the inert matter becomes active only when there is the directive action of intelligence in it." [1]

The Vedānta contends that only an intelligent agent can set inert matter in motion, and since Puruṣa as defined in Sāṁkhya is

[1] *Vedāntasūtra,* ii, II, 2.

without the power of agency, another principle must be postulated that has the attribute of acting as an agent. Without this additional principle, two important problems arise in the Sāṁkhya system. First, how is the process of cosmic evolution started; and, secondly, how do we account for the phenomenon of Pralaya (annihilation of the world at the end of each cycle) when nature is at rest and there is no manifestation. There are other objections raised by the Vedāntist which concern the contradiction of terms; but only these two questions are directed toward the inherent structure of the system as a whole.

The Vedānta argues that only the existence of an intelligent agent can account for the mysterious super-imposition of Puruṣa and Prakrti, the primal impulse of nature, the regulation of the eternal cycle of events. This primal cause cannot be said to inhere in Prakṛti, for it would still exist as a force in liberated souls, since it is their very essence; therefore, they would always be present, and the process of cosmic evolution would never cease as it does during Pralaya. Even if they were dormant, as it is contended, during Pralaya, there is nothing to prevent them from awakening at some arbitrary time and from re-starting the process of evolution. The primal cause cannot be a modification of Prakṛti, for then it would be an effect; and an effect cannot affect itself, no more than fire can burn fire. The primal cause cannot be a modification of Puruṣa, because, by definition, Puruṣa is changeless; therefore, the primal cause must be an intelligent agent separate and apart from Puruṣa and Prakṛti in order to account for the beginning, continuance, and dissolution of each cycle of time. In no other way is it possible to explain the first beginning.

The Vedānta's principal objection to the Vaiśeṣika system is seen in the following Sūtra:

"On both assumptions (whether the Adṛṣṭa is in the atom or in the soul) there is no motion, and, consequently, there is absence of the origination of the world." [2]

Here again is the question of what is the cause of the original

[2] *Ibid.*, ii, II, 12.

or primal motion in nature. The Vaiśeṣika system taught that the original impulse was caused by the Adṛṣṭa of the soul. This is a Sanskrit term meaning "unseen, invisible, unknown"; that which is beyond the reach of observation or consciousness, as, for instance, the merit or demerit attaching to a man's conduct in one state of existence and the corresponding reward or punishment with which he is visited in another. In other words, it is our potential moral worth resulting from past conduct. It is the potential energy stored in the soul which will manifest itself as kinetic energy when the proper conditions obtain. For example, when we indulge in some particular form of pleasurable activity, there remains within us a latent desire to repeat that form of action at another time; and as soon as the environment provides an opportunity, we shall repeat that form of action. There are some forms of this latent energy that must remain latent for a long period of time before manifestation, in the same way that some seeds must remain latent for several years before they are ready to germinate. So with human beings, there are some latent effects that will not be manifest until another life-time; these effects are called Adṛṣṭa; and this latent effect, or Adṛṣṭa, is what the Vaiśeṣika doctrine says is the cause of the initial impulse in nature.

The Vedāntists raise the question: Does this potential energy reside in the aṇu or in the soul. They argue that, by definition, it does not reside in the aṇu; and it cannot be in the soul, for then it would be impossible for this potential energy to start action in something that is separate and apart, such as an aṇu. The Vaiśeṣika system says that the primal motion originates in the aṇu when it comes into the proximity of the soul with potential energy to start the action. The Vedāntists contend that this is not reasonable, for both are, by definition, without parts; and there can be no contact between things having no parts. During Pralaya, the souls are dormant, so they cannot originate motion; therefore, there could never be a first beginning. On the other hand, what is there to prevent them from awakening from this dormant condition at any arbitrary time and starting up the process of cosmic evolution? Because of these problems, the Vedānta maintains that it is necessary to postulate another category in order to account for the primal motion in nature.

The Vedānta raises other minor objections in its refutation of the standard systems, but for the most part these objections pertain to the contradiction of terms used by the other systems in establishing their position. So far as the order of cosmic evolution is concerned, the Vedānta accepts the order as outlined in the Sāṁkhya and explained in the Vaiśeṣika. These systems assume the existence of a first cause and devote their efforts to presenting the pattern of cosmic evolution and the interrelation of its parts. They were presenting an interpretation of nature for minds who were not interested in inquiring into the nature of the first cause. Fundamentally, all systems are in perfect accord; but each has its special contribution to the whole. The outstanding contribution of the Vedānta, aside from its analysis of the reasoning used by the other systems, is the additional category called Brahman, which causes the initial impulse in nature.

Brahman

The Ultimate Principle, Brahman, is defined in the *Sūtra* as follows:

"He, from whom proceeds the creation, preservation, and reconstruction of the universe, is Brahman." [3]

The word Brahman is derived from the Sanskrit root *bṛh,* "to grow, increase, expand, swell"; that which has reached its ultimate evolution, development, expansion, or growth. There are two other related terms that students will encounter in their readings which should be called to their attention at this time. In composition the term Brahma is frequently used instead of Brahman. This form is the nominative neuter ending and is used to indicate the One Universal Soul or divine essence and source from which all created things emanate and to which they return. It is the Self-existent, the Abso-

[3] *Ibid.,* i, I, 2.

lute, the Eternal, and is not generally an object of worship, but, rather, of meditation and knowledge. The personal form which is deified for the purpose of worship is spelt Brahmā, ending in the long "ā" which is the nominative masculine ending. This term is used when the personal spirit is intended. The mixing of the universal and individual spirit is a constant source of confusion, and it is paramount that the student learn early to differentiate between them, otherwise the philosophy will always seem to be a source of contradiction.

The Ultimate Principle (Brahman) is the creator, maintainer, and destroyer of everything in the universe, from the smallest miscroscopic germ to the largest celestial body. As such, it is the instrument and material cause of all manifest phenomena. In its transcendental aspect, it has two conditions, one in which it is at rest and in the other in which it is active, but at no time is it ever non-existent. Its passive condition is called in Sanskrit Asat, "non-being." This is the subtle condition of nature when the infinite variety of forms have become submerged into the eternal source from which they came. This is not a state of non-existence any more than there is a non-existence of clay when the various forms into which it has been cast have been destroyed. The clay still exists, but there is no being or manifestation of the forms which it is capable of assuming. This condition is called Pralaya, the time of universal dissolution, reabsorption, destruction, or annihilation of all manifest phenomena which takes place at the end of each world-cycle. Its active condition is called Sat, "being." During this period, it has three attributes, universal being, consciousness, and bliss, called Sat-Cit-Ānanda. Here it exists as pure light and serves as the support of everything in the universe. Its transcendental aspect can never be comprehended by the human mind; it can be understood only as a logical necessity, for there must be a support for manifest existence; and in order to evade the logical fallacy of *regressus ad infinitum,* no support can be postulated for the Ultimate Principle. For the same reason, it is the uncaused cause.

The problem arises, How is this Ultimate Principle, which is unlimited and undifferentiated, able to become limited? This is much the same as is witnessed in the phenomenon of electricity, which is unlimited, yet manifests in the limited forms of light, heat, motive power, without ever becoming exhausted. The immanent aspect of the Ultimate Principle has two inseparable forms: one without qualities, existing as pure spirit, called Nirguṇa; the other with qualities, existing as pure matter, called Saguṇa. These guṇas or qualities are the same as explained in Sāṁkhya. Spirit and Matter, also referred to as Name and Form, are called Ātman and Prakṛti in Vedānta.

In the immanent aspect of the Ultimate Principle the problem arises, How do things seemingly so different in this world arise from that which is so perfect? The principle that the cause must always be found in the effect applies only to the substance, and not to the forms. For example, the yarn used to weave a rug is the same in weight and chemical analysis before and after the rug is woven. Only the form has changed; so it is with the Ultimate Principle; it assumes an infinite variety of forms, but in essence it is ever the same.

In the transcendental aspect of the Ultimate Principle, the problem arises, Why is it that the Ultimate Principle is not tainted with the stains of worldly corruption observed in this world when all things are finally absorbed into the universal reservoir during the period of Pralaya? Particularly so when all things are supposed to be the same. It is explained that the defects of the world pertain to the transient forms and have nothing to do with the universal substance. For example, no amount of dirt can ever alter the chemical purity of the gold in a gold ring. So with the Ultimate Principle; the stains of worldliness belong only to its forms, never to its essence, which is infinite purity.

Ātman

The term Ātman, so frequently used in the Vedānta, is translated as "Soul or Self." Here it means the Universal Soul. Sometimes the word Paramātman is used to specify the soul of the universe, the highest and greatest vital principle, the Supreme Spirit.

Ātman is identified with Puruśa, existing as Pure Spirit and serving as the efficient or instrumental cause of the manifest world. It is without parts and, therefore, actionless, changeless, uncreated, eternal, and without the power of agency. It brings about all change by its mere presence, as the sun brings forth the spring flowers. This universal self is also known as Cit in the sense that it is universal consciousness, in contrast with universal matter, which is called Acit, "without consciousness." It is the One Universal, Infinite Consciousness without limitation, incapable of being extended or divided, permeating all space and manifesting itself in all things.

When a part of the Universal Breath becomes ensconced in the protoplasmic environment which it animates, it is called jīva. This term means "life" and has reference to the individual and personal soul, as distinguished from the Universal Soul. It is that which animates the inanimate; the eternal spirit unconscious of its true nature; the universal spirit limited by the internal organ. Therefore, the only difference between man and God is only one of degree, for ultimately they are one in the same way that the space inside a cup is the same as the space outside. There is only a difference of extent. Man is, therefore, only a spark of the infinite.

Māyā

The term Māyā, so commonly used in the Vedānta, means "delusion." It is that force which creates in nature the illusion of non-perception, as manifest in the diversified forms of the objective world. It is the dividing force in nature, the finitising principle, that which measures out the immeasurable and creates forms in the formless. It is postulated to account for the variety of things in the manifest world when in reality all is one. It is not a substance, but only a means of operation. It has two functions, one to conceal the real, the other to project the unreal. It pervades the universe, but its presence is inferred only from its effect.

It is identified with Prakṛti, Universal Matter, for it exists as the material cause of the universe. When nature is in a state of equilibrium, Universal Matter is called Prakṛti; but the first disturbance, the first conceived motion away from that original triune condition of equipoise, is called Māyā, because there has been no change in substance, but only in form; therefore, it is an illusion. As such, it is the material substratum of creation; it brings forth the universe by undergoing mutations. The world is regarded as Māyā because it has no reality, but is only an appearance of fleeting forms. The real is never affected by the unreal any more than the ground is made wet by a mirage.

When the universal force called Māyā operates in the mind of the individual, it is called Avidyā, "ignorance," especially in the spiritual sense. It is the subjective aspect, while Māyā is the objective aspect. It is an impersonal force in the consciousness of all individuals, producing the phenomena of illusion as demonstrated, for instance, when we look at a rope and think it is a snake. It is called Avidyā, "without knowledge," because knowledge will dissipate all the illusions of perception, as the sun dissipates the morning mist

Literature

The *Vedāntasūtra* of Bādarāyaṇa was not the only interpretation of the Upaniṣads, for others existed at that time. There were, for instance, Āśmarathya, holding that the soul was not absolutely different from nor absolutely like Brahma; Auḍulomi, holding the opinion that the soul is different until it is merged on final release; and Kāśakṛtsna, contending that the soul is absolutely identical with Brahma, which only presents itself as the soul. Bādarāyaṇa's viewpoint, therefore, is the outcome of the various schools of thought of his day. Today it is the accepted classic of the Vedānta system.

The *Sūtra* consists of about 560 sūtras divided into four books as follows:

1. Book one discusses the theory of Brahma, and the ultimate principle, reconciling all previous views.

2. Book two discusses all the objections against the viewpoint and shows the relationship of the world and soul with the ultimate principle, and how all eventually merge into it.
3. Book three discusses the theory of ways and means of attaining knowledge of the ultimate principle, that is, Brahmavidyā.
4. Book four discusses the theory of the departure of the soul after death.

Each book is divided into four parts called pādas; the sūtras of each section are related by what are called adhikaraṇas.

The sūtras are so concise and recondite that without commentary they are scarcely to be understood. They refuse to be caught in any definite interpretation. It is thought that Bādarāyaṇa wrote them in this manner so that they would have universal appeal and not be limited to any definite time or place, thereby serving as the source of knowledge for all peoples during all ages. The literature that has arisen from this source has been discussed in the introduction.

KĀŚMĪR ŚAIVISM

Kāśmīr Śaivism is a system of idealistic monism based on the *Śivasūtra.* It derives its name from the tradition that the *Śivasūtra* was supposedly revealed in Kāśmīr by Śiva himself. Because this system deals with the three-fold principle of God, Soul, and Matter, it is also called Trikśāsana, Trikaśāstra or simply Trika. The terms Kāśmīr Śaivism and Trika may be used interchangeably.

The Father of Kāśmīr Śaivism was Vasugupta to whom the Śivasūtra is assigned. There are several accounts relating how the *Śivasūtra* was revealed to Vasugupta, but in no instance is it to be understood that Śiva materalized and whispered it into the ear of Vasugupta; instead, it means that Vasugupta received the sūtras by inspiration rather than by intellectual analysis. That is, after a lifetime devoted to study and meditation, he finally awakened the inner depths of consciousness through the practice of Yoga and saw reality in all its fullness. Afterwards he recorded his experience much in the same way as a traveler returning from a foreign land leaves a written account of his journey.

Little is known of the life of Vasugupta aside from the fact that he lived during the end of the 8th century and the beginning of the 9th century. His retirement was spent in a small hermitage below the holy Mahādeva peak in the lovely valley of the Hārwan stream behind the Shālimar garden near Srīngar, the capital of Kāśmīr.

Purpose

The purpose of the *Śivasūtra* was to preserve for man the principles of monism which had existed in the literature called the Tantras. According to tradition, these principles had existed since time immemorial in the minds of the ancient ṛṣis (seers) who were the repositories of all spiritual knowledge. With the appearance of this new age, Kali Yuga, came the disappearance of these enlightened minds and the vanishing of their knowledge. The result was a turning toward a dualistic and pluralistic interpretation of Nature, losing sight of the monastic aspect of the Ultimate Reality. In order to revive an understanding of Truth in its ultimate form, it is believed that Śiva revealed the *Śivasūtra* to Vasugupta in order to lead man back to the path of monism.

Scope

Kāśmīr Śaivism accepts the fundamental premise that pure consciousness is the spiritual substance of the universe. However, it differs from the Sāṁkhya and the Vedānta systems in its interpretation of the three basic problems: (1) What is the nature of the ultimate reality; (2) What is the cause of its first movement; and (3) What is the nature of its manifest form? The concepts involved can be briefly stated.

What is the nature of the ultimate reality? To solve this problem the Sāṁkhya system postulates two independent realities, Puruṣa and Prakṛti, and thus constructs a dualism. The Vedānta system postulates a single ultimate reality, Brahman, and then supports this solution by the introduction of another principle called Māyā, which is held to be not real, yet not unreal, which is counter to logic. Therefore, the monism offered by Vedānta is tainted with the suggestion of a dualism. Kāśmīr Śaivism meets the problem by constructing a pure monism which postulates a single reality with two aspects, one Transcendental and the other Immanent. The former is beyond all manifestations, and the latter pervades the universe of manifest phenomena. Both are real, for the effect cannot be different from the cause. In this way Śaivism reconciles the dualism of the Sāṁkhya with the monism of the Vedānta. However, it is said that logic can never construct an unassailable monism; therefore, final proof of these two aspects can be had only by the spiritual experience of Samādhi (union) attained through the practice of Yoga.

What is the cause of its first movement? The Sāṁkhya says that it is due to the association of Puruṣa and Prakṛti, but no reason is given for the cause of the association. The Vedānta contends that only an intelligent agent can set universal consciousness in motion; so it postulates the additional category Brahman, translated as the Supreme Lord. Both systems tell where the initial impulse originates, but neither explains the cause. To solve this problem, Kāśmīr Śaivism teaches that consciousness eternally alternates between two phases, rest and action, that is, transcendental and immanent. The transcendental phase is a period of potentiality technically called Pralaya, "dissolution and reabsorption." It is the passive phase of consciousness. Here all the forms of manifest phenomena are dissolved and their essence is reabsorbed by the universal consciousness. During the period of potentiality, called Pralaya, all manifestations are dormant in the same way that the characteristics of an oak tree are dormant in an acorn. After a latent period, the universal seeds of potentiality begin to germinate, and consciousness becomes active. The active phase of consciousness is here called Sṛṣṭi, that is, the creation of the universe. This phase of manifestation is also called Ābhāsa, the root *bhās*, "to appear or shine", therefore, the shining forth. Each phase of action is said to generate the seeds of potentiality that will germinate during the period of rest to bring the next phase of action into being, in the same way that the flowering of an apple tree produces the seeds for the growth of another tree. A complete cycle consisting of a Sṛṣṭi and a Pralaya—that is, a creation and a dissolution, is technically called a Kalpa which is said to last 4,320,000,000 years, after which another will follow. This periodic rhythm of consciousness is without absolute beginning or final end. The movement is governed by the Law of Karma, which is based on the principle that for every action there is a reaction. It is popularly known as the Law of Cause and Effect. So the first movement of consciousness is a reaction from past action. All Nature is regulated by this universal law from the lowest form of life to the highest celestial being; so Brahman, the deification of the ultimate principle by the Vedānta system, is governed by the Law of Karma, the cause of the initial impulse.

What is the nature of its manifestation? All three schools of thought acknowledge the existence of the manifest world, but each interprets differently the relationship between the ultimate reality of pure consciousness and the manifest world of matter. The Sāṁkhya doctrine contends that there are two independent realities, Spirit and Matter; therefore, the manifest world is the appearance of unconscious matter as separate and independent reality. The Vedānta doctrine contends there is only one ultimate reality which never changes; therefore, the manifest world is merely an appearance. In accord with this concept, the process of the evolution of consciousness is called Vivarta, derived from *vi-vart,* "to turn round, go astray," used in this sense to mean error or illusion; therefore, the manifest world is said not to exist any more than does the water in a mirage. Kāśmīr Śaivism contends that there is only one reality, but it has two aspects; therefore, the manifestation is real. This is based on the argument that the effect cannot be different from its cause. The world of matter is only another form of consciousness in the same way that the web of a spider is a part of its substance in another form. In this system the process of the evolution of consciousness is called Ābhāsa, "a shining forth." This is founded on the belief that the ultimate consciousness never changes, but always remains transcendent and undiminished in the same way that a candle lighted from another candle does not diminish the light of the first candle.

Kāśmīr Śaivism postulates thirty-six categories to explain the process of cosmic evolution, thus providing the most complete analysis of Nature yet devised by any system of philosophy. The first twenty-four categories, from Pṛthivī (Earth) to Prakṛti (Matter), are the same as those postulated by the Sāṁkhya system; the remaining twelve categories show how Puruṣa (Spirit) is derived from higher principles. Each principle follows inevitably from the preceding one in accord with the law of logical necessity. The stages are technically called Tattvas, "thatness, truth, reality," that is, the true principle or essence from which each stage is derived. Since the first twenty-four stages, from Pṛthivī to Prakṛti, are the same, only the last twelve, from Puruṣa to the Ultimate Reality in its transcendental aspect will be discussed here. For the others, reference may be made to the chapter on the Sāṁkhya.

Philosophy

The transcendental aspect of Nature is called Parāsaṁvit. The term is derived from the root *vid,* "to know," and means Pure Consciousness, the Supreme Experience. Another term commonly used is Paramaśiva, the Supreme Śiva, "in whom all things lie"; therefore, the deity that personifies the ultimate form of consciousness.

The Transcendental aspect of pure consciousness exists as a logical necessity, for there must be a condition beyond which further analysis cannot go in order to evade the logical fallacy of *regressus ad infinitum.* Since something cannot come out of nothing, this Ultimate Reality must contain all things in their fullness. Therefore, in order to account for feeling, it must be Universal Consciousness (Cit); in order to account for joy it must be Universal Bliss (Ānanda); in order to account for desire, it must be Universal Desire (Icchā); in order to account for knowledge, it must be Universal Intelligence (Jñāna); in order to account for action, it must be Universal Action (Kriyā). The technical term used to describe the eternal substance in which all things inhere is Caitanya, which means the changeless aspect of pure consciousness, the Universal Intelligence or Spirit. It is technically defined as Sat-Cit-Ānanda, that is, Being-Consciousness-Bliss. This does not mean that Being is a Consciousness *of* Bliss, but that Being is Conscious *and* Bliss *as such.* This represents the perfect condition of the supreme ideal, when Nature rests in Herself, when there is no feeling of a want to be satisfied, when there is no feeling of a need to go forth. It is the transcendental condition of universal potentiality.

Caitanya is, therefore, pure consciousness and can be defined as the boundless plenum in which the universe is born, grows, and dies; the continuum of experience that pervades, sustains, and vitalizes all existence; the source of all things; the spiritual substance of all things; the foundation upon which all things appear; the one and only reality. It is by definition without parts (Niṣkala), and, therefore, unproduced, indestructible, and motionless, for all these necessitate the displacement of parts. It must also be eternal and all-pervading, and therefore, with no inside or outside; it is without attributes (Nirguṇa), and, therefore, beyond time and space; it is beyond the mind, and, therefore, not a subject of knowledge. It is a principle of pure experience and can be realized only by the ecstasy of spiritual illumination.

To account for the phenomenon of manifestation affirmed by experience, this doctrine postulates the immanent aspect of pure consciousness; the aspect of change and action. All change is said to take place on the surface of consciousness as a wave appears on the surface of the ocean, and this appearance must consist of consciousness as a wave consists of water. To manifest means, by definition, to appear or become evident to the mind, here the universal mind. To appear means to be perceived, which implies the perceived and the perceiver, that is, subject and object. In this universal condition both factors must be consciousness, for there is nothing else. Consciousness, then, in its immanent aspect, by definition becomes visible to Itself as subject and object.

The two factors, subject and object, in the active aspect of consciousness are technically called Aham (I) and Idam (This). They are as closely related as wetness is to water; the removal of one destroys the other. They are consciousness and the power of consciousness. They appear simultaneously and are eternally related. During the period of universal dissolution, they are in a condition of equilibrium. When the balance is upset and the process of cosmic evolution begins, the first appearance is the dual factor of Aham (I) and Idam (This) which characterizes the immanent or active aspect of consciousness.

The subject and object must be considered separately for the purpose of explanation, but it must always be borne in mind that they are both present, only one is more evident in the same way that a picture has two sides, a front and a back, but only one side can be seen at a time. These two factors are the first two tattvas in the process of cosmic evolution, and are technically called the Śiva Tattva and the Śakti Tattva.

The Śiva Tattva

The first factor in the process of cosmic evolution is called the Śiva Tattva. The term Śiva is used to deify the ultimate condition of consciousness in its Immanent aspect for the purpose of worship. Consciousness in this condition is technically called Cit, the static aspect of consciousness in the manifest world. Consciousness must be considered here in the broadest possible sense of the term, as the power to know, to feel, and to act. Actually there is no English equivalent for Cit. Only study and reflection will reveal its full connotation.

By definition a manifestation necessitates a subject and object. The Śiva Tattva is postulated to account for the Subject (Aham) of the dual relationship of universal manifestation. In this condition, consciousness is the subject, knower, experiencer; it is the static center of all things; it is the static support of all things; it is the substratum of all change, as is the bed of a river. It can never be seen, but it can be known by its effects.

In this condition the emphasis is on the Aham (I) without any awareness of the existence of Idam (This). It is pure consciousness; the ideal universe of perfect equilibrium has vanished, and consciousness has begun to stir. The Śiva Tattva is the Cit aspect of the universal condition of Sat-Cit-Ānanda.

Since the Śiva Tattva represents the passive aspect of pure consciousness, it is dependent upon the active aspect of consciousness to bring it into being. To account for this aspect of consciousness, the next category is postulated.

The Śakti Tattva

The second factor in the process of cosmic evolution is called the Śakti Tattva. The term Śakti is derived from the root *śak,* "to be able, to be capable of"; therefore, the power of consciousness to act. It is the kinetic aspect of consciousness.

By logical necessity the Śakti Tattva is postulated to account for the Object (Idam) of the dual relationship of universal manifestation. It accounts for the universal cause of all motion and change observed throughout the manifest world. Śakti is the universal stream of consciousness that brings all things into being and destroys all things at the end of each cycle of time. As Śiva is the Cit-aspect of the universal condition of Sat-Cit-Ānanda, Śakti is the Ānanda-aspect. When this condition is predominant, a condition of supreme bliss is experienced.

The Śakti Tattva represents the force that negates universal consciousness by producing a strain on the surface of consciousness. It polarizes consciousness into the positive and negative, the Aham and Idam, the Subject and Object. It is the universal energy that brings all things into being, and, as such, it is considered as the feminine aspect of Nature, the Mother of the Universe.

The first two tattvas, Śiva Tattva and Śakti Tattva, are unproduced, and therefore, eternal. During the period of Pralaya, universal dissolution, they exist in the universal sea of pure consciousness in a state of equilibrium, ever ready to manifest once the balance is upset. Since they are unproduced, they are not considered as stages in the process of the evolution of consciousness. They are merely an appearance on the surface of consciousness as a swell on the surface of the ocean before the manifestation of a wave.

Śakti, Cosmic Energy, is said to have three principal modes to account for the three fundamental psychological steps that precede the determination of every action. They are technically called Icchā, the power of Will; Jñāna, the power of Knowledge; and Kriyā, the power of Action. One follows the other in logical succession; and with the predominance of each respective mode in the process of the evolution of consciousness, the first three tattvas produced come into being.

The Sadāśiva Tattva

The third stage in the process of cosmic evolution is called the Sadāśiva Tattva. This term is compounded of *sadā* "always," and *śiva,* "happy or prosperous"; therefore, "always happy or prosperous." This stage is also called the Sadākhya Tattva, the state in which there is the first notion of Being.

By logical necessity, in any manifestation there must be a first step forward. The Sadāśiva Tattva is postulated to account for that phenomenon in universal manifestation. It is, therefore, the first evolute of consciousness. As a produced thing, it must, by definition, have parts; those parts are the dual relationship of *I am This.* Here the emphasis is on the Aham (I). The subject (Aham) is said to become aware of itself in relation to its object (Idam). In the universal condition the entire experience is subjective, for there is no inner and outer, as in the world known to us.

This category accounts for the power of Universal Desire, technically called the Icchā Śakti, the Will-aspect of Śakti, or consciousness. It manifests itself as a vague and indistinct feeling, an undefined and unformulated idea that eludes the mind. It is the condition that precedes any determinate action. It is referred to as the state of Divine Wonder.

As produced tattva, it is destructible, and, therefore, not eternal. As the first evolute produced in the process of the evolution of consciousness, it is the last evolute dissolved in the involution of consciousness at the time of universal reabsorption.

The Īśvara Tattva

The fourth stage in the process of cosmic evolution is called the Īśvara Tattva. The term Īśvara means "Lord." It is used to deify that condition in Nature when all is recognized as One.

This tattva is postulated to account for that condition when the subject (Aham) recognizes the object (Idam). Here the relationship is *This am I,* with the emphasis on the *This* (Idam). It is the stage of complete self-identification, as when one awakens from a sound sleep. Here This (Idam) is said to emerge into full view, and the Divine Glory of his being is recognized.

This category accounts for the power of Universal Knowledge, technically called the Jñāna Śakti, the Knowledge-aspect of Śakti, or consciousness. It is knowledge as such without reference to any emotion; it is pure awareness without reaction. There is no desire to go toward or away. It is the knowledge that precedes ultimate action.

The Sadvidyā Tattva

The fifth stage of cosmic evolution is called the Sadvidyā Tattva. This term is compounded of *sat,* "true," and *vid,* "to know," and means to have true knowledge. It is also called Śuddhā Vidyā Tattva, meaning the tattva of pure knowledge.

This tattva is postulated to account for the complete unity in the dual relationship of *I am This.* It is, therefore, the condition of complete recognition without emphasis either on the subject (Aham) or on the object (Idam).

This category accounts for power of universal action, technically called Kriyā Śakti, the Action-aspect of Śakti, or consciousness. In the preceding tattvas, action has been absent. In the Sadāśiva Tattva, consciousness was lost in the ecstasy of divine wonder while embracing Itself as the subject (Aham); in the Isvara Tattva, consciousness was overcome by exaltation while gazing at Itself as the object (Idam). In the Sadvidyā Tattva, consciousness looks first at Aham (I) and then at Idam (This), which necessitates movement; therefore, this tattva is said to manifest that aspect of universal consciousness that creates all things.

The first five tattvas, from Śiva Tattva to Sadvidyā Tattva, are classified for the purpose of worship as the Pure category (Śuddha Tattva). They represent the manifestation of the universal aspect of consciousness in contrast to the limited aspect to follow. They are called Pure because the dual relationship of subject and object is a single unit, that is, the object is seen as a part of the subject. In the condition to follow, the subject and object are separated, so that the object is seen as something separate and apart from the subject. The force that separates them is another mode of Śakti, the active aspect of consciousness. This force is technically called Māyā Śakti, the power of consciousness to separate and divide.

The Māyā Tattva and Its Evolutes

The sixth category in the process of cosmic evolution is called the Māyā Tattva. The term Māyā means "delusion." Here it is used to mean the veiling, obscuring force of Nature. As such, it displays universal consciousness as a duality.

The category of Māyā is postulated to account for the manifestation of form out of the formless, the finite out of the infinite. The same principle was postulated in the Vedānta system, but there it was said to be not real or not unreal, that is, not part of the Ultimate, yet not something else. In this doctrine, Kāśmīr Śaivism, Māyā is considered not as a separate reality, but as the gross power of consciousness, and is referred to as Māyā Śakti. During the period of universal dissolution (Pralaya), it is in its subtle aspect. At no time is it ever non-existent; it is merely non-active, that is, dormant; therefore, it is eternal and unproduced.

Māyā is defined as the finitising principle, that which limits the universal conditions of consciousness and produces the states of limited experience. It is said to cast asunder the Divine Unity of the Godhead and brings Mind and Matter into being.

The reason why Māyā exerts its influence at this stage is found in the law of Nature that every period of action is followed by a period of rest, as witnessed by the fact that sleep always follows action. When Nature goes to sleep after the experience of universal manifestation, the five evolutes of Māyā appear; therefore, the world of limited experience is the cosmic dream of nature.

The Kañcukas

The five evolutes of Māyā are called the Kañcukas, derived from the root *kañj*, "to bind." Here it means the contraction by the power of Māyā of the five universal modes of consciousness, namely, Cit-Ānanda-Icchā-Jñāna-Kriyā. These five forms of universal power as displayed in the five preceding tattvas, Śiva, Śakti, Sadāśiva, Īśvara, and Sadvidyā gave rise to the universal experience of: Eternal Existence (Nityatva), All-Pervasiveness (Vyāpakatva), All-Completeness (Pūrṇatva), All-Knowledge (Sarvajñatva), and All-Powerfulness (Sarvakartṛtva). When these five universal conditions are limited by Māyā, the five Kañcukas come into being. They are Time, Space, Desire, Limited Knowledge, and Limited Power, their technical names being Kāla, Niyati, Rāga, Vidyā, and Kalā.

Kāla limits the universal condition of Eternal Existence; therefore, it is the origin of Time, the determinate when, that is, now and then.

Niyati is derived from *ni-yam*, "to regulate, to restrain." It is the power that limits the universal condition of All-Pervasiveness; therefore, it is the origin of Space, the determinate where, that is, here and there.

Rāga is derived from the root *rañj*, "to color," meaning the feeling of interest and desire. It is the power that limits the universal condition of All-Completeness; therefore it is the origin of Desire.

Vidyā is derived from the root *vid*, "to know." It is the power that limits the universal condition of All-Knowledge; therefore. it is the origin of Limited Knowledge.

Kalā means a small part of anything, from the Indo-European base *gele–"to strike, hew, break off." It is the power that limits the universal condition of All-Powerfulness; therefore, it is the origin of Limited Power.

The following outline will best show the relationship of these terms:

Tattva	Śakti	Universal Experience	Kañcukas	Limited Experience
Śiva	Cit	Eternal Existence (Nityatva)	Kāla	Time
Śakti	Ānanda	All-Pervasiveness (Vyāpakatva)	Niyati	Space
Sadāśiva	Icchā	All-Completeness (Pūrṇatva)	Rāga	Desire
Īśvara	Jñāna	All-Knowledge (Sarvajñātva)	Vidyā	Limited Knowledge
Sadvidyā	Kriyā	All-Powerfulness (Sarvakartṛtva)	Kalā	Limited Power

The result of Māyā and its evolutes, the Kañcukas, is the production of Puruṣa and Prakṛti. At this stage, the Subject (Aham) and the Object (Idam) are completely severed and look upon each other as mutually exclusive. Here the dual world of the mind and matter is permanently established.

For the purpose of worship, the tattvas from Māyā to Puruṣa are classified as the Pure-Impure Category (Śuddhāśuddha Tattva). They are so termed because they represent that condition in Nature which exists between the world of Pure Unity (Śuddha Tattva), consisting of the pure categories from Śiva Tattva to Sadvidyā Tattva, and the world of Impure Duality (Aśuddha Tattva), made up of the remaining twenty-four tattvas from Prakṛti to Pṛthivī.

To summarize, all the tattvas may be outlined as follows:

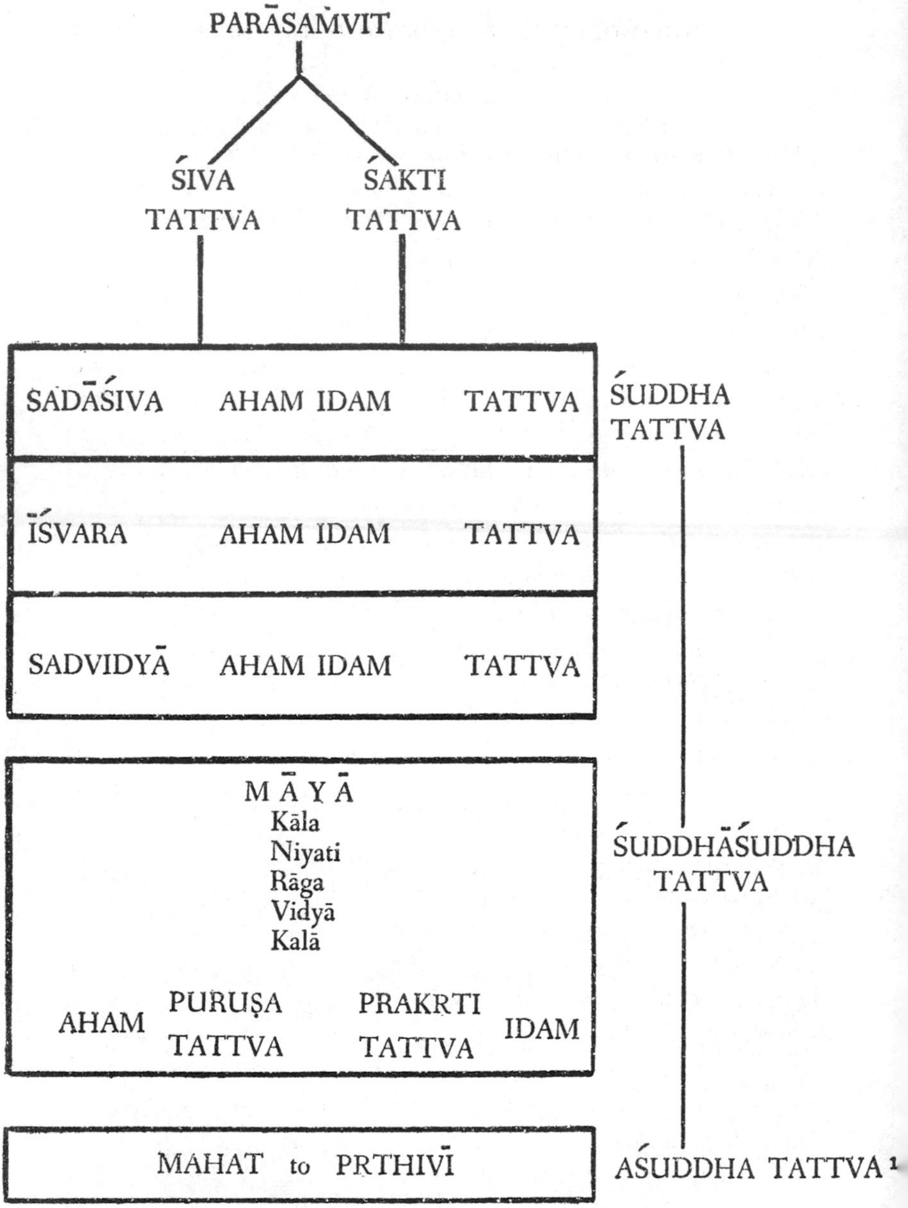

[1] For details see the Sāmkhya chart.

Literature

The literature of Kāśmīr Śaivism is classified under three broad divisions: (1) *The Āgamaśāstra*, (2) *The Spandaśāstra*, and (3) *The Pratyabhijñāśāstra.* Their chief feature and a few of the principal and still existing works are as follows:

The Āgamaśāstra is regarded as of superhuman authorship. It lays down the doctrine and the practices of the system as revelations which are believed to have come down (āgama) through the ages, being handed down from teacher to pupil. The most important Tantras belonging to this group are *Mālinī Vijaya, Svacchanda, Vijñāna Bhairava, Ucchuṣma Bhairava, Mṛgendra, Mataṅga, Netra, Naiśvāsa, Svāyambhuva,* and *Rudrayāmala.* With the passage of time there developed a tendency toward a dualistic interpretation of these works; therefore the *Śivasūtra* was revealed by Śiva to Vasugupta to stop the spread of this dualistic teaching. According to some authorities, Vasugupta wrote an explanatory work of the *Śivasūtra* called the *Spandāmṛta,* both of which he transmitted to his pupils who promulgated his teachings.

The Spandaśāstra elaborates in greater detail the doctrines of the *Śivasūtra* but does not undertake to discuss the philosophy upon which they are based. The founder of this branch of the literature was Kallaṭa Bhaṭṭa (c. 850–900 A.D.), the famed pupil of Vasugupta. His first treatise is entitled *Spandasūtra* and is generally called the *Spandakārikā.* It is believed that Kallaṭa Bhaṭṭa made liberal use of the *Spandāmṛita* of Vasugupta, making only a few additions and alterations of his own. Kallaṭa Bhaṭṭa wrote a short Vṛtti or commentary on the *Spandakārikā* which is called *Spanda Sarvasva.* Other commentaries which he wrote are *Tattvārthacintamaṇi* and *Madhuvāhinī,* both of which are lost. By means of these works, Kallaṭa Bhaṭṭa spread the teachings of Vasugupta.

The pupils who continued the tradition of Kallaṭa Bhaṭṭa form a line of spiritual succession. Kallaṭa Bhaṭṭa handed down the *Śivasūtra* with the commentaries to his cousin, Pradyumna Bhaṭṭa; he in turn to his son, Prajñārjuna; he to his pupil Mahādeva; he to his son,

Śrīkaṇṭha Bhaṭṭa; and he to Bhāskara (c. 11th cent.). The interpretation of the *Śivasūtra* as taught by Kallaṭa Bhaṭṭa is preserved in the commentary by Bhāskara, called the *Śivasūtravārttika*. From this work, we learn that Kallaṭa Bhaṭṭa developed only the doctrines of the *Śivasūtra*. Two other outstanding commentators who have contributed to the *Spanda* branch of the literature are Utpala Vaiṣṇava, author of *Spandapradīpikā*; and Rāmakaṇṭha (c. 900–925 A.D.), author of *Spandavivṛti* and also of commentaries on the *Mataṅgatantra* and the *Bhagavadgītā* from the Śaiva point of view.

The Pratyabhijñāśāstra is regarded as the philosophy proper of Kāśmīr Śaivism, for this branch of the literature treats specifically the philosophical reasons for the doctrines of the *Śivasūtra*. No religion can survive in India unless it is supported by philosophical reasons; so it was necessary to formulate the philosophical system upon which the doctrines were based. The founder of this branch of the literature was Somānanda (c. 850–900 A.D.) another distinguished pupil of Vasugupta. He is said to have written an exhaustive philosophical treatment of the doctrines of Vasugupta, supporting them by reason and refuting all opponents. The first work of Somānanda which laid the foundation of this branch of literature was the *Śivadṛṣṭi*. This was considered the basic text of Kāśmīr Śaivism; however, it is no longer extant. Somānanda composed a Vṛtti or commentary on the *Śivadṛṣṭi*. This, too, is lost.

The work of Somānanda was carried on in greater detail by the line of famed disciples to follow. The first was Utpalacaraya (c. 900–950 A.D.), author of the *Pratyabhijñāsūtra*, which embodied the teachings of his master, Somānanda. The importance of this treatise is seen from the fact that its name has been used for this branch of the literature, and has specific reference to the philosophy of Kāśmīr Śaivism. Utpala is said merely to have summarized the teachings of Somānanda in the *Pratyabhijñāsūtra*. This work with its commentaries and the other works it has inspired, now constitutes perhaps the greater portion of the existing writings on Kāśmīr Śaivism. The pupil of Utpalācharya was his son, Laksmana (c. 950–1000 A.D.), who is remembered because of his gifted pupil, Abhinava

Gupta (c. 993–1015 A.D.) who became the great Śaiva author. The well known commentaries of Abhinava Gupta are *Mālinīvijayavārttika*, *Parātriṁśikāvivaraṇa*, *Śivadṛṣṭyālocana*, *Pratyabhijñāvimarśinī* (*Laghvīvṛtti*, or Shorter Commentary), and *Pratyabhijñāvivṛtivimarśinī* (*Bṛihatīvṛtti* or Longer Commentary). Besides these he wrote the famous *Tantrāloka*, *Tantrasāra*, *Paramārthasāra*, and many others.

Other outstanding teachers and their works are Kṣemarāja (11th cent.), author of *Śivasūtravṛtti*, *Śivasūtravimarśinī*, and *Pratyabhijñāhṛidaya*. He also made contributions to the *Spanda* literature with *Spandasaṅdoha* and *Spandanirṇaya*. Besides these he wrote commentaries on several of the Tantras. Next followed his pupil, Yogarāja (12th cent.), author of a commentary on the *Paramārthasāra* of Abhinava Gupta. The labours of Yogarāja were carried on by Jayaratha (12th cent.) who wrote a commentary on the *Tantrāloka* of Abhinava Gupta. The last of this line was Śivopādhyāya (18th cent.), author of a commentary on the *Vijñānabhairavatantra*. With Śivopādhyāya the history of the literature of Kāśmīr Śaivism comes to a close. The faith still endures, and a few scholars continue to study the ancient literature, but no new contributions are being made.

GENERAL WORKS

Āchārya, Śrī Ānanda, *Brahmadarsanam or Intuition of the Absolute*. New York, Macmillan Co., 1917.

Ballantyne, J. R., *Hindu Philosophy*. Calcutta, J. Ghose and Co., 1879.

———, *The Aphorisms of the Nyāya and Vaiśeṣika and the other systems of Indian Philosophy.*

———, *The Vedānta-Sara.* Madras, Christian Literature Society for India, 1898.

Banerjea, K. M., *Dialogues on Hindu Philosophy, comprising the Nyāya, the Sāṅkhya, the Vedānta; to which is added a discussion of the authority of the Vedas.* London, Williams and Norgate, 1861.

Barnett, L. D., *Brahma Knowledge.* London, John Murray, 1911.

Barua, Benimadhab, *A History of Pre-Buddhistic Indian Philosophy.* Calcutta University Press, 1921.

Bennett, Allan, *The Wisdom of the Aryas.* London, Kegan Paul, Trench, Trübner & Co., 1923.

Bhattacharyya, Hari Mohan, *Studies in Philosophy.* Adyar, Madras, Theosophical Publishing House, 1915.

Bose, Ram Chandra, *Hindu Philosophy.* New York, Funk & Wagnalls, 1884.

Brown, Brian, *The Wisdom of the Hindus.* New York, Brentano's, 1921.

Colebrooks, H. T., *Essays on religion and philosophy of the Hindus.* New ed. London, 1858.

———, *Papers on the Nyāya and Vaiśeṣika and the other systems of Indian Philosophy.*

Cowell, E. B., and Gough, A. E., *The Sarva Darśana Saṁgraha or Review of the Different Systems of Hindu Philosophy,* by Madhava Āchārya. London, Kegan Paul, Trench, Trübner & Co., 1904.

Dasgupta, S. N., *Hindu Mysticism.* Chicago, Open Court, 1927.

———, *A History of Indian Philosophy.* 3 vols., Cambridge, The University Press, 1922.

Desa, S. A., *A Study of the Indian Philosophy.* Bombay, Thacker & Co., 1906.

Deussen, Paul, *Allgemeine Geschichte der Philosophie mit be-*

sonderer Berücksichtigung der Religionen. Leipzig, F. A. Brockhaus, 1894.

———, *The Philosophy of the Upanishads.* Edinburgh, T. & T. Clark, 1908.

Elliot, Sir Charles, *Hinduism and Buddhism.* 3 Vols., London, Edward Arnold & Co., 1921.

Farquhar, J. N., *A Primer of Hinduism.* London, Oxford University Press, 1912.

———, *Outline of the Religious Literature of India.* London, 1920.

———, *The Crown of Hinduism.* Oxford University Press, 1915.

Garbe, Richard, *Philosophy of Ancient India.* Chicago, Open Court, 1899.

Gough, A. E., *The Philosophy of the Upanishads, and Ancient Indian Metaphysics.* London, Kegan Paul, Trench, Trübner and Co., Ltd., 1903.

Grousset, René, *Les philosophies indiennes, les systèmes.* 2 Vols., Paris, Desclee, de Brouwer et c^ie^, 1931.

Harrison, Max Hunter, *Hindu Monism and Pluralism.* London, Oxford University Press, 1932.

Hastings, James, ed., *Encyclopaedia of Religion and Ethics.* New York, Charles Scribner's Sons, 1916.

Hiriyanna, M., *Outlines of Indian Philosophy.* London, Geo. Allen & Unwin, Ltd., 1932.

Iyengar, Srinivasa, *Outlines of Indian Philosophy.*

Keith, A. Berriedale, *A History of Sanskrit Literature.* Oxford, The Clarendon Press, 1928.

———, *Classical Sanskrit Literature.* Oxford, The Clarendon Press, 1928.

———, *The Religion and Philosophy of Veda and Upanishads.* (Harvard Oriental Series, Vols. 31 and 32), Cambridge, Mass., 1925.

Macdonell, Arthur A., *A History of Sanskrit Literature.* New York, Appleton & Co., 1914.

MacDonald, K. S., *The Brahmanas of the Vedas.* Madras, Christian Literature Society for India, 1901.

Masson-Oursel, Paul, *Esquisse d'une histoire de la philosophie indienne.* Paris, P. Geuthner, 1923.

McLaurin, Hamish, *Eastern Philosophy for Western Minds.* Boston, The Stratford Co., 1933.

Monier-Williams, Sir Monier, *Brahmanism and Hinduism.* New York, Macmillan and Co., 1891.

———, *Indian Wisdom.* London, Luzac & Co., 1893.

Mudaliyar, S. Sabaratna, *Essentials of Hinduism*. Madras, Maykandan Press, 1915.

Müller, Max, *The Six Systems of Indian Philosophy*. London, Longmans, Green and Company, 1928.

Nath, Rai Bahadur Lala Baij, *Ancient and Modern Hinduism*. Meerut, Office of the Vaishya Hitkari, 1899.

Prasad, Jwala, *Introduction to Indian Philosophy*. Allahabad, The Indian Press, Ltd., 1928.

Radhakrishnan, S., *Indian Philosophy*. 2 Vols., London, George Allen & Unwin, Ltd., 1927.

———, *The Hindu View of Life*. London, George Allen & Unwin, Ltd., 1927.

———, *The Philosophy of the Upanishads*. London, George Allen & Unwin, Ltd., 1924.

Ranade, R. D., *A Constructive Survey of Upanishadic Philosophy*. Poona, Oriental Book Agency, 1926.

Seal, Brajendranath, *The Positive Sciences of the Ancient Hindus*. London, Longmans, Green & Co., 1915.

Sen, Guru Prosad, *An Introduction to the Study of Hinduism*. Calcutta, Thacker, Spink & Co., 1893.

Shastri, Prabhu Dutt, *Essentials of Eastern Philosophy*. New York, Macmillan & Co., 1928.

Sircar, Mahendranath, *Hindu Mysticism According to the Upaniṣads*. London, Kegan Paul, Trench, Trübner & Co., Ltd., 1934.

Sri Ramakrishna Centenary Memorial, *The Cultural Heritage of India*. 3 Vols., Belur Math, Calcutta, pub. by Swami Avinashananda.

Strauss, Otto, *Indische Philosophie*. Munich, E. Reinhardt, 1925.

Vaswani, T. L., *The Aryan Ideal*. Madras, Ganesh & Co., 1922.

Vivekananda, *The Complete Works of Swami Vivekananda*. 5 Vols., Almora, Advaita Ashrama, 1915.

Wilkins, W. J., *Modern Hinduism*. London, T. Fisher Unwin, 1887.

Winternitz, M., *A History of Indian Literature*. Calcutta University Press, 1927.

———, *Some Problems of Indian Literature*. Calcutta, Calcutta University Press, 1925.

Nyāya

Athalye, Y. V., ed., *Tarkasaṁgraha of Annambhaṭṭa, and Govardhana's Nyāyabodhinī*. Bombay, Government Central Book Depot, 1897.

Bahulikar, Balwant Narhar, tr., *The Tarka-sangraha of Annambhatta*, with the author's Dīpika. Poona, Gungadhar N. Bahulikar, 1903.

Ballantyne, J. R., *Lectures on the Nyāya Philosophy*. Allahabad, Presbyterian Mission Press, 1849.

Ballantyne, J. R., ed., *The aphorisms of the Nyāya philosophy by Gautama*, with illustrative extracts from the commentary by Viśwanātha, in Sanskrit and English. 3 Vols., Allahabad, Presbyterian Mission Press, 1850, 1853, 1854.

Bhattacharyya, Vidhushekhara, *The Nyāyapraveśa*. Part II, Tibetan text, compared with Sanskrit and Chinese versions and edited with an introduction, comparative notes and indexes, Baroda, Central Library, 1927.

Bodas, *Introduction to Tarkasaṁgraha.*

Cowell, E. B., ed. and tr., *Udayana's Kusumanjali, with the commentary of Hari Dāsa Bhaṭṭāchārya.* Calcutta, Baptist Mission Press, 1864.

Dvivedi, Maṇilāl Nabhubhāi, ed., *The Tarkakaumudī by Laugākshi Bhāskara.* Bombay, Government Central Book Depot, 1886.

Frauwallner, E. von, *Dignāgas Ālambhanaparīkṣā*. Text, Übersetzung und Erläuterungen, *Wiener Zeitschrift für die Kunde des Morgenlandes*, 37, 1930.

Hultzsch, E. von, tr., *Annambhaṭṭas Tarkasaṁgraha*. Ein Kompendium der Dialektik und Atomistik, mit des Verfassers eigenem Kommentar, genannt Dīpikā, Berlin, Weidmannsche Buchhandlung, 1907.

Jhā, Gangānātha, tr., *The Nyāya-sūtras of Gautama with the Bhāṣya of Vātsyāyana and the Vārtika of Udyotakara, with notes from the Nyāyavārtikatātparyaṭīka of Vāchaspati Miśhra and Tātparyapariśuddhi of Udayanāchārya.* 3 Vols. Indian Thought Series, 7, 9, 12, 1912.

———, tr., *Ślokavārttika* [*Kumārila*]. Calcutta, Bibliotheca Indica, New series, 1900–08.

Keith, Arthur Berriedale, *Indian Logic and Atomism, an exposition of the Nyāya and Vaiśeṣika Systems.* Oxford, Clarendon Press, 1921.

Parab, Kāśīnāth Pāṇdurang, ed., *The Tarkasangraha of Annam Bhatta* with his own gloss (Dīpikā) and an English translation. Bombay, Nirṇayasāgar Press, 1876.

Poussin, L. de la Vallée, edited with appendices, Tibetan translation of the *Nyāyabindu of Dharmakīrti* with the commentary of Vinitadeva (Sanskrit text of ṭīkā lost), Calcutta, Asiatic Society of Bengal, Bibliotheca Indica work 171, Nos. 1179, 1374, 1908–13.

Randle, H. N., ed. and tr., *Fragments from Diṅnāga.* London, Royal Asiatic Society, Prize Publication Fund, 9, 1926.

Röer, E., tr., *Division of the categories of the Nyāya philosophy, with a commentary by Viswanatha Panchanana.* Calcutta.

Śāstri, Haraprasād, *Six Buddhist Nyāya Tracts.*

Śāstrī, Keśava, tr., *The Nyāyasūtra and Vātsyayana's Nyāyabhāṣya.* The Pandit, N. S. 2, 1877–78.

Sastri, S. Kuppuswami, *A Primer of Indian Logic According to Annambhaṭṭa's Tarkasamgraha.* Madras, P. Varadachary and Co. 1932.

Sen, Saileśvar, *A Study of Mathurānātha's Tattva-cintāmaṇirahasya.*

Stcherbatsky, Th., *Buddhist Logic.* 2 Vols., Leningrad, Academy of Sciences of the USSR, Bibliotheca Buddhica, 26, 1930–32.

———, *Dignāga's theory of perception.* Journal of the Taisho University, Vols. 6–7, 1930.

Takakusu, J., *I-tsing.* Oxford, Clarendon Press, 1896.

Tucci, Giuseppe, tr., *Pre-Diṅnāga Buddhist texts on Logic from Chinese Sources.* Baroda, Oriental Institute, 1929.

Vidyābhāsna, Satisachandra, *A History of Indian Logic: ancient, mediaeval, and modern schools.* Calcutta, Calcutta University, 1921.

Vidyābhūṣana, Satīśa Chandra, tr., *The Nyāya Sūtras of Gotama.* Allahabad, Pāṇini Office, SBH Vol. 8, Nos. 24, 52, 53, 1913.

Vidyāsagara, Pandit Jivānanda, ed. and tr., *Tarkasañgraha by Anna Bhaṭṭa.* Calcutta, Sarasudhanidhi Press, 1872.

Viśvanātha Pancānana, *Bhāṣāpariccheda or Kārikāvalī.* Edited with commentary by Mukunda Śarmā Jhopa, Bombay, Nirṇayasāgara Press, 1911.

Yamaguchi, Susumu, en collaboration avec Henriette Meyer, *Dignāga.* Examen de l'objet de la connaissance (Ālambhanaparīkṣā). Textes tibétain et chinois et traduction des stances et du commentaire. *Journal Asiatique,* 214, 1929.

Vaiśeṣika

Chatterji, Jagadīsha Chandra, *Hindu Realism.* Allahabad, The Indian Press, 1912.

Dhole, Heeralal, *The Vedantasara, A Manual of Adwaita Philosophy.* Calcutta, Author, 1888.

Faddegon, *The Vaiśeṣika System.*

Gough, A. E., tr., *Vaiśeṣika-Sūtras with extracts from Commentaries.* Benares, Lazarus & Co., 1873.

Jhā, Gangānāth, *Praśastapāda's Padārthadharmasaṁgraha with Śrīdhara's Nyāyakandalī.*
Keith, A. B., *Indian Logic and Atomism and exposition of the Nyāya and Vaiśeṣika Systems.* Oxford, Clarendon Press, 1921.
Mishra, Umesha, *Conception of Matter according to Nyāya-Vaiśeṣika,* Allahabad, Pub. author, 1936.
Ray, Praphulla Chandra, *A History of Hindu Chemistry.* Calcutta, (2 Vols.) Chuckervertty, Chatterjee & Co. Ltd., 1925.
Röer, E., *Bhāsāpariccheda and Siddhāntamiktāvali of Viśvanātha.*
———, tr., *Die Lehrsprüche der Vaiśeṣika-Philosophie von Kaṇāda. Zeitschrift der Deutschen Morgenländischen Gesellschaft,* 21–22, 1867–68.
Sinha, Nandalal, *The Vaiśeṣika Sūtras.* Tr. Vol. VI, Sacred Books of the Hindus, Allahabad, The Panini Office, 1923.
Sirkar, Kishori Lal, *The Hindu System of Physics.* Calcutta, Pub. by Author, 1911.
Ui, H., *The Vaiśeṣika Philosophy according to the Daśapadārtha-Śāstra.* London, Royal Asiatic Society, 1917.

Sāṁkhya

Ballantyne, James R., tr., *The Sāṁkhya Aphorisms of Kapila.* London, Trübner & Co., 1885.
Banerjee, S. C., *Sāṁkhya Philosophy.* Calcutta, Hare Press, 1898.
Colebrooke, Henry Thomas, tr., *The Sāṁkhya Kārikā by Īśwara Krishna.* Bombay, Tookaram Tatya, 1887.
Davis, John, *The Samkhya System of Īśwara Krishna—An Exposition of the System of Kapila.* London, Kegan Paul, Trench, Trübner & Co., Ltd., 1894.
Garbe, Richard, *Die Sāṁkhya Philosophie.* Leipzig, H. Haessel Verlag, 1917.
———, ed., *The Sāṁkhya-Pravacana-Bhāsya by Vijnāna Bhiksu.* Cambridge, Mass., Harvard University Press, Vol. 2. Harvard Oriental series, 1895.
———, *Sāṁkhya Sūtravṛitti.* Calcutta, Asiatic Society of Bengal, 1888.
Ghosh, Jajneswar, *Sāṁkhya and Modern Thought.* Calcutta, The Book Company, Ltd., 1930.
———, ed., *The Sāṁkhya Sūtras of Pancasikha & other Ancient Sages.* Calcutta, pub. by Sanatkumar Ghosh, 1934.
Jhā, Gangānātha, tr., *Tattva-Kaumudī of Vāchaspati Miśra.* Bombay, Tattva Vivechaka Press, 1896.

Johnston, E. H., *Early Sāṁkhya*. London, The Royal Asiatic Society, 1937.

Keith, A. Berriedale, *The Sāṁkhya System*, Calcutta, Association Press; London, Oxford University Press, The Heritage of India Series, 1918.

Lawl, Jag Mohan, *The Sāṁkhya Philosophy of Kapila*. Edinburgh, Orpheus Publishing House, 1921.

Majumdar, Abhay Kumar, *The Sāṁkhya Conception of Personality*. Calcutta, University Press, 1930.

Sastri, S. S. Suryanarayana, ed. and tr., The *Sāṁkhyakārikā of Īśvara Kṛṣṇa*. Madras, University of Madras, 1935.

Sinha, Nandalal, *The Sāṁkhya Philosophy*.

Yoga

Ballantyne, J. R., and Govind Shastri Deva, tr., *The Philosophy of Yoga*, Patanjaḷi's Text. Bombay Theosophical Publishing Fund, 1885.

Behanan, K. T., *Yoga: A Scientific Evaluation*. New York, Macmillan, 1937.

Bernard, Theos, *Haṭha Yoga*. New York, Columbia University Press, 1944.

———, *Heaven Lies Within Us*. New York, Scribner's, 1939.

Bhishagratna, Kaviraj Kunja Lal, ed., *The Sushruta Samhita*. Calcutta, Author, 1907.

Brahma, N. K., *The Philosophy of Hindu Sādhanā*. London, Kegan Paul, Trench, Trübner & Co., Ltd., 1932.

Brown, G. W., *The Human Body in the Upanishads*. Jubbulpore, 1921.

Dasgupta, S. N., *A Study of Patanjali*. Calcutta, University of Calcutta, 1920.

———, *Yoga Philosophy*. Calcutta, University of Calcutta, 1930.

———, *Yoga as Philosophy and Religion*. London, Kegan Paul, Trench, Trübner & Co., Ltd., 1924.

Dvivedi, Manilal Nabhubhai, *The Yoga Sutras of Patanjali*, Bombay, Tookaram Tatya, 1890.

Garbe, Richard, *Sāṁkhya und Yoga*. Strassburg, Grundriss der Indo-Arischen Philologie und Altertumskunde, 1896.

Ghosh, Jajneswar, *A Study of Yoga*. Calcutta, 1933.

Hauer, J. W., *Der Yoga als Heilweg*. Stuttgart, 1932.

Jhā, Gangānāth, tr., *The Yoga-Darshana*, comprising *The Sūtras* of

Patañjali—With the *Bhāsya of Vyāsa.* Adyar, Madras, Theosophical Publishing House, 1934.

———, tr., *Yoga-Sāra-Sañgraha of Vijñāna Bhikṣu.* Adyar, Madras, Theosophical Publishing House, 1933.

Johnston, Charles, *The Yoga Sutras of Patanjali.* New York, Quarterly Book Dept., 1912.

Marques-Riviere, J., *Tantrik Yoga.* London, Rider & Co.

Prasāda, Rāma, tr., *The Yoga Sūtras of Patañjali with the commentary of Vyāsa and the Gloss of Vāchaspati Miśra.* Allahabad, pub. by Sudhindranath Vasu, in the *Sacred Books of the Hindus,* Vol. IV, 1924.

Stephen, Daniel R., *Patanjali for Western Readers.* London, Theosophical Pub. House, 1919.

Vidyārṇava, Rai Bahadur Srisa Chandra, *Yoga Śāstra—An Introduction to the Yoga Philosophy.* (Also contains the *Siva Samhita* and the *Gheranda Samhita*), Allahabad, pub. by Maj. B. D. Basu, 1925.

Woods, James Haughton, tr., *Yoga System of Patañjali.* Cambridge, Harvard University Press, in the Harvard Oriental Series, Vol. 17, 1914.

Mīmāṁsā

Edgerton, Franklin, tr., *The Mīmāṁsā Nyāya Prakāśa; or Āpadevī: a treatise on the Mīmāṁsā system by Āpadeva.* New Haven, Yale University Press, 1929.

Jhā, Gaṅgānāth, *Slokavārttika.* Calcutta, Asiatic Society of Bengal, 1907.

———, *Prabhākara School of Pūrva Mīmāṁsā.*

Keith, A. Berriedale, *Karma Mīmāṁsā.* Calcutta, Association Press, 1921.

Sandal, Pandit Mohan Lal, tr., *Introduction to the Mīmāṁsā Sūtras of Jaimini.* S.B.H. Vol. XXVIII, Part I. Allahabad, pub. by Major B. D. Basu, The Panini Office, 1925.

———, tr., *The Mīmāṁsā Sūtras of Jaimini,* S.B.H. Vol. XXVII, Part I. Allahabad, pub. by Dr. Sudhindre Nath Basu, The Panini Office, 1923.

Sastri, P., *Introduction to Pūrva Mīmāṁsā.*

Sirkar, *The Mīmāṁsā Rules of Interpretation.*

Vedānta

Āchārya, Śrī Ānanda, *Brahmadarsanam or Intuition of the Absolute.* New York, The Macmillan Co., 1917.
Aiyar, B. R. Rajam, *Rambles in Vedānta.* Madras, S. Ganesan, 1925.
Aiyar, C. N. Krishnaswāmī, *Sri Mādhwa and Mādhwaism.* Madras, G. A. Natesan & Co.
———, *Śrī Sankarāchārya.* Madras, G. A. Natesan & Co.
Aiyar, R. Krishnaswāmi, *Thoughts from the Gītā.* Tinnevelly, pub. by the Author, 1933.
———, *Thoughts from the Vedānta.* Srirangam, Sri Vani Vilas Press, 1923.
Aiyar, G. Ramachandra, *Ātma-Vidyā or A Few Thoughts on the Science of the Self.* Srirangam, Sri Vani Vilas Press, Kaliyuga 5011.
Badarayana, *The Aphorisms of the Vedānta Philosophy.* Mirzapore, Orphan School Press, 1851.
Belvalkar, S. K., *Vedānta Philosophy.* Poona, Bilvakunja Publishing House, 1929.
Bhashyacharya, Pandit N., *The Age of Sri Sankaracharya.* Adyar, Madras, Theosophical Publishing House, 1915.
Bon, Tridandi Swami B. H., *Sree Chaitanya.* Bombay, The Popular Book Depot, 1940.
Buch, Maganlal, *The Philosophy of Shankara.* Baroda, pub. by A. G. Widgery, 1921.
Chatterji, Mohini M., *Viveka-Chūdāmaṇi or Crest-Jewel of Wisdom.* Adyar, Madras, Theosophical Pub. House, 1932.
Das, Ras-Vihari, *The Essentials of Advaitism.* Lahore, Motilal Banarsi Dass, 1933.
Dasgupta, Surendranath, *Indian Idealism.* Cambridge, The University Press, 1933.
Deussen, Paul, *The System of the Vedānta.* Tr. by Charles Johnston. Chicago, The Open Court Publishing Company, 1912.
Dhole, Heeralal, ed., *The Vedantasara—A Manual of Adwaita Philosophy.* Calcutta, Heeralal Dhole, 1888.
Dvivedi, Manilal Nabhubhai, *Monism or Advaitism?* Bombay, Subodha-Praka'sa Press, 1889.
———, *The Imitation of Sankara.* Bombay, pub. by Author, 1895.
Govindācārya, E. T., *Rāmānuja's commentary on the Bhagavad Gita.*
Guénon, René, *Man & His Becoming According to The Vedānta.* London, Rider & Co., 1928.

Iyer, S. Sundarm, *Absolute Monism; or Mind Is Matter & Matter Is Mind.* Madras, National Press, 1887.

Majumdar, Sridhar, *The Vedānta Philosophy.* Bankipore, pub. by Surendra Nath Bhattacharya, 1926.

Mallik, Girindra Narayan, *The Philosophy of Vaisnava Religion.* Lahore, Motilal Banarsi Das, 1927.

Mehta, S. S., *A Manual of Vedānta Philosophy.* Bombay, pub. by Author, 1919.

Müller, Max, *Three Lectures on the Vedānta Philosophy.* London, Longmans, Green and Company, 1894.

Narasinham, P., *The Vedāntic Absolute and the Vedāntic Good. Mind,* N. S. 82 and 93.

Raman, N. Venkata, *Sankaracharya The Great and His Successors in Kanchi.* Madras, Ganesh & Co., 1923.

Ramanujachari, Diwan Bahadur V. K., *The Three Tatvas.* Kumbakonam, pub. by the Author, 1932.

Sandal, Pandit Mohan Lal, *Philosophical Teachings of the Upanisads.* S.B.H. Extra Volume No. 5., Allahabad, pub. by Major B. D. Basu, at the Paṇini Office, 1926.

———, *The Siddhanta Darsanam.* S.B.H. Vol. XXIX. Allahabad, pub. by Major B. D. Basu, at the Paṇini Office, 1925.

Sastri, Kokileswar, *An Introduction to Adwaita Philosophy.* Calcutta, pub. by University of Calcutta, 1926.

Śāstri, A. Mahādeva, *The Vedānta Doctrine of Śrī Śankarāchārya.* Madras, Thompson and Co., 1899.

———, *Bhagavadgītā with Śaṁkara's Commentary.*

Shāstrī, Prabhu Dutt, *The Doctrine of Māyā.* London, Luzac and Co., 1911.

Swami, Śrimad Vidyāranya, *The Panchadasī.* Bombay, Rajaram Tukaram Tatya, 1912.

Thibaut, George, *The Vedānta-Sūtras.* With the commentary of Ramanuja, Oxford, Clarendon Press, 1904.

———, *The Vedānta-Sūtras.* With the commentary by Sankarakarya, Oxford, Clarendon Press, 1890.

Vidyārṇava, Rai Bahadur Śrīśa Chandra, *Studies in the Upaniṣads.* S.B.H., Vol. XXII, Part I, Allahabad, pub. by Dr. L. M. Basu, The Paṇini Office, 1933.

———, *Studies in the Vedānta Sūtras.* S.B.H., Vol. XXII, Part II, Allahabad, pub. by Dr. L. M. Basu, The Paṇini Office, 1933.

———, *The Vedānta-Sūtras of Bādarāyana.* With Commentary of Baladeva. S.B.H. Vol. V, Allahabad, pub. by Dr. L. M. Basu, The Paṇini Office, 1934.

Kāśmīr Śaivism

Avalon, Arthur, *The Great Liberation,* Madras, Ganesh & Co., 1927.

———, *Principles of Tantra.* 2 Vols. London, Luzac & Co., 1914, 1918.

———, *The Serpent Power, 3rd Ed.* Madras, Ganesh & Co., 1931.

Barnett, L. D., *The Heart of India.*

Carpenter, J. E., *Theism in Mediaeval India.* London, William and Morgate, 1921.

Chatterji, Jagadish Chandra, *Kashmir Shaivaism,* Srinagar, Kashmir; The Kashmir Series of Texts and Studies, 1914.

Leidecker, Kurt F., *The Secret of Self-recognition (Pratyabhijñāhṛdayam).* Adyar Library, Madras, 1938.

Das, Sudhendu Kumar, *Śakti or Divine Power.* Calcutta, University of Calcutta, 1934.

Nallasvāmi Pillai, *Studies in Śaiva Siddhānta.*

Padmanābhācārya, *Life and Teachings of Śrī Madhva.*

Pope, *Tiruvāśagam.*

Shivapadasundaram, S., *The Śaiva School of Hinduism,* London.

Woodroffe, Sir John, *The Garland of Letters.* Madras; Ganesh & Co., 1922.

———, *Shakti and Shāktā.* Madras, Ganesh & Co., 1920.

Abbreviations

cf.	—compare	OH Germ.	—Old High German
Eng.	—English	op.	—opposite or opposed to
fr.	—from	part.	—participle
ger.	—gerund	pass.	—passive
Germ.	—German	perf.	—perfect
I-E	—Indo-European	pr.	—prefix
Lat.	—Latin	prep.	—preposition
Mod.	—Modern	q.v.	—quod vide (Lat. which see)
neg.	—negative		

Symbols

<—derived from	$\surd$—root
>—equivalent or equal to	*—hypothetical

GLOSSARY

Ābhāsa (fr. prep. *ā*, to + √*bhās*, to shine), 'the shining forth,' (in Kāśmīr Śaivism), the immanent or active phase of consciousness (also called *sṛṣṭi*, q.v.); (in Vedānta) the immanent aspect of the Ultimate Principle (Brahman, q.v.), the manifest world is said to be merely an appearance (*ābhāsa*); (in Nyāya) fallacious reasoning.

Abhāva (fr. neg. part., *a* + *bhāva*, becoming <√*bhū*, to become), non-existence, a means of correct knowledge (*pramāṇa*, q.v.), defined as the deduction of the existence of one of two opposite things from the non-existence of the other; (in Nyāya) this is included in inference (*anumāna*).

Abheda (fr. neg. part. *a* + *bheda*, cleavage <√*bhid*, to split), 'not different,' non-dualism, monism.

Abhidhātrī (in Mīmāṁsā) that which indicates the material used in the sacrifice.

(The etymology of the component parts of the technical compound words used in the outline of the Jaimini's method of interpretation of Vedic texts has not been given for the reason that these words so seldom occur in philosophical literature. Only the meaning in the Mīmāṁsā has been given.)

Ācāra (compounded of prep. *ā* + *cāra*, movement <√*car*, to go), conduct, behaviour; custom, traditional or immemorial usage; an established rule of conduct, institution, precept.

Ācārya, 'knowing or teaching the *ācāra*, q.v., or rules,' a spiritual guide or teacher; a title affixed to name of learned Brāhmans and great teachers.

Acit (fr. neg. part. *a* + *cit*, q.v.), 'without consciousness,' (in Vedānta) universal matter.

Acitta (neg. part, *a* + *citta*, perf. pass. participle of *cit*, q.v.), without intellect; unnoticed, unexpected; not an object of thought, inconceivable.

Ādhibhautika (fr. *adhibhūta*, supreme being, compounded of prep, *adhi*, above + *bhūta*, q.v.), proceeding from extrinsic causes, such as other men, beasts, birds, or inanimate objects; (in Sāṁkhya) one of the threefold causes of misery, viz. (1) *ādhyātmika*, (2) *ādhibhautika*, and (3) *ādhidaivika*, qq.v.

Ādhidaivika (fr. *adhideva,* supreme god, compounded of prep. *adhi,* above + *deva,* god), proceeding from supernatural causes, such as influences of the atmosphere or planets; (in Sāṁkhya) one of the threefold causes of misery, viz. (1) *ādhyātmika,* (2) *ādhibhautika,* and (3) *ādhidaivika,* qq.v.

Adhikaraṇa (fr. prep. *adhi,* above + *karaṇa* making <√*kar,* to make), a topic, subject; section, consisting of five parts, viz. (1) thesis (*viṣaya*), (2) doubt (*saṁśaya*), (3) anti-thesis (*pūrvapakṣa*), (4) synthesis or right conclusion (*siddhānta*), and (5) agreement or consistency (*saṁgati*), qq.v.

Adhyātma (fr. prep. *adhi,* above + *ātman,* q.v.), the Supreme Spirit; concerning self or individual personality.

Adhyātmaśāstra (compounded of *adhyātma* + *śāstra,* qq.v.), another name for the *Vaiśeṣikasūtra,* q.v., so called because it is a treatise about the Supreme Spirit (*Adhyātma*).

Ādhyātmika (fr. prep. *adhi,* above + *ātmika,* relating to the soul <*ātman,* q.v.), proceeding from intrinsic causes, such as disorders of the body and mind, (in Sāṁkhya) one of the threefold causes of misery, viz. (1) *ādhyātmika,* (2) *ādhibhautika,* and (3) *adhidaivika,* qq.v.

Adhyāya (fr. preps. *adhi,* above + *ā,* to + *aya,* going <√*i,* to go), a lesson, lecture, chapter.

Adṛṣta (neg. part. *a* + *dṛṣṭa,* seen, perf. pass. participle of √*darś,* to see), 'unseen, invisible, unknown'; that which is beyond the reach of observation or consciousness, as, for instance, the merit attaching to a man's conduct in one state of existence and the corresponding reward or punishment with which he is visited in another; potential worth resulting from past conduct; latent effect.

Advaita (fr. neg. part. *a,* + *dvaita,* dualism <*dvi,* two), 'non-dualism,' the doctrine of monism advocated by Śaṁkara, q.v., which contends that only the Ultimate Principle (*Brahman,* q.v.) has any actual existence, and that all phenomenal existence is an illusion (māyā, q.v.).

Āgama (fr. pr. *ā,* to + √*gam,* to come), 'that which has come down,' another name for tantra, q.v.

Āgamaśāstra (compounded of *āgama* + *śāstra,* qq.v.), the traditional branch of the literature of Kāśmīr Śaivism, believed to have been handed down (āgama) through the ages from teacher to pupil; the *Śivasūtra,* q.v., belongs to this branch of the literature.

Ahalyā, according to tradition, the wife of Gautama, founder of the Nyāya philosophy. Some authorities claim this was not his wife.

Ahalyāsthāna (compounded of *Ahalyā* + *sthāna,* standing < √*sthā,* to stand), the legendary burial place of the wife of Gautama, founder of the Nyāya philosophy; it is located two miles east of Gautamasthāna, the birth place of Gautama. According to some authorities, this was not his wife.

Aham, the personal pronoun 'I.'

Ahaṁkāra (compounded of *aham,* I + *kāra,* making, action < √*kar,* to do, make), 'I-maker,' (in Sāṁkhya) the individuating principle, responsible for the limitations, division, and variety in the manifest world; (in Yoga) the ego, a self-conscious principle.

Aitihya (fr. *iti-ha,* thus, indeed), tradition, a means of correct knowledge (*pramāṇa,* q.v.), defined as an assertion which has come down from the past without any indication of the source from which it first originated; (in Nyāya) this is included in verbal testimony (*śabda*).

Ākāśa (fr. prep. *ā,* to + *kāśa,* appearance < √*kāś,* to shine, to appear), Ether as an element, (in Vaiśesika) the fifth Eternal Reality (*Dravya,* q.v.); (in Sāṁkhya) the first Sense-Particular (*Mahābhūta,* q.v.), the principle of vacuity; its Special Property (*Viśeṣa,* q.v.) is Sound (*Śabda,* q.v.).

Akṣa (fr. I-E √*ogu,* eye), the eye; sensual perception.

Akṣapāda (compounded of *aksa,* eye + *pāda,* foot), 'Eye-Footed,' another name for Gautama (Gotama), founder of the Nyāya philosophy; this name is said to be descriptive of Gautama's habit of directing his eyes toward his feet when walking, a natural way to carry the head when contemplating during the course of a stroll.

Amṛta (fr. neg. part. *a* + √*mar,* to die), immortal, a god.

Ānanda (prep. *ā,* to + √*nand,* to rejoice, be pleased, be delighted), bliss; (in Vedānta) one of the three attributes of the Ultimate Principle (*Brahman,* q.v.); (in Kāśmīr Śaivism) universal bliss.

Aṅga (in Mīmāṁsā) that which leads up to the completion of the principal action (*apūrva,* q.v.), the subordinate part of a Vedic sacrifice.

Antahkaraṇa (compounded of *antar,* internal + *karaṇa,* sense-organ < √*kar,* to do, make), the internal organ; Mind in the collective sense, including intelligence (*buddhi,* q.v.), ego (*ahaṁkāra,* q.v.), and mind (*manas,* q.v.).

Aṇu (<**al-nu* <I-E √*ale,* to grind, crush), fine, minute, atomic, (in Vaiśeṣika) a positional reality that has no length, breadth, or thickness; cf. paramāṇu.

Āṇubhāva (compounded of *aṇu,* q.v., + *bhāva,* becoming <√*bhū,* to become), becoming an atom.

Anumāna (fr. prep. *anu,* according to + *māna,* concept <√*man,* to think), inference, a means of correct knowledge (*pramāṇa,* q.v.), defined as that knowledge which is preceded by perception.

Anuṣṭhānasādeśya (in Mimāṁsā) the equality of place according to the performance.

Anuvāda (Mīmāṁsā), a statement made by the text which is in keeping with the existing state of facts.

Ānvīkṣikī (fr. anvīkṣā, compounded of prep. *anu,* according to + *īkṣā,* looking, sight <√*īkṣ,* to see + I-E base **ogu,* to see), logic, another name used for the Nyāya.

Apāna (fr. prep. *apa,* away + *ana,* breath), one of the five vital airs (*vāyu,* q.v.) of the inner body; its movement is downward, opposed to *prāṇa* which moves inward; its seat is the anus.

Āpas (fr. the root word *ap,* water), Water as an element, (in Vaiseṣika) the second Eternal Reality (*Dravya,* q.v.); (in Sāṁkhya) the fourth Sense-Particular (*Mahābhuta,* q.v.), the principle of liquidity, its function is contraction, its Special Property (*Viśeṣa,* q.v.) is Flavour (*Rasa*), its General Qualities (*Sāmānya Guṇas,* q.v.), are Form (*Rūpa*), Touch (*Sparśa*), and Sound (*Śabda*), qq.v.

Apavarga (fr. prep. *apa,* away + *varga,* division <√*varj,* to turn), release, (in Nyāya) an object of Right Knowledge (*Prameya,* q.v.) and defined as absolute deliverance from pain.

Apūrva (in Mīmāṁsā), the invisible result of action to mature in another life; therefore the principal part of Vedic sacrifice; when a text lays down a new injunction for the attainment of an object which one cannot know by any other means.

Ārādupakāraka (in Mīmāṁsā), actions which are enjoined without any reference to any substance or divinity, leading directly to the ultimate result; it is the essence of the sacrifice.

Āraṇyakas, 'forest treatises," so called because they were composed by forest-dwelling Brahmanical sages; they are the theological portion of the Brāhmaṇas, q.v.; in tone and content they form a transition to the Upaniṣads, q.v., which are attached to them.

Arjuna, name of the third of the Pāṇḍava princes of the Mahābhārata, q.v.; son of Indra and Kuntī qq.v.; in the Bhagavadgītā, q.v., he receives a divine revelation from Kṛṣṇa, q.v.

Artha (fr. √*arth,* to strive to obtain, desire, wish), aim, purpose; (in Nyāya) an object of Right Knowledge (*Prameya,* q.v.) and defined as the object of the senses (*Indriyas*, q.v.), viz. sound (*śabda*), touch (*sparśa*), form (*rūpa*), flavour (*rasa*), and odour (*gandha*); wealth, as one of the three objects of human pursuit (*Trivarga*, q.v.).

Arthakrama (in Mīmāṁsā), the order determined by the object for the performance of the minor parts of a Vedic sacrifice; see *prayogavidhi*.

Arthāpatti (compound of *artha*, motive + prep. *ā*, to + *patti*, movement <√*pad*, to fall), presumption, a means of correct knowledge (*pramāna*, q.v.), defined as the deduction of one thing from the declaration of another thing; (in Nyāya) this is included in inference (*anumāna*).

Arthāpattisama (fr. *arthāpatti*, q.v., + *sama*, same), an inference by which the quality of an object is attributed to another object because of their sharing some other quality in common.

Arthavāda (compounded of *artha* + *vāda*, qq.v.), explanatory passages; (in Mīmāṁsā) passages in praise or blame of a Vedic command or prohibition, one of the five divisions under which the contents of the Vedas, q.v., are classified.

Āsana (fr. √*ās*, to sit), 'sitting,' posture; one of the stages in the practice of Yoga, q.v.

Asat (neg. part. *a* + *sat*, q.v.), 'non-being,' (in Vedānta) the passive condition of the transcendental aspect of the Ultimate Principle (Brahman); cf. *sat*.

Aṣṭa eight.

Aśuddha (fr. neg. part. *a* + *śuddha*, q.v.), impure; (in Kaśmīr Śaivism) the twenty + four categories (*tattva*, q.v.) from *Prakṛti* to *Pṛthivī* are classified for the purpose of worship as the Impure Category (*Aśuddha Tattva*); they are *Prakṛti, Mahat, Ahaṁkāra, Manas*, ten *Indriyas*, five *Tanmātrās*, and five *Mahābhūtas*, qq.v.; so called, because they represent the world of Impure Duality; see also *Śuddha* and *Śuddhāśuddha*.

Ātma, in composition for *ātman*, q.v.

Ātman (etymology doubtful, cf. Anglo-Sax *æfm*, breath, soul, OH Germ. *ātum*, Mod. Germ. *Atem*, breath), the soul, self, principle of life and sensation, or abstract individual; (in Nyāya) an object of Right Knowledge (*Prameya*, q.v.) and said to be the abode of desire (*icchhā*), aversion (*dveṣa*), effort (*prayatna*), pleasure *sukha*), pain (*duḥkha*), and knowledge (*jñāna*); (in *Vaiśeṣika*) the eighth Eternal Reality or Substance (*Dravya*, q.v.).

Atharvaveda, one of the four Vedas, q.v.

Aulūka (fr. *ulūka,* an owl), another name for Kaṇāda, founder of the Vaiśeṣika philosophy; this name is said to be descriptive of Kaṇāda's habit of meditating all day and seeking food during the night like an owl, a common practice of yogis.

Aulūkya, a follower of the Vaiśeṣika doctrine.

Aulūkyadarśana, name of the Vaiśeṣika system.

Avāntaraparakaraṇa (in Mīmāṁsā), when the context relates to the rewards of the subordinate part of the sacrifice.

Avatār (fr. pr. *ava,* off, away, down + √*tṛ,* to pass across, through, or over), descent of a deity.

Avayava (fr. prep. *ava,* off + **yava* < √*yav,* to unite), members of a syllogism, viz. (1) proposition (*pratijñā*), (2) reason (*hetu*), (3) example (*udāharaṇa*), (4) application (*upanaya*), and (5) conclusion (*nigamana*), qq.v.; (in Nyāya) one of the sixteen categories.

Avidyā (fr. neg. part. *a* + *vidya,* knowing < √*vid,* to know, 'ignorance,' especially in the spiritual sense; (in Vedānta) caused by the operation of *Māyā,* q.v.

Avyakta (fr. neg. part. *a* + prep. *vi,* apart + *akta,* anointed, perf. pass. participle of √*añj,* to anoint), 'unmanifest matter,' another name for *prakṛti,* q.v.

Āyur (for *āyus* in composition), life, vigour, health.

Āyurveda (compounded of *āyur* + *veda,* qq.v.), the science of medicine; the two most ancient and outstanding authorities are Caraka and Suśruta.

Bādarāyaṇa, the founder of the Vedānta philosophy; author of the *Vedāntasūtra*; his actual date is quite unknown; the dates given range from 500 B.C. to 200 A.D.; some scholars contend that Bādarāyaṇa is an alias for Vyāsa, q.v., the celebrated mythical sage who is regarded as the one who originally compiled and arranged the Vedas and other portions of Hindū sacred literature.

Bauddhas (Buddhists), adherents of the school of philosophy founded by Gautama Buddha.

Bhagavadgītā ('Song of the Divine One,' i.e. Kṛṣṇa), a celebrated philosophic epic poem, inserted in the Mahābhārata, q.v., containing a dialogue between Kṛṣṇa and Arjuna, qq.v., which clearly indicates the relationship between morality and absolute ethical values in the Hindū philosophy of action (Karma Yoga); it is considered to be one of the most influential philosophical poems of Sanskrit literature; its exact date is quite unknown.

Bhakti (fr. √*bhaj,* to love, worship, adore), worship, faith, religious devotion as a way of salvation.

Bhāṣya (fr. √*bhās,* to speak, talk, say, tell), commentary. an explanatory work.

Bhaṭṭa (Prākrit form of *bhartār,* a bearer < √*bhar,* to bear), a title of respect used by humble persons addressing a prince; but also affixed or prefixed to the name of learned Brāhmans.

Bhaṭṭācārya (compounded of *bhaṭṭa* + *ācārya,* q.v.), another name frequently used for Kumārilabhaṭṭa who founded the second important school based on the Mīmāṁsā philosophy; however this title may be given to any learned Brāhman or great teacher.

Bhāṭṭas, adherents of Bhaṭṭācārya (also known as Kumārilabhaṭṭa) who founded the second important school based on the Mīmāṁsā philosophy.

Bhāva (fr. √*bhū,* to become, be), becoming, being, existing, occurring, appeared.

Bhāvana (fr. √*bhū,* to become, to be), forming in the mind, conception, apprehension, imagination, supposition, fancy, thought, meditation; (in Nyāya) that cause of memory which arises from direct perception, demonstration, argument, ascertainment.

Bheda (fr. √*bhid,* to split, cleave, divide), 'different,' dualism.

Bhedābheda (compounded of *bheda,* cleavage + neg. part. *a* + *bheda*), 'different, yet not different,' dualism (*bheda*) and non-dualism (*abheda*).

Bhedābhedavādin (compounded of bhedābheda, q.v. + *vādin,* saying < √*vad,* to speak), one who follows the doctrine of dualism (*bheda*) and non-dualism (*abheda*).

Bhedana (fr. √*bhid,* to split), breaking, splitting, dividing.

Bhedavādin (compounded of *bheda,* cleavage < √*bhid,* to split + *vādin,* saying < √*vad,* to speak), a dualist.

Bhoga (fr. √*bhuj,* to enjoy), enjoyment.

Bhūta (past. pass. participle of √*bhū,* to become, be), one of the five gross elements (*mahābhūtas,* q.v.) as perceived by the senses.

Bhutārthavāda (in Mīmāṁsā), a statement made which is neither against the existing state of facts nor is it in conformity with it.

Bhuvana (fr. √*bhū,* to become, be), a being, living creature, man, mankind; the world, earth.

Brahmā, name of one of the gods of the Hindū Trimūrti or Trinity, viz. Brahmā, 'the creator,' Viṣṇu, 'the preserver,' Śiva, 'the destroyer'; the personal god, see Brahman.

Brahman (fr. √*bṛh,* to grow, increase, expand, swell), 'evolution, 'development,' 'expansion,' or 'growth'; that which has reached its ultimate evolution, development, expansion, or growth; (in Vedānta) the Ultimate Principle, the creator, maintainer, and destroyer of everything in the universe; the Self-existent, the Absolute, the Eternal, the Universal Spirit; not generally an object of worship, but, rather, of meditation and knowledge; its three attributes are universal being, consciousness, and bliss (*Saccitānanda*, q.v.). It should be observed that in composition the term Brahmă, spelt with short *ă*, the nominative neuter gender, is used for the Universal Spirit, while Brahmā, spelt with long *ā*, the nominative masculine ending, is used for the individual spirit or personal god; this latter form is also identified with Primal Nature (*prakṛti*, q.v.) of the Sāṁkhya system.

Brāhmaṇa, the precept portion of the Veda, q.v., its contents can be classified under two heads, (1) *vidhi*, ritualistic rules, and (2) *arthavāda*, explanations; the Brahmaṇas include the Āraṇyakas and Upaniṣads, qq.v.

Brahmamīmāṁsā (compounded of *brahma* + *mīmāṁsā*, qq.v.), another name for the *Vedāntasūtra*, q.v., so called because the central topic is an investigation of the Universal Spirit (Brahman).

Brahmasūtra (compounded of *brahma* + *sūtra*, qq.v.), another name for the *Vedāntasūtra*, q.v., so called because the central topic is the Universal Spirit (Brahman, q.v.).

Buddhi (fr. √*budh*, to wake up, recover consciousness, observe), intelligence, (in Nyāya) an object of Right Knowledge (*Prameya*, q.v.) and defined as the power of forming and retaining conceptions and general notions, the faculty of the mind to discern, judge, comprehend, apprehend, and understand the meaning of right knowledge.

Buddhitattva (compounded of *buddhi* + *tattva*, qq.v.), the principle of intelligence.

Caitanya (fr. *cetana*, visible, conspicuous, conscious, intelligent < √*cit*, q.v.), consciousness, intelligence; (in Kāśmīr Śaivism) the changeless aspect of pure consciousness, the Universal Intelligence of Spirit; defined as *Saccitānanda*, q.v.; name of a Vaiṣṇava reformer, born about 1485.

Cakṣus (fr. √*cakṣ*, to see < √ *kāś*, to shine, to be visible), the power to see, one of the five abstract knowing-senses (*jñānendriyas*, q.v.).

Caraka, the author of an ancient work on Indian medicine (*Āyurveda*, q.v.).

Cārvāka, founder of a materialistic school of philosophy; his doctrines are embodied in the lost *Bārhaspatyasūtra;* the name Cārvāka is applied to any adherent of this school.

Catur, four.

Ceṣṭā (fr. √*ceṣṭ,* to move the limbs, struggle, strive), motion, gesture; behaviour, manner of life.

Chala (etymology uncertain), equivocation, (in Nyāya) one of the sixteen categories and defined as opposition offered to a proposition by means of (1) playing upon words (*vācas*), (2) generalizations (*sāmānyas*), and (3) metaphors (*upacārās*), qq.v.

Cintā (fr. √*cit,* to think with nasal infix), thought, care, anxiety, consideration.

Cintāmaṇi (compounded of *cintā,* thought + *maṇi,* gem), 'thought-gem,' name of various treatises and commentaries.

Cit (fr. √*cit,* to perceive, know, appear), universal consciousness; (in Kāśmīr Śaivism) the static aspect of consciousness in the manifest world, called the *Śiva Tattva,* qq.v.

Citta (fr. √*cit,* to perceive, know, appear), individual consciousness; (in Vedānta) one aspect of the Universal Mind; (in Yoga) the Mind in the collective sense, composed of three categories, viz. intelligence (*buddhi,* q.v.), ego (*ahaṁkāra,* q.v.), and mind (*manas,* q.v.).

Dakṣiṇa, right; south (as being on the right side of a person looking eastward); upright.

Dakṣiṇācāra (compounded of *dakṣiṇa* + *ācāra,* qq.v.), the 'right' way among the worshippers of Śakti, q.v.; said to be not so monistic as *Vāmācāra,* q.v.

Dakṣiṇācārin, one who worships *Śakti,* q.v., according to the 'right' way; cf. *Vāmācārin.*

Dama (fr. √*dam,* to tame, subdue, conquer), 'taming, subduing,' self-restraint or control of conduct, restraining the senses from external actions; (in Vedānta) one of the six acquirements (*ṣaṭsampat,* q.v.).

Darśana (fr. √*darś,* to see), view, doctrine, or philosophical system, see Ṣaḍ Darśana.

Daśa, ten.

Deśika (fr. √*diś,* to point out, show), a guide, a Guru or spiritual teacher.

Devadatta (compounded of *deva,* god + *datta,* given < √*dā,* to give), 'god-given'; one of the five vital airs (*vāyu,* q.v.) of the outer body; it performs the function of yawning.

Dhanaṁjaya (compounded of *dhana,* prize, treasure + *jaya,* winning <√*jay,* to conquer), one of the five vital airs (*vāyu,* q.v.) of the outer body; it performs the function of hiccuping.

Dhāraṇā (fr. √*dhar,* to hold), concentration; one of the stages in the practice of Yoga, q.v.

Dharma (fr. √*dhar,* to hold, bear, support, maintain, preserve), Law; when used in the metaphysical sense, it means those universal laws of Nature that sustain the operation of the Universe and the manifestations of all things; when applied to the individual, it has reference to that code of conduct that sustains the soul, and produces virtue, morality, or religious merit leading toward the development of man.

Dhyāna (fr. √*dhyai,* to think of, consider, meditate on), meditation; next to the last stage in the practice of Yoga, q.v.

Dik (fr. √*diś,* to point out, show), Space, (in Vaiśeṣika) the seventh Eternal Reality (*Dravya,* q.v.), it has reference to that power or force that holds all discrete things in their respective positions in relation to each other as they appear in Space (*Ākāśa,* q.v.).

Dīrgha, long in space and time.

Dīrghatapas (compounded of *dīrgha* + *tapas,* qq.v. penance), 'Long-Penance,' another name for Gautama (Gotama), founder of the Nyāya philosophy, descriptive of his long penances during his periods of study.

Doṣas (fr. √*duṣ,* to be bad, to sin), faults, (in Nyāya) an object of Right Knowledge (*Prameya,* q.v.), and defined as the cause of all action; they are (1) Attraction, which consists of lust, greed, craving, longing, and covetousness; (2) Aversion, which consists of anger, envy, jealousy, and implacability; (3) Delusion, which consists of false knowledge, doubt, pride, and carelessness; (in Suśruta, q.v.) the three humours of the body, viz. air (*vāyu*), fire (*pitta*), and phlegm (*kapha*).

Dravya (etymology uncertain), Substance, (in Vaiśesika), the first Predicable (*Padārtha*), which is the foundation of the universe and is resolved into nine Eternal Realities, viz. (1) Earth (*Pṛthivī*), (2) Water (*Āpas*), (3) Fire (*Tejas*), (4) Air (*Vāyu*), (5) Ether (*Ākāśa*), (6) Time (*Kāla*), (7) Space (*Dik*), (8) Soul (*Ātman*), (9) Mind (*Manas*).

Dṛṣṭānta (compound of *dṛṣṭa,* past pass. participle of √*darś,* to see + *anta,* end), illustration, (in Nyāya) a familiar example, one of the sixteen categories and defined as that thing about which an ordinary man and an expert entertain the same opinion.

Duḥkha (probably late and artificial formation with *dus,* bad + *kha,* hole, axle-hole on the analogy of *sukha,* q.v.), pain, (in Nyāya) an object of Right Knowledge (*Prameya,* q.v.) and defined as an impediment that hinders the progress of the soul.

Dva (original stem of dvi), two.

Dvaita (fr. *dvi,* two + suffix *-ta*), 'dualism,' the doctrine advocated by Madhva, q.v., which denies that the Ultimate Principle (*Brahman,* q.v.) is the cause of the world, and contends that the soul is a separate principle having an independent existence of its own, and is only associated with the Ultimate Principle.

Dvaitādvaita (compounded of *dvaita* + *advaita,* qq.v.), dualism and non-dualism.

Dvaitādvaitamārga (compounded of *dvaita* + *advaita* + *mārga,* qq.v), the path of dualism and non-dualism.

Dvāpara (compounded of *dvā* = *dvi,* two + *para,* last; having two as its highest [number]), the third of the four ages (*yugas,* q.v.); a fourth less righteous and briefer than the preceding, enduring 864,000 years.

Dveṣa (fr. √*dviṣ,* to hate, loathe), hatred, dislike, repugnance, enmity to.

Dvivedin (compounded of *dvi,* two + *veda,* q.v.), one who is familiar with two Vedas.

Dvyaṇuka (compounded of *dvi,* two + *anuka,* relating to *aṇu,* q.v.), a binary or a form consisting of two variables associated in such a manner as to combine along a common axis; this form is described as a line which is a series of related positions or association of points (*aṇus,* q.v.) so co-ordinated as to have a single axis; it has extended position with length and breadth, but no thickness.

Eka, one.

Ekapadarūpa (in Mīmāṁsā), the meaning indicated by one sentence.

Ekābhidhānarūpa (in Mīmāṁsā), the meaning denoted by one word.

Gandha (fr. *gandh,* to injure, hurt), the subtle element (*tanmātra,* q.v.) of odour.

Gautama (also Gotama), the founder of the Nyāya philosophy; author of the *Nyāyasūtra;* his actual date is quite unknown; however the outstanding authorities place him about 550 B.C.; he is also called Akṣapāda or Eye-Footed, and Dīrghatapas or Long-Penance, qq.v.

Gautamasthāna (compounded of *Gautama* + *sthāna,* position, place <√*sthā,* to stand), the legendary birth place of Gautama, founder of the Nyāya philosophy, located twenty-eight miles north-east of Darbhanga in North Behar.

Ghrāṇa (fr. √*ghrā,* to smell), the power to smell, one of the five abstract knowing-senses (*jñānendriyas,* q.v.).

Guṇa (fr. **gr-nó,* <I-E base **gere,* to twist, wind), quality, property, attribute; (in Vaiśeṣika) attribute, the second Predicable (*Padārtha,* q.v.); (in Sāṁkhya) one of the three constituents of Cosmic Substance (*Prakṛti,* q.v.), Illuminating (*Sattva,* q.v.), Activating (*Rajas,* q.v.), and Restraining (*Tamas,* q.v.).

Guṇakarma (in Mīmāṁsā), the secondary action of a sacrifice.

Guṇavāda (in Mīmāṁsā), a statement made by the text that is contradictory to the existing state of the affair and means of proof; new qualities.

Gurū (fr. I-E base **ʒuere,* heavy, weighty), a spiritual teacher.

Haṁsa (etymology uncertain), a goose, swan, flamingo; a poetical or mythical bird said to be able to separate milk from water; therefore, a symbol of discrimination; the soul as symbolized by the pure white colour of the swan; sometimes used to represent the 'Supreme Spirit'; affixed to the name of holy men who have attained enlightenment, and other outstanding men.

Hetu (fr. √*hi,* to impel, drive), cause, reason, (in Nyāya) the second member (*avayava,* q.v.) of the five-membered syllogism and defined as the vehicle of inference (*anumāna,* q.v.) used to prove the proposition.

Hetuvidyā (compounded of *hetu* + *vidyā,* qq.v.), 'science of causes,' dialectics, logic, another name used for the Nyāya.

Hetvābhāsa (compounded of *hetu* + *ābhāsa,* qq.v), fallacies, viz. the erratic, the contradictory, the equal to the question, unproved, and the mistimed; (in Nyāya) one of the sixteen categories.

Idam, the demonstrative pronoun 'this.'

Iti, in this manner, thus; it is equivalent to 'as you know'; in quotations it serves the purpose of inverted commas; it may form an adverbial compound with the name of an author, e.g. *itipāṇini,* thus according to Pāṇini, q.v.

Itihāsa (compounded of *iti* + *ha* + *āsa,* so indeed it was), historical literature.

Indra (the etymology is much disputed), god of the atmosphere and sky; the Indian Jupiter Pluvius or lord of rain (who in Vedic mythology reigns over the deities of the intermediate region or atmosphere; he fights against and conquers with his thunderbolt [*vajra*] the demons of darkness, and is in general a symbol of generous heroism; Indra was not originally lord of the gods of the sky, but his deeds were most useful to mankind, and he was therefore addressed in prayers and hymns more than any other deity, and ultimately superseded the more lofty and spiritual Varuṇa; in later mythology Indra is subordinated to the triad Brahman, Viṣṇu, and Śiva, but remained the chief of all other deities in the popular mind).

Indriyabuddhi (compounded of *indriya* + *buddhi,* qq.v.), perception by the senses, the exercise of any sense, the faculty of any organ.

Indriyas (fr. *indra,* q.v.), sense-powers; they are divided into two groups, five abstract knowing-senses or powers of cognition called *Jñānendriyas,* and five abstract working-senses or capacities for action called *Karmendriyas.* The abstract knowing-senses (*Jñānendriyas*) are the power to hear (*śrotra*), the power to feel (*tvak*), the power to see (*cakṣus*), the power to taste (*rasana*), and the power to smell (*ghrāṇa*). The abstract working-senses (*Karmendriyas*) are the power to express (*vāk*), the power to pro-create (*upastha*), the power to excrete (*pāyu*), the power to grasp (*pāṇi*), and the power to move (*pāda*); (in Nyāya) an object of Right Knowledge (*Prameya,* q.v.).

Indriyasaṁyama (compounded of *indriya* + *saṁyama,* qq.v.), the restraint of the senses.

Indriyārtha (compounded of *indriya* + *artha,* qq.v.), an object of sense, viz. sound (*śabda*), touch (*sparśa*), form (*rūpa*), flavour (*rasa*), and odour (*gandha*).

Iṣṭa 1. (past. pass. participle of √*iṣ,* to endeavour to obtain, strive, seek for; to desire, wish, long for, request), wished, desired, liked, cherished, reverenced, respected.

Iṣṭa 2. (past. pass. participle of √*yaj,* to worship, offer, sacrifice), sacrificed, worshipped with sacrifices, sacred rite, sacrament.

Īśvara (fr. √*īś,* to be master, get in one's power, command, possess, dispose of), lord, supreme deity; (in Kāśmīr Śaivism) the fourth category (*tattva,* q.v.), postulated to account for that condition when the subject (*Aham*, q.v.) recognizes the object (*Idam*, q.v.), the stage of complete self-identification; sometimes used as an affix for proper names, e.g. *Īśvarakṛṣṇa*, q.v.

Īśvarakṛṣṇa (compound of *Īśvara* + *kṛṣṇa*, q.v.) name of the author of the Sāṁkhyakārikā, the classic textbook on the Sāṁkhya system.

Jaimini, the founder of the Mīmāṁsā philosophy; author of the *Mīmāṁsāsūtra*; his actual date is quite unknown; however the style of his writings assigns him to the Sūtra period which extended from 600–200 B.C.; according to tradition he was a pupil of Bādarāyaṇa, founder of the Vedānta philosophy.

Jalpa (etymology uncertain), controversy, polemics, (in Nyāya) one of the sixteen categories and defined as a defense or attack of a proposition by means of equivocation (*chala*, q.v.), futility (*jāti*, q.v.), disagreement in principle (*nigrahasthāna*, q.v.), for the sole purpose of gaining victory, and with no desire to gain further knowledge.

Jāti (fr. √*jan*, to beget, be born), futility, (in Nyāya) one of the sixteen categories and defined as offering objections founded on mere similarity or dissimilarity without consideration of the universal connection between the middle term and the major term.

Jijñāsā (desiderative noun from √*jñā*, to know), inquiry, (in Nyāya) the first member of the additional five-membered syllogism introduced by later commentators to establish the object to be examined, defined as that which investigates the proposition.

Jijñāsana (desiderative noun from √*jñā*, to know), desire of knowing, investigation.

Jīva (fr. √*jīv*, to live), the principle of life, the individual soul as distinguished from the Universal Soul, called Puruṣa, q.v., in the Sāṁkhya system.

Jīvakośa (compounded of *jīva*, life + *kośa*, sheath <I-E base *(*s*) *geu-ke*, to cover, envelop), a case or sheath enveloping the personal soul.

Jīvātman (compounded of *jīva* + *ātman*, qq.v.), the individual spirit, cf. *paramātman*.

Jñāna (fr. *jñā*, to know, knowledge, esp. the knowledge derived from meditation on the Universal Spirit; (in Kāśmīr Śaivism) Universal Knowledge.

Jñanakāṇḍa (compounded of *jñāna* + *kāṇḍa*, qq.v), that portion of the Veda which relates to knowledge of the one Spirit.

Jñānatattva (compound of *jñāna* + *tattva*, qq.v.), true knowledge.

Jñānendriyas (compounded of *jñāna* + *indriya,* qq.v.), the five abstract knowing-senses, viz. the power to hear (*śrota*), the power to feel (*tvak*), the power to see (*cakṣus*), the power to taste (*rasana*), and the power to smell (*ghrāṇa*); they function respectively through the organs of ears, skin, eyes, tongue, and nose.

Kaivalya (fr. *kevala,* exclusively one's own), complete absorption in the thought of the universal unity, absolute happiness, beatitude.

Kalā (fr. I-E base *(*s*) *gele,* to cut, split), Limited Power, (in Kāśmīr Śaivism) one of the five Kañcukas, q.v.; it is the power that limits the universal condition of All-Powerfulness (*Sarvakartṛtva,* q.v.); therefore, it is the origin of Limited Power.

Kāla (etymology uncertain), Time, (in Vaiśeṣika) the sixth Eternal Reality (*Dravya,* q.v.); (in Kāśmīr Śaivism) one of the five Kañcukas, q.v., it is the power that limits the universal condition of Eternal Existence (*Nityatva,* q.v.); therefore, it is the origin of Time, the determinate when, that is, now and then.

Kali Yuga (probably fr. I-E base, **s*(*s*)*gele,* to cut, split), the present age, last of the four ages (*yugas,* q.v.); it began at midnight between the 17th and 18th of February 3102 B.C.; it is a fourth less righteous and briefer than the preceding, enduring 432,000 years; it is characterized by strife, discord, quarreling, and contention; at the end of this age the world is to be destroyed.

Kalpa (etymology uncertain), a day of Brahmā, a period of 1000 yugas, q.v.; it consists of a creation (*sṛṣṭi,* q.v.) and a dissolution (*pralaya,* q.v.); said to last 4,320,000,000 solar years; a month of Brahmā is supposed to contain thirty such Kalpas; according to the Mahābhārata, q.v., twelve months of Brahmā constitute his year, and one hundred such years his lifetime; fifty years of Brahmā's are supposed to have elapsed, and we are now in the *śvetavārāhakalpa* of the fifty-first year.

Kāma (fr. √*kam,* to wish, desire, long for; to love), wish, desire, love; pleasure, as one of the three objects of human pursuit (*trivarga,* q.v.).

Kaṇāda (compounded of *kaṇa,* atom + √*ad,* to eat), 'Atom-Eater,' the founder of the Vaiśeṣika philosophy; author of the *Vaiśeṣika-sūtra*; he is assigned to the third century B.C.; he is also called Aulūka, from *ulūka,* meaning owl; other names are Kaṇabhuj and Kaṇabhakṣa, but his real name seems to be Kaśyapa.

Kañcukas (fr. √*kañc,* to bind), the five evolutes of Māyā, q.v., (in Kāśmīr Śaivism) produced when the five universal conditions of consciousness are limited by Māyā, they are (1) Time (*Kāla*), (2) Space (*Niyati*), (3) Desire (*Raga*), (4) Limited Knowledge (*Vidyā*), and (5) Limited Power (*Kalā*), qq.v.

Kāṇḍa (fr. **gol-ndo* >I-E base **gele*, to strike, hew, cut off), any part or portion, section, chapter, division of a work or book, any distinct portion or division of an action or of a sacrificial rite; a separate department or subject (e.g. *karmakāṇḍa*).

Kapila, the founder of the Sāṁkhya philosophy; author of the *Sāṁkhyapravacanasūtra*; his actual date is quite unknown; however, the weight of authority places him in the sixth century B.C.

Kara (fr. √*kar*, to do, make, perform), a doer, maker, performer.

Kārikā (fr. √*kar*, to do, make, perform), a concise statement in verse on the doctrines of philosophy or grammar.

Karmakāṇḍa (compounded of *karman* + *kāṇḍa*, qq.v.), that portion of the Veda which relates to ceremonial acts and sacrificial rites.

Karman (in composition karma, fr. √*kar*, to do, make, perform), action, (in Vaiśeṣika) the third Predicable (*Padārtha*, q.v.); as Law, the principle of causality, popularly known as the Law of Cause and Effect, based on the principle that for every action there is a reaction.

Karmendriyas (compound of *karman* + *indriya*, qq.v.), the five abstract working-senses, viz. the power to express (*vāk*), the power to procreate (*upastha*), the power to excrete (*pāyu*), the power to grasp (*pāṇi*), and the power to move (*pāda*); their physical organs are the voice, sex-organs, anus, hands, and feet.

Kartṛ (fr. √*kar*, q.v.), one who does, makes or performs; name used for Brahmā, Viṣṇu, or Śiva as the creator of the world.

Kārya (fut. pass. participle of *kar*, to do, make, perform), 'to be done'; motive, object, aim, purpose.

Kāśmīr Śaivism (fr. *śiva*, q.v.), a Hindū philosophical system based on the *Śivasūtra*, founded by Vasugupta (9th cent.); so called, because the *Śivasūtra* was supposed to have been revealed to Vasugupta by Śiva in Kāśmīr; because it deals with the three-fold principle of God, Soul and Matter, it is also called Trika; it constructs a pure monism which postulates a single reality with two aspects, one Transcendental (*Parāsaṁvit*) and the other Immanent; in its analysis of the Immanent aspect of Nature, it recognizes thirty-six *tattvas* (categories), viz. *Śiva* (Static aspect of Consciousness), *Śakti* (Kinetic aspect of Consciousness), *Sadāśiva* (Universal Will), *Īśvara* (Universal Knowledge), *Sadvidyā* (Universal Action), *Māyā* (Limiting Principle) which gives rise to the five limited principles of *Kāla* (Time), *Niyati* (Space), *Rāga* (Desire), *Vidyā* (Limited Knowledge), *Kalā* (Limited Power), out of which evolve *Puruṣa* (Spirit), and the remaining twenty-four *tattvas* (categories) which are the same as those postulated in the Sāṁkhya system, q.v.; the literature of Kāśmīr Śaivism is classified under three broad divisions: the *Āgamaśāstra,* q.v., or traditional literature which includes the *Śivasūtra;* the *Spandaśāstra,* q.v., which discusses the doctrines of the *Śivasūtra,* and the *Pratyabhijñāśāstra,* q.v., which emphasizes the philosophical reasons for the doctrines of the *Śivasūtra.* The first leading exponent of this latter branch of literature was Somānanda who wrote *Śivadṛṣṭi,* which is no longer extant; however, his pupil Utpalācārya has summarized the teachings of Somānanda in the *Pratyabhijñasūtra.* This work, with its commentaries and the other works it has inspired, now constitutes perhaps the greater portion of the existing writings on Kāśmīr Śaivism.

Kavi (fr. I-E base **geue,* to observe, regard), a wise man, poet.

Kavirāja (compounded of *kavi* + *rajan,* king), 'king of poets,' a practitioner of Indian medicine (*Āyurveda,* q.v.).

Kavya (formed on *kavi,* q.v.), a sacrificial priest, an oblation to deceased ancestors.

Kevalakramapara, (in Mīmāṁsā) a text indicating an order or sequence only for the performance of the minor parts of a Vedic sacrifice; see *prayogavidhi.*

Krāntā (past. pass. participle of √*kram,* to step, stride, go, proceed, go through), one of the regions of ancient India; according to the Tantras, q.v., India had been divided into three regions called *krāntās,* viz. (1) *Viṣṇukrāntā,* extending from the Vindhya Mountain to Cattala (Chittagong), thus including Bengal; (2) *Rathakrāntā,* from the same mountain to Mahāchina (Tibet), including Nepal; and (3) *Aśvakrāntā,* from the same mountain to 'the great ocean,' apparently including the rest of India.

Kriyā (fr. √*kar,* to do, make), action; (in Kāśmīr Śaivism) universal action.

Kriyārūpa (in Mīmāṁsā) the action enjoined by a sacrifice.

Kṛkara (onomatopoetic word), 'a kind of partridge'; one of the five vital airs (*vāyu,* q.v.) of the outer body; it performs the function of hunger and thirst.

Kṛṣṇa, the eighth avatar, q.v., of Viṣṇu and one of the most widely worshiped of the Hindū deities; in the epic literature he is the hero of innumerable exploits; frequently a proper name.

Kumbhaka (fr. *kumbha*, jar, pitcher < I-E base *qeu-m-b(h)e, bend, curve), breath suspension, one of the three parts of prāṇayāma, q.v.

Kuntī, name of Pṛthā, daughter of a Yādava prince named Śūra who gave her to his childless cousin Kuntī, by whom she was adopted; she afterwards became one of the wives of Pāṇḍu; she had three sons, Yudhiṣṭhira, Bhīma, and Arjuna.

Kūrma, 'tortoise'; one of the five vital airs (vāyu, q.v.) of the outer body; it performs the function of opening the eyes.

Laghu, light, short.

Laghuvṛtti (compounded of *laghu* + *vṛtti*, qq.v), 'short commentary.'

Lakṣa (fr. √*lakṣ*, to mark, sign; probably < √*lag*, to adhere, stick, cling), a mark, sign, characteristic; one hundred thousand.

Lakṣaṇa (fr. *lakṣa*, q.v.), a mark, sign, symbol, characteristic, attribute, quality; (often confounded with *lakṣmaṇa*, q.v.).

Lākṣaṇikī (in Mīmāṁsā), an inferred prohibition for the performance of a Vedic sacrifice.

Lakṣmaṇa (fr. *lakṣa*, q.v.), having marks or signs or characteristics; endowed with auspicious signs or marks; name of various authors and other persons.

Lakṣmī (fr. *lakṣa*, q.v.), name of the goddess of fortune and beauty; frequently in later mythology regarded as the wife of Viṣṇu.

Laya (fr. √*lī*, late form of √*rī*, be dissolved, melt, become fluid), melting, dissolution, disappearance or absorption in; (in Yoga) making the mind inactive or indifferent.

Layakāla (compounded of *laya* + *kāla*, qq.v.), time of dissolution or destruction.

Lekhā (fr. √*likh*, later form of *rikh*, to scratch), delineating, drawing, painting, writing.

Līlā (probably reduplicated fr. the I-E onomatopoetic base *lā), play, sport, pastime.

Liṅga (etymology unknown), the phallic symbol under which Śiva, q.v., is principally worshipped, cf. *yoni*; (in Nyāya) the invariable mark that proves the existence of anything; (in Mīmāṁsā) the secondary sense of a word inferred from another word or collection of words.

Liṅgaśarīra (compounded of *liṅga* + *śarīra*, qq.v.), the subtle body, the invisible vehicle of the soul (*jīva*, q.v.); it is constant and does not change throughout the cycles of life and death; however, it is not eternal, for it is eventually re-absorbed into the elements of which it is composed; it consists of eighteen elements, viz.

(1) Intelligence (*buddhi*), (2) Ego (*ahaṁkāra*), (3) Mind *manas*), (4) five Knowing-senses (*jñānendriyas*), (5) five Working-senses (*karmendriyas*), and (6) five Subtle Elements (*tanmātras*), qq.v.; it is also called *Sūkṣmaśarīra*, q.v.; op. *sthūlaśarīra*, q.v.

Lingāyat, the Southern school of Śaivism, q.v., characterised by wearing a Liṅga, q.v., around their necks, also called liṅgavats, Liṅgaits, and sometimes Jaṅgamas.

Loka (fr. √*lok*, connected with √*ruc*, to shine, beam, display splendor), a sphere; world; universe; three Lokas are commonly enumerated, viz. heaven, earth, and the atmosphere or lower regions; but a fuller classification gives seven worlds, viz. (1) Earth (*bhūrloka*), (2) Sky (*bhuvarloka*), (3) Heaven (*svarloka*), (4) Middle Region (*maharloka*), (5) Place of Re-births (*janarloka*), (6) Mansion of the Blessed (*taparloka*), and (7) Abode of Truth (*satyaloka* or *brahmaloka*).

Madhva, leader of a Vaiṣṇava sect who founded the doctrine of dualism (*dvaita*, q.v.) based on the *Vedāntasūtras*, q.v.; he is also known as Ānandatīrtha; he was a Kanarese Brāhman, born in the year 1199 in a village near Udipi of the South Kanara district about sixty miles north of Mangalore; he founded a temple for Kṛṣṇa, q.v., at Udipi, where he taught until his death at the age of seventy-nine.

Māgha, the month of the Hindū calendar when the full moon is in the constellation Maghā; it corresponds to our January-February.

Mahābhārata, 'the great war of the Bharatas,' name of the great epic poem in about 215,000 lines describing the acts and contests of the sons of the two brothers Dhṛtarāṣṭra and Pāṇḍu, descendants of Bhārata, who were of the lunar line of kings reigning in the neighborhood of Hastināpura; the poem consists of eighteen books with a supplement called Harivaṅśa. It is all ascribed to Vyāsa, q.v.

Mahābhāṣya (compounded of *mahā* + *bhāṣya*, q.v.), 'Great Commentary,' name of Patañjali's commentary on the grammar of Pāṇini.

Mahābhūtas (compounded of *mahā*, great + *bhūta*, qq.v.), 'great elements,' the Sense-particulars of the Sāṁkhya system, viz., ether (*ākāśa*, q.v.), air (*vāyu*, q.v.), fire (*tejas*, q.v.), water (*āpas*, q.v.), and earth (*pṛthivī*, q.v.), these terms are not to be understood literally; their existence is dependent upon the subtle elements (*tanmātras*, q.v.).

Mahāprakaraṇa (in Mīmāṁsā), when the context relates to the rewards of the principal part of the sacrifice.

Maharṣi (compounded of *maha*, great + *ṛṣi*, q.v.), a great saint or sage.

Mahat, see *mahātattva*.

Mahātattva (compounded of *mahā*, great + *tattva*, q.v.), or simply Mahat, 'the Great Principle,' Cosmic Intelligence, (in Sāṁkhya) the first motion that arises in the supreme ideal universe, the first stage away from the original condition, the first product of the Cosmic Substance (*prakṛti*, q.v.).

Manana (fr. √*man*, to think), thinking, discriminative understanding, the second stage of self-culture.

Manas (fr. √*man*, to think, believe, imagine, suppose, conjecture), mind; in the widest sense of the word, it means all the mental powers, such as intellect, intelligence, understanding, perception, conscience, and will; in its limited use, it means the capacity for reflection, inference, testimony, doubt, ready wit, dream, cognition, conjecture, memory, desire, and feeling of pleasure and pain; (in Nyāya) it is an object of Right Knowledge (*Prameya*, q.v.); (in Vaiśeṣika) it is the ninth Eternal Reality or Substance (*Dravya*, q.v.), the internal organ of cognition and perception through which thoughts enter or by which objects affect the Soul (*Ātman*); (in Sāṁkhya) it is the Cosmic Mind, the principle of cognition; (in Yoga) it is the individual mind, the power of attention, selection, and rejection.

Manastva (compounded of *manas*, q.v., + abstract formative *-tva*), the state or condition of mind.

Maṇi (etymology doubtful), a jewel, gem.

Manogata (compounded of *manas*, q.v., + *gata*, past pass. participle of √*gam*, to go), 'mind-gone,' a thought, idea, wish, desire.

Mantra (fr. √*man*, to think), 'instrument of thought,' the ideal, inaudible sounds constituting one aspect of the universe, and when visualized or written as letters, or vocalized as syllables, constituting a universal terminology; also that portion of the Veda, q.v., which contains songs of praise to the gods; (in Mīmāṁsā) a text which helps one to remember the procedure of a sacrifice.

Manu (etymology doubtful), a man, thought of as the progenitor of the human race.

Manusaṁhitā (compounded of *manu* + *saṁhitā*, qq.v.), name of the collection of laws commonly known as 'the laws or institutes of Manu.'

Mārga (etymology ambiguous), a road, path, way; (with the Buddhists) the way or path pointed out by Buddha for escape from the misery of existence.

Maṭha (etymology uncertain), a cloister, temple.

Matvarthalakṣaṇābhayāt (in Mīmāṁsā), a figure of speech in which the *matup* affix is used.

Māyā (fr. I-E base **māie,* <**mā,* to motion with hand), delusion; the veiling, obscuring force of Nature, displaying universal consciousness as duality, thus producing error and illusion; it is postulated to account for the manifestation of all phenomena; (in Vedānta) it is said to be not real, yet not unreal; (in Kāśmīr Śaivism) it is regarded as the gross power of consciousness, and is referred to as *Māyā Śakti,* q.v.

Mīmāṁsā (fr. desiderative of √*man,* to reflect upon, consider, examine, investigate), literally, 'examination of the Vedas,' the popular name of the first part of the third division of Hindū philosophy, technically called *Pūrva-mīmāṁsā* (early examination) or *Karma-mīmāṁsā* (examination of the effect of actions); founded by Jaimini, whose actual date is quite unknown; concerns itself chiefly with the correct interpretation of Vedic ritual and texts; the second part of this division of Hindū philosophy is commonly known as Vedānta, q.v., technically called *Uttara-mīmāṁsā.*

Mīmāṁsāsūtra (compounded of *mīmāṁsā* + *sūtra,* qq.v.), the aphorisms of the Mīmāṁsā philosophy, ascribed to Jaimini, q.v.

Miśra (fr. I-E base **meike,* to mix), an affix of respect frequently used with proper names; name of various authors and other outstanding men.

Mokṣa (fr. *mokṣ,* desiderative of √muc, to set loose, free, release), emancipation, liberation, release from worldly existence.

Mokṣaśāstra (compounded of *Mokṣa* + *śāstra,* qq.v.), another name for the *Vaiśeṣikasūtra,* q.v., so called because it teaches the doctrine of liberation (*mokṣa*).

Mṛta (past pass. participle of √*mar,* to die), dead, deathlike.

Mukhyakrama (in Mīmāṁsā), the sequence of the subsidiaries or the subordinate parts to the order in the principal part of a Vedic sacrifice; see *prayogavidhi.*

Mukta (perf. pass. participle of √*muc,* to set loose, free, release), liberated, delivered, released, emancipated from worldly existence.

Mukti (fr. √*muc,* to set loose, free), final liberation or emancipation of the soul from worldly existence, final beatitude.

Muktvā (ger. of *muc,* to set loose, free), having attained final emancipation.

Mumukṣu (fr. desiderative of √*muc,* to set loose, free), anxious for liberation from mundane existence or final beatitude.

Mumukṣutva (fr. *mumukṣu,* q.v., + abstract formative *-tva*), right desire, which consists of earnestness to know the Ultimate Principle and thereby to attain liberation; (in Vedānta) one of the four qualifications listed by Śaṁkara for a student of philosophy, viz. (1) right discrimination (*viveka,* q.v.), (2) right dispassion and indifference (*vairāgya,* q.v.), (3) right conduct (*ṣaṭsampat,* q.v.), and (4) right desire (*mumukṣutva*).

Muni (fr. √*man,* to think), a saint, sage, seer, ascetic, monk, devotee, hermit (esp. one who has taken the vow of silence).

Nāga, 'snake'; one of the five vital airs (*vāyu,* q.v.) of the outer body; it performs the function of eructation.

Naiyāyikas, followers of the Nyāya philosophy.

Nāma (etymology uncertain), name; a characteristic mark or sign, as opposed to reality.

Nāmadheya (fr. *nāma,* name + √*dhā,* to put), a name title, appellation; the ceremony of giving a name to a child; (in Mīmāṁsā) a proper name used in defining the matter enjoined to it, one of the five divisions under which the contents of the Vedas, q.v., are classified.

Nāmarūpa (compounded of *nāma,* name + *rūpa,* form), name and form, meaning the phenomenal world.

Nava, nine.

Nigama (fr. pr. *ni,* down, into + √*gam,* to go), a work or treatise in which Śiva asks the questions and Pārvatī answers them, cf. *agama.*

Nigamana (fr. *Nigama,* q.v.), the summing up of an argument, conclusion, (in Nyāya) the last member (*avayava,* q.v.) of the five-membered syllogism and defined as that which shows the convergence of the four means of right knowledge (*pramāṇa* q.v.) toward the same object.

Nigrahasthāna (compounded of pr. *ni,* down, into + *graha,* seizure < √*grabh,* to seize + *sthāna,* position, place < √*sthā,* to stand), disagreement in principle, (in Nyāya) one of the sixteen categories; it is said to arise when one misunderstands, or does not understand at all, in which instance one is privileged to stop the argument.

Nimeṣa (fr. pr. *ni,* down, into + **meṣa,* a winking, opening of the eyes < √*miṣ,* to wink, open the eyes), 'shutting the eyes'; another term for the disappearance of the universe (*pralaya,* q.v.); op. *unmeṣa,* q.v.

Nindā (fr. √*ni[n]d,* to revile, scoff, blame), censure, blame.

Nirguṇa (fr. *nir,* without + *guṇa,* q.v.), without attribute, devoid of all qualities or properties.

Nirṇaya (fr. pr. *nis,* away, without + √*nī,* to lead), removal, ascertainment, (in Nyāya) one of the sixteen categories and defined as the removal of doubts by the hearing of two opposite views.

Nirvacana (fr. pr. *nis,* out + *vacana,* speaking < √*vac,* to speak), explanation, interpretation, etymology.

Nirvāṇa (fr. pr. *nis,* out + *vāna,* blown < √*vā,* to blow), 'extinction of the flame of life,' final emancipation from matter and re-union with the Supreme Spirit (*Brahman,* q.v.).

Niṣedha (fr. pr. *ni,* down, into + √*sidh,* to repel, scare or drive away), prohibition; (in Mīmāṁsā) a negative precept which prevents a man from doing a thing which is injurious or disadvantageous to him, one of the five divisions under which the contents of the Vedas, q.v., are classified.

Niṣkala (fr. pr. *niṣ,* away, without + *kalā,* q.v.), without parts, undivided.

Nitya (fr. pr. [*e*]*ni,* in + formative *-tya*), innate, native; perpetual, eternal; invariable, fixed, necessary.

Nityatva (fr. *nitya,* q.v., + abstract formative *-tva*), 'alwaysness' or 'eternity,' (in Kāśmīr Śaivism) the universal experience of Eternal Existence.

Niyama (fr. pr. *ni,* down, into + √*yam,* to hold together or back, check, curb, control, restrain), self-culture, regulation; the second prerequisite to the study and practice of Yoga, q.v.; ten rules of inner control (*niyamas*) are listed in the classic text, *Haṭhayogapradīpikā,* viz. penance, contentment, belief in God, charity, adoration of God, hearing discourses on the principles of religion, modesty, intellect, meditation, and sacrifice; see also yama; (in Mīmāṁsā) the restrictive rule, when the text lays down one mode of doing a thing that could be done in several ways.

Niyati (fr. pr. *ni,* down, into √*yam,* to control, restrain, hold), Space, (in Kāśmīr Śaivism) one of the five Kañcukas, q.v., it is the power that limits the universal condition of All-Pervasiveness (*Vyāpakatva,* q.v.); therefore, it is the origin of Space, the determinate where, that is, here and there.

Nyāya (compounded of pr. *ni,* down, into + *āya,* arrival, approach <√*nī,* to lead), one of six *Darśanas* (philosophical systems), founded by Gautama (also Gotama, c. 550 B.C.); so called, because it "goes into" all subjects, physical or metaphysical, according to the syllogistic method; it is the science of logical proof, and furnishes a correct method of philosophical inquiry into the objects and subjects of human knowledge; it is also called Tarkavidyā, "science of reasoning," or Vādavidyā, "science of discussion."

Nyāyśāstra (compounded of *nyāya* + *śāstra,* qq.v.), the doctrine of the Nyāya school of philosophy.

Nyāysūtra (compounded of *nyāya* + *sūtra,* qq.v.), the aphorisms of the Nyāya philosophy, ascribed to Gautama, q.v.

Nyāyavidyā (compounded of *nyāya* + *vidyā,* qq.v.), 'science of discussion,' logic; another name for Nyāya, q.v.

Nyāyavṛtti (compounded of *nyāya* + *vṛtti,* qq.v.), a commentary on the *Nyāyasūtra,* q.v.

Pada, a step, footstep, mark, sign, place, position, abode.

Pāda, the foot, a foot as a measure, (in Sāṁkhya) the power to move, one of the five abstract working-senses (*karmendriyas,* q.v.).

Padārtha (compounded of *pada* + *artha,* qq.v.), the meaning of a word; (in Vaiśeṣika) predicable, that which may be predicated or affirmed of existing things, category; six are given, viz. (1) Substance (*dravya*), (2) Attribute (*guṇa*), (3) Action (*karman*), (4) Generality, (*sāmānya*), (5) Particularity (*viśeṣa*), and (6) Combination (*samavāya*), qq.v.

Pañca, six.

Pañcalakṣaṇa (compounded of *pañca,* five + *lakṣaṇa,* q.v.), possessing five characteristics; said of the Purāṇas, q.v.

Pāṇi (Prākrit form for **parṇi,* cognate with Lat. *palma* [>Eng. palm]), the power to grasp, one of the abstract working-senses (*karmendriyas,* q.v.).

Pāṇini, name of the most eminent of all native Sanskrit grammarians, author of Astādhyāyī, and supposed author of *Dhātupāṭha, Gaṇapāṭha, Liṅgānuśāsana,* and *Śikṣā;* he was a *Gāndhāra* and a native of Śalātura, situated in the Northwest near Attok and Peshawar; he lived after Gautama Buddha, probably 5th cent., and is regarded as an inspired Muni or sage; his grandfather's name was Devala and his mother's name was Dākṣī.

Paṇḍita (etymology uncertain), a learned man, scholar, teacher, (esp.) a Brahman versed in Sanskrit, and in the science, laws, and philosophy of the Hindūs.

Patañjali, the founder of the Yoga philosophy; author of the *Yogasūtra;* he is assigned to various periods ranging from the third century B.C. to the fourth century A.D. (the earlier date is more probable); the name of a celebrated grammarian (author of the famous commentary called the *Mahābhāṣya* on the grammar of Pāṇini); some authorities argue that they are the same individual.

Pāṭhakrama (in Mīmāṁsā), when the order of the execution of things for the performance of the minor parts of a Vedic sacrifice is governed by their order in the text; see *prayogavidhi.*

Pāthasādeśya (in Mīmāṁsā), equality of place in the text.

Para (fr. $\sqrt{}$*par,* to pass, bring over), distant, far, opposite, ulterior, farther than, beyond; former, ancient; later; final, last; more than, better or worse than; superior or inferior, highest, supreme, chief (in comparative meanings).

Parakriyā (in Mīmāṁsā), the action of one individual.

Parāsaṁvit (compounded of *parama* + *saṁvid,* qq.v.), the Transcendental aspect of Nature, (in Kāśmīr Śaivism) Pure Consciousness, the Supreme Experience, also called *Paramaśiva,* q.v.; the technical term for this form of consciousness is *Caitanya,* q.v., which means the changeless aspect of pure consciousness, the Universal Intelligence or Spirit.

Parama (superlative of *para,* q.v.), most distant, most prominent, most excellent; highest point, highest degree; supreme.

Paramabrahman (compounded of *parama* + *brahma,* qq.v.), the Supreme Spirit.

Paramādvaita (compounded of *parama* + *advaita,* qq.v.), 'the highest being without a second,' pure non-duality.

Paramahaṁsa (compounded of *parama,* q.v., + *haṁsa,* goose, swan, flamingo), an ascetic of the highest order, a holy man who has subdued all his senses by abstract meditation.

Paramamokṣa (compounded of *parama* + *mokṣa,* qq.v.), final liberation.

Paramānanda (compound of *parama* + *ānanda,* qq.v.), highest bliss.

Paramāṇu (compounded of *parama* + *aṇu* qq.v.), 'atom,' the smallest possible division of matter, beyond which further division is impossible, or that whole which has no parts; a positional reality with no magnitude, that is, no length, breadth, or thickness; (in Vaiśeṣika) the ultimates of all things, the first four Eternal Realities (*dravyas*, q.v.), viz. (1) Earth (*pṛthivī*), (2) Water (*āpas*), (3) Fire (*tejas*), and (4) Air (*vāyu*), qq.v.

Paramapada (compounded of *parama* + *pada*, qq.v.), the highest state or position, final beatitude.

Paramaśiva (compounded of *parama* + *śiva*, qq.v.), 'in whom all things lie,' (in Kāśmīr Śaivism) the Supreme Śiva, the deity that personifies the ultimate form of consciousness, another name for the Transcendental Aspect of Nature (*Parāsaṁvit*, q.v.).

Paramātman (compounded of *parama* + *ātman*, qq.v.), the Supreme Spirit, the Universal Spirit, cf. *jīvātman.*

Paramatattva (compounded of *parama* + *tattva*, qq.v.), the highest truth.

Paramārtha (compounded of *parama* + *artha*, qq.v.), the highest truth, spiritual knowledge; any excellant or important object; the best kind of wealth.

Parameśa (compounded of *parama*, q.v., + *īśa*, lord, master < √*iś*, to own, possess), the Supreme Lord, name of Viṣṇu.

Parameśvara (compounded of *parama* + *īśvara*, qq.v.), the Supreme Lord; a name frequently used for Śiva, Viṣṇu, and Indra; also used as a proper name for illustrious men.

Parisaṁkhyā (in Mīmāṁsā), an implied prohibition in the performance of a Vedic sacrifice.

Pārvatī (fr. *parvata*, mountain, mountain-range), a Hindū goddess, consort of Śiva; so named because she was the daughter of Himavat, king of the snowy mountains (Himalayas, fr. *hima*, snow + *ālaya*, abode).

Paryudāsa (in Mīmāṁsā), a negative precept that applies to a person who is undertaking to perform a sacrifice.

Pāśa (fr. √*paś*, to bind), a snare, trap, noose, chain, fetter; especially the noose as attribute of Siva or Yama.

Paurāṇikas (fr. *purāṇa*, q.v.), adherents of a school founded by Loma Harṣaṇa, based on legend and mythology (*Purāṇa*, q.v.).

Pāyu (etymology quite uncertain), the power to excrete, one of the five abstract working-senses (*karmendriyas*, q.v.).

Phala (fr. √*phal*, to burst), fruit, (in Nyāya) an object of Right Knowledge (*Prameya*, q.v.), is defined as the product of all activity.

Prabhākara (compounded of *prabhā*, splendour, radiance <pr. *pra*,

before, first + √*bhā*, to shine + *kāra*, making, maker <√*kar*, to do, make), name of the founder of the first important school based on the Mīmāṁsā philosophy.

Pradhāna (fr. pr. *pra*, before, first + *dhāna*, containing, receptacle <√*dhā*, to put, set, place before), 'primary matter,' another name for *prakṛti*, q.v.

Pradhānakarma (in Mīmāṁsā), the primary action of a sacrifice.

Pradīpikā (fr. pr. *pra*, before first + *dīpikā*, flaming <√*dīp*, to shine), an explanation, commentary.

Prakaraṇa (in Mīmāṁsā), when the meaning of a sentence or a clause depends upon the context in which it is used.

Prakṛti (fr. pr. *pra*, before, first + *kar*, to make), Cosmic Substance, Primal Nature; the second principle postulated by the Sāṁkhya system, the primary source of all things; the unevolved which does evolve, the uncaused cause of phenomenal existence; it is eternal, indestructible, and all-pervasive; it is formless, limitless, immobile, and immanent; it consists of three constituents (*guṇas*, q.v.), viz. sattva, rajas, and tamas, qq.v.; it is also called *pradhāna* and *avyakta*, qq.v.; (in Vedānta) it is known as Māya, q.v.

Pralaya (fr. pr. *pra*, before, first + *laya*, q.v.), the dissolution and reabsorption of the universe at the end of a Kalpa, q.v.; (in Kāśmīr Śaivism) this is the transcendental phase of consciousness, the passive phase, the potential period when all manifestations are dormant; op. *sṛṣṭi*, q.v.

Pramaṇa (fr. pr. *pra*, before, first + *māna*, opinion <√*man*, to think), means of acquiring right knowledge; one of the sixteen categories listed in the Nyāya philosophy; each school has its theory of knowledge; perception (*pratyakṣa*) is the only means admitted by the Cārvākas; verbal testimony (*śabda*) is the only means admitted by the Mīmāṁsās; perception (*pratyakṣa*), and inference (*anumāna*) are admitted by the Vaiśeṣikas and Bauddhas (Buddhists); perception (*pratyakṣa*), inference (*anumāna*), and verbal testimony (*śabda*) are accepted by the Sāṁkhyas; a fourth, called comparison (*upamāna*), is added by the Naiyāyikas; a fifth, called presumption (*arthāpatti*), is added by the Prābhākaras; a sixth called non-existence (*abhāva*), is added by the Bhāṭṭas and Vedāntins; a seventh and eighth, called probability (*sambhava*) and tradition (*aitihya*), are added by the Paurāṇikas, qq.v.

Prameya (fr. pr. *pra*, before, first + *meya*, measurable <√*mā*, to measure), an object of right knowledge, (in Nyāya) twelve are listed, viz. Soul (*Ātma*), Body (*Śarīra*), Senses (*Indriya*), Objects

(*Artha*), Intelligence (*Buddhi*), Intellect (*Manas*), Activity (*Pravṛtti*), Fault (*Doṣa*), Rebirth (*Pretyabhāva*), Fruit (*Phala*), Pain (*Duḥkha*), and Release (*Apavarga*), qq.v.; one of the sixteen categories listed in the Nyāya philosophy.

Prāṇa (fr. pr. *pra*, before, first + *ana*, breath <√*an*, to breathe), the breath of life, vital air; one of the five vital airs (*vāyu*, q.v.) of the inner body; its movement is inward; its seat is the heart.

Prāṇāyāma (compounded of *prāṇa*, breath + *yāma*, cessation, end <√*yam*, to sustain, hold), breath control by means of inhalation (*pūraka*, q.v.), suspension (*kumbhaka*, q.v.), and exhalation (*recaka*, q.v.), one of the stages in the practice of Yoga, q.v.

Praśaṁsā (fr. pr. *pra*, before, first + √*śaṁs*, to praise), praise, commendation.

Pratijñā (fr. pr. *prati*, *towards*, against + √*jñā*, to know), declaration, proposition, (in Nyāya) the first member (*avayava*, q.v.) of the five-membered syllogism and defined as the enunciation of the object of knowledge to be proved as set forth in the Śāstras, q.v., or by verbal testimony (*śabda*, q.v.).

Pratiṣedha (in Mīmāṁsā), a negative precept of general applicability.

Pratyabhijñā (fr. preps. *prati*, towards, against + *abhi*, to, unto, towards + √*jñā*, to know), 'recognition,' the rediscovery or realization that the Universal and individual spirits are one; another name for Kāśmīr Śaivism.

Pratyabhijñāśāstra (compounded of *pratyabhijñā* + *śāstra*, qq.v.), that branch of the literature of Kāśmīr Śaivism that treats specifically the philosophical reasons for the doctrines of the *Śivasūtra*, q.v.; the founder of this branch of literature was Somānanda (c. 850–900 A.D.), author of *Śivadṛṣṭi*, which became the basic text of Kāśmīr Śaivism; however, his work was carried on in greater detail by his famed pupil, Utpala (c. 900–950 A.D.), author of the *Pratyabhijñāsūtra*, which has given its name to this branch of the literature.

Pratyāhāra (fr. preps. *prati*, towards, against + *ā*, to + √*har*, to take, hold back), withdrawal of the senses (*indriyas*, q.v.) from external objects; one of the stages in the practice of Yoga, q.v.

Pratyakṣa (fr. pr. *prati*, towards, against + *akṣa*, q.v.), perception, a means of correct knowledge (*pramāṇa*, q.v.), defined as that knowledge which arises from the contact of a sense with its object.

Pravṛtti (fr. pr. *pra*, before, first + *vṛtti*, mode of life or conduct, behaviour, general usage, mode of being, nature, character <√*vart*, to turn, occur, proceed, be, exist), activity, (in Nyāya) an object of Right Knowledge (*Prameya*, q.v.) and is defined as that which sets the mind, body, and voice in motion.

Pravṛttikrama (in Mīmāṁsā), the order of a procedure, once begun, will apply to others as well as in the performance of the minor parts of a Vedic sacrifice; see *prayogavidhi*.

Prayāga (fr. pr. *pra*, before, first + *yāga*, sacrifice, oblation <√*yaj*, to sacrifice, worship), 'place of sacrifice,' name of a celebrated place of pilgrimage at the confluence of the Gaṅga and Yamunā rivers, now called Allāhabād.

Prayāja (fr. pr. *pra*, before, first + *yāja*, sacrifice <√*yaj*, to sacrifice, worship), 'pre-sacrifice,' preliminary offering; a principal ceremony or sacrifice.

Prayatna (fr. pr. *pra*, before, first + *yatna*, endeavour <√*yam*, to reach), effort, endeavour.

Prayogavidhi (in Mīmāṁsā), the injunction that lays down the order of performance of the subsidiary or minor parts; the succession or order (*krama*) is of six kinds, viz. *śrutikrama, arthakrama, pāṭhakrama, sthānakrama, mukhyakrama,* and *pravṛttikrama*, qq.v.

Prayojana (fr. pr. *pra*, before, first + *yojana*, adjoining, yoking <√*yuj*, to join, yoke), purpose, (in Nyāya) one of the sixteen categories and defined as that with an eye to which one proceeds to act; also the fourth member of the additional five-membered syllogism introduced by later commentators to establish the object to be examined, defined as that which ascertains if the object is something to be sought, avoided, or ignored.

Preta (fr. pr. *pra*, before, first + *ita*, past participle of *i*, to go), departed, deceased, dead; the spirit of a dead person.

Pretya (compounded of pr. *pra*, before, first + ger. of √*i*, to go), having died, after death, in the next world, in the life to come, hereafter.

Pretyabhāva (compounded of *pretya* + *bhāva*, qq.v.), the state after death, future life, (in Nyāya) an object of Right Knowledge (*Prameya*, q.v.) and defined as the reappearance of the animating principle in physical form after having passed away.

Pṛthā, name of a daughter of Sūra and adopted daughter of Kuntī and one of the wives of Pāṇḍu; mother of Yudhiṣṭhira, Bhīma, and Arjuna.

Pṛthivī (fr. I-E base **plēte*, broad, flat, spread out; cf. √*prath*, to spread, extend), Earth as an element, (in Vaiśeṣika) the fir-

Eternal Reality (*Dravya,* q.v.); (in Sāṁkhya) the fifth Sense-Particular (*Mahābhūta,* q.v.), the principle of solidarity, its function is cohesion, its Special Property (*Viśeṣa,* q.v.) is Odour (*Gandha,* q.v.), its General Qualities (*Sāmānya Guṇas,* q.v.) are Flavour (*Rasa*), Form (*Rūpa*), Touch (*Sparśa*), and Sound (*Śabda*), qq.v.

Pūraka (fr. √*par,* to fill), inhalation, one of the three parts of *prāṇāyāma,* q.v.

Purākalpa (in Mīmāṁsā), the action of many individuals or a nation; these are the historical descriptions of one individual or many individuals and are indicated by the particles *iti, āha* or *ha.*

Purāṇa (fr. *purā,* before, formerly, of old), one of eighteen or more sacred treatises, legendary in character and discussing five principal topics (*pañcalakṣaṇa,* q.v.), viz. the creation of the universe, its destruction and renovation, the genealogy of gods and patriarchs, the reigns of the Manus, and the history of the solar and lunar races; interspersed are ethical, philosophical, and scientific observations; they are supposed to have been compiled by the poet Vyāsa, q.v.

Pūrṇa (past pass. participle of *par,* to fill, sate, nourish), filled, finished, completed, satisfied.

Purṇatva (fr. *pūrṇa,* q.v., + abstract formative *-tva*), fulness, (in Kāśmīr Śaivism) the universal experience of All-Completeness.

Puruṣa (etymology quite uncertain), Cosmic Spirit; the first principle postulated by the Sāṁkhya system to account for the subjective aspect of nature; it is the ultimate principle that regulates, guides, and directs the process of cosmic evolution, the efficient cause of the universe that gives the appearance of consciousness to all manifestations of matter (*prakṛti,* q.v.); it is pure spirit, eternal, indestructible, and all-pervasive; it is without activity and attribute, without parts and form; it is the unevolved which does not evolve, the uncaused which is not the cause of any new mode of being.

Pūrva, first, earlier, former, prior, previous.

Pūrvamīmāṁsā (compounded of *pūrva* + *mīmāṁsā,* qq.v.), 'inquiry into or interpretation of the first or Mantra portion of the Veda'; name of the system of philosophy founded by Jaimini (as opposed to *uttaramīmāṁsā,* founded by Bādarāyaṇa, which is an inquiry into the later or Upaniṣad portion of the Veda); pūrvamīmāmsā is generally called simply the Mīmāṁsā, q.v.

Pūrvapakṣa (compounded of *pūrva,* q.v., *pakṣa,* wing, side of an argument *I-E base *pāge, pōge,* side), the first objection to an assertion in any discussion, the anti-thesis; the third division of a topic (*adhikaraṇa,* q.v.).

Rāga (fr. √*ra* (*ñ*)*j,* to be coloured), desire, (in Kāśmīr Śaivism) one of the five Kañcukas, q.v.; it is the power that limits the universal condition of All-Completeness (Pūrṇatva, q.v.); therefore, it is the origin of Desire.

Rajas (fr. √*ra*(*ñ*)*j,* to be coloured, affected, or moved), energy, activity; (in Sāṁkhya) one of the three constituents (*guṇas,* q.v.) of the Cosmic Substance (*prakṛti,* q.v.), viz. the activating aspect of Nature without which the other constituents could not manifest their inherent qualities; (in Yoga) the quality of egoism or selfishness.

Rāmānuja, the renowned Vaiṣṇava leader who founded the doctrine of qualified non-dualism (*viśiṣṭādvaita,* q.v.) based on the *Vedāntasūtras,* q.v. He was born 1027 A.D. in Śriperuṁbudūr, a town located a few miles west of Madras, and, according to tradition, he lived to be 120 years of age; most of his life was spent at Śrīraṅgam; his great commentary (*Śrībhāṣya*) on the *Vedāntasūtras* is the classic text for the Vaiṣṇavas today.

Rāmāyaṇa (compounded of *Rāma* + *āyana,* approach fr. pr. *ā* to + *yāna,* travel, journey < √*yā* to go), name of Vālmīki's celebrated epic poem, describing the 'goings' of Rāma and his wife Sītā in about 24,000 verses divided into seven books; the first and last are believed to be comparatively modern additions, but the date of the original books is probably the 3rd or 4th cent. B.C.; Rāma's character is described as that of a perfect man, who bears suffering and self-denial with superhuman patience.

Rasa (fr. √*ras,* to taste), the subtle element (*tanmātra,* q.v.) of flavour.

Rasana (fr. *rasa,* q.v.), the power to taste, one of the five abstract knowing-senses (*jñānendriyas,* q.v.).

Recaka (fr. √*ric,* to empty, set free, give up), exhalation, one of the three parts of *prāṇāyāma,* q.v.

Ṛgveda, one of the four Vedas, q.v.

Ṛṣi (probably fr. √*ras,* to roar, yell, cry, pointing to a forgotten shamanistic period), an inspired poet or sage.

Rūḍhi (in Mīmāṁsā), a word, not compounded with any other word and with a conventional meaning which must be learned from past authorities, such as Pāṇini, q.v.; it has the inherent power to convey a sense.

Rūpa (etymology uncertain), the subtle element (*tanmātra,* q.v.) of form.

Śabda (possibly fr. I-E onomatopoetic base *kop,* to make a noise), verbal testimony, a means of correct knowledge (*pramāṇa,* q.v.), defined as the instructive assertion of a reliable person; the only means (*pramāṇa*) admitted by Jaimini in the Mīmāṁsā system; here Śabda means the Word or the first sound in Nature, and is claimed to be eternal; (in Sāṁkhya) the subtle element (*tanmātra,* q.v.) of sound.

Saccitānanda (compounded of *sat* + *cit* + *ānanda,* qq.v.), 'being—consciousness—bliss'; (in Vedānta) the three attributes of the Ultimate Principle (*Brahman,* q.v.); (in Kāśmīr Śaivism) it represents the perfect condition of the supreme ideal, the transcendental condition of universal potentiality.

Sadākhya (fr. pr. *sadā,* always, ever + √*khyā,* to behold, see), another name for the third category (*tattva,* q.v.) in Kāśmīr Śaivism, see Sadāśiva.

Ṣad Darśana (fr. numeral *ṣaṣ,* six and √*darś,* to see); the six 'insights,' views, doctrines, or philosophical systems, viz. Nyāya by Gautama; Vaiśeṣika by Kaṇāda; Sāṁkhya by Kapila; Yoga by Patañjali; (Pūrva) Mīmāṁsā by Jaimini; Uttara-Mīmāṁsā or Vedānta by Bādarāyaṇa, qq.v.

Sadāśiva (fr. pr. *sadā,* always, ever + *śiva,* q.v.), 'always prosperous'; (in Kāśmīr Śaivism) the third category (*tattva,* q.v.), postulated to account for the first evolute of consciousness. Here the subject (*Aham,* q.v.) has just become aware of itself in relation to its object (*Idam,* q.v.); also called the *Sadākhya Tattva.*

Sādhaka (fr. √*sādh,* to go straight to the goal, be successful), one who practices spiritual exercises (*sādhana,* q.v.).

Sādhana (fr. √*sādh,* to go straight to the goal, be successful), that which produces success (*siddhi,* q.v.) or the result sought, be it material or spiritual advancement; spiritual exercises.

Sadhu (fr. √*sādh,* to go straight to the goal, be successful), an ascetic, holy man.

Sadvidyā (compounded of *sat* + *vidyā,* qq.v.), 'having true knowledge'; (in Kāśmīr Śaivism) the fifth category (*tattva,* q.v.), postulated to account for the complete unity in the dual relationship of *I am This,* the condition of complete recognition without emphasis either on the subject (Aham, q.v.) or on the object (Idam, q.v.); also called the Śuddha Vidyā *Tattva.*

Saguṇa (fr. pr. *sa,* with + *guṇa,* q.v.), with attribute having qualities or properties, qualified.

Sahasra, one thousand.

Śaivism (fr. *śiva,* q.v.), name of one of the three great divisions of modern Hindūism (the other two being Vaiṣṇavism and Śāktism, qq.v.); the Śaivas identify Śiva—rather than Brahma and Viṣṇu—with the Supreme Being, and are exclusively devoted to his worship, regarding him as the creator, preserver, and destroyer of the universe.

Śakti (fr. √*śak,* to be strong, able), power, energy, capacity, strength; (in Kāśmīr Śaivism) the second category (*tattva,* q.v.), representing the power of consciousness to act; therefore, the kinetic aspect of consciousness; (in Śāktism, q.v.) *śakti* is portrayed as the female aspect of the Ultimate Principle, deified as the wife of Śiva, q.v.

Śāktism (fr. *śakti,* q.v.), name of one of the three great divisions of modern Hindūism (the other two being Śaivism and Vaiṣṇavism, qq.v.); the Śāktas worship Śakti—rather than Śiva and Viṣṇu—and regard it as the embodiment of the power that supports all that lives and which upholds the universe; Śakti is portrayed as the female aspect of the Ultimate Principle, and deified as the wife of Śiva.

Śakya (fr. √*śak,* to be strong, able), able, capable.

Śakyaprāpti (compounded of *śakya,* q.v., + *prāpti,* attainment, acquisition + pr. *pra,* before, first + √*āp,* to reach), capacity; (in Nyāya) the third member of the additional five-membered syllogism introduced by later commentators to establish the object to be examined, defined as that which determines if the example warrants the conclusion.

Śama (fr. √*śam,* to become quiet, cease, be extinguished), tranquility or control of thought by withdrawing the mind from worldly affairs, abstraction from external objects through intense meditation; (in Vedānta) one of the six acquirements (*ṣaṭsampat,* q.v.).

Samādhāna (fr. prs. *sam,* together + *ā,* to + *dhāna,* receptacle < √*dhā,* to put, place, set; bear, hold), balanced mental equipoise; freedom from much sleep, laziness, and carelessness; abstract contemplation; profound absorption; (in Vedānta) one of the six acquirements (*ṣaṭsampat,* q.v.).

Samādhi (fr. prs. *sam,* together + *ā,* to + **dhi,* a placing < √*dhā,* to put, place), 'putting together,' profound meditation; the final stage in the practice of Yoga, q.v., in which the individual becomes one with the object of meditation, thus attaining a condition of superconsciousness and unqualified blissfulness, which is emancipation (*mokṣa,* q.v.).

Samākhyā (in Mīmāṁsā), when it is necessary to break compound words up into their component parts in order to ascertain their meaning.

Samāna (fr. pr. *sam,* together + *āna,* breath <√*an,* to breathe), one of the five vital airs (*vāyu,* q.v.) of the inner body; it separates things; its seat is in the region of the navel.

Sāmānya (fr. *sama,* same), general, universal, common; (in Nyāya) generalization, one of the three forms of equivocation (*chala,* q.v.); (in Vaiśeṣika) generality, genus, the fourth Predicable (*Padārtha,* q.v.).

Samavāya (fr. prs. *sam,* together + *ava,* off +*aya,* a going <√*i,* to go), combination, co-inherence, concomitance; (in Vaiśeṣika) the sixth Predicable (*Padārtha,* q.v.), expressing the relation which exists between a substance and its qualities, between a whole and its parts.

Sāmaveda, one of the four Vedas, q.v.

Sambhava (fr. pr. *sam,* together + *bhava,* being, existence <√*bhū,* to be), probability, a means of correct knowledge (*pramāṇa,* q.v.), defined as cognizing the existence of a thing from that of another thing in which it is included; (in Nyāya) this is included in inference (*anumāna*).

Saṁgati (fr. pr. *sam,* together + *gati,* going <√*gā,* to go), going together, agreement, consistency; the fifth division of a topic (*adhikaraṇa,* q.v.); it must comply with three requirements, viz. (1) consistency with the entire treatise (*śāstrasaṁgati*), (2) consistency with the whole chapter (*adhyāyasaṁgati*), and (3) consistency with the whole part (*pādasaṁgati*).

Saṁgraha (fr. pr. *sam,* together + √*graha,* seizure), a compendium, summary, catalogue, list, epitome, abridgment, short statement.

Saṁhita (perf. pass. participle of *sandhā,* fr. pr. *sam,* together + √*dhā,* to put, place), put together, joined, attached; fixed, settled.

Saṁhitā (fr. *saṁhita,* q.v.), collection, especially any collection of hymns forming the Vedas; any methodically arranged collection of texts or verses.

Śaṁkara, a celebrated teacher whose name is almost synonymous with Vedānta; he founded the doctrine of non-dualism (*advaita,* q.v.) based on the *Vedāntasūtras,* q.v.; it is generally believed that he lived between A.D. 788 and 820; his birth place is said to have been Kāladi, on the west coast of the peninsula in the Malabar; his family was of the learned but hardworking Nambūdri sect of Brāhmans; all accounts describe him as having led an erratic, controversial life; he founded four monasteries (*maṭhas*), viz. at Śṛṅgeri in the South, Badarīnāth in the North, Pūri in the East, and Dvārakā in the West; he is believed to have died in the Himalayan village of Kedārnāth.

Sāṁkhyā (fr. pr. *saṁ*, together + √*khyā*, to reckon or count up, sum up, enumerate, calculate), the oldest school of Hindū Philosophy, giving the first systematic account of the process of cosmic evolution, founded by Kapila (?6th cent. B.C.), so called, because in its analysis of the universe it "enumerates" twenty-five tattvas (categories), viz. *Puruṣa* (Cosmic Spirit), *Prakṛti* (Cosmic Substance), *Mahat* (Cosmic Intelligence), *Ahaṁkāra* (Individuating Principle), *Manas* (Cosmic Mind), *Indriyas* (ten Abstract Sense Powers), *Tanmātras* (five Subtle Elements), and *Mahābhūtas* (five Sense-Particulars), qq. v.; the oldest account of the Sāṁkhya system is given in the *Sāṁkhyapravacanasūtra* and the *Tattvasamāsa*, ascribed to the sage Kapila; the oldest extant systematic exposition of the Sāṁkhya system is the *Sāṁkhyakārikā* by Īśvarakṛṣṇa which claims to be merely a condensation of an earlier text called the *Ṣaṣṭitantra*, of which only scanty fragments are extant.

Sāṁkhyakārikā (compounded of *saṁkhya* + *kārikā* q.v.), name of a collection of seventy-two memorial verses or stanzas by Īśvarakṛṣṇa (also called *sāṁkhyasaptati*; the oldest extant systematic exposition of the Sāṁkhya system).

Sampat (in composition for *sampad*, fr. pr. *sam*, together + **pad*, a falling < √*pad*, to fall), success, accomplishment; a condition or requisite of success.

Saṁsāra (fr. pr. *sam*, together + *sāra*, flowing < √*sar*, to flow), 'going about,' the passage of the soul in the cycle of births and deaths; the round of existence; transmigration, metempsychosis.

Saṁśaya (fr. pr. *sam*, together + **śaya* < √*śī*, to fall out or away, disappear, vanish), doubt, (in Nyāya) one of the sixteen categories and defined as a conflicting judgment about the precise character of an object, arising from the recognition of properties common to many objects, or of properties not common to any of the objects, from conflicting testimony, and from irregularity of perception and non-perception; also the second member of the additional five-membered syllogism introduced by later commentators to establish the object to be examined, defined as that which questions the reason, the second division of a topic (*adhikaraṇa*, q.v.).

Saṁśayavyudāsa (compounded of *saṁśaya* + *vyudāsa*, qq.v.), removal of all doubt, (in Nyāya) the firth member of the additional five-membered syllogism introduced by later commentators to establish the object to be examined, defined as that which makes certain that the opposite of the proposition is not true.

Saṁskāra (fr. pr. *sam*, together + (*s*)*kāra*, action < √(*s*)*kar*, to put together, form well, compose), mental impression, memory; the effects of *karma*, q.v.

Saṁskṛta (pref. pass. par. of *saṁskar*, to put together; cf. *saṁskāra*), the Sanskrit language.

Saṁvid (fr. pr. *sam*, together + *vid*, knowledge < √*vid*, to know), consciousness, knowledge, understanding.

Saṁyama (compounded of *sam*, together + *yama*, q.v.), restraint, self-control, forbearance.

Saṁyoga (compounded of *sam*, together + *yoga*, q.v.), conjunction, combination, union, absorption.

Sannidhipāṭha, (in Mīmāṁsā) when the meaning is regulated by the text which is near.

Sannipatyopakāraka, (in Mīmāṁsā) actions enjoined with respect to the substance, producing visible and invisible results.

Sapta, seven.

Sara (etymology doubtful), the core, essence, heart of anything; the real meaning; a compendium, summary, epitome.

Śarīra (etymology doubtful), the body, (in Nyāya) an object of Right Knowledge (*Prameya*, q.v.) and defined as the site of motion (*ceṣṭā*), of the senses (*indriyas*), and of the objects (*arthas*) of pleasure and pain.

Śārīrakamīmāṁsa (compounded of *śārīraka* + *mīmāṁsā*, qq.v.), another name for the *Vedāntasūtra*, q.v., so called because the central topic is an inquiry into the embodied spirit (*śārīraka*).

Sarva, whole, entire, all, every.

Sarvajña (compounded of *sarva*, q.v., + *jña*, knowing < √*jña*, to know), all-knowing, omniscient.

Sarvajñatva (compounded of *sarvajña*, q.v., + abstract formative *-tva*), 'all-knowingness' or 'omniscience,' (in Kāśmīr Śaivism) the universal experience of All-Knowledge.

Sarvakara (compounded of *sarva* + *kara*, qq.v.), 'maker of all,' name of Śiva.

Sarvakartṛ (compounded of *sarva* + *kartṛ*, qq.v.), the maker or creator of all.

Sarvakartṛtva (compounded of *sarvakartṛ* + abstract formative *-tva*), 'all-makingness,' (in Kāśmīr Śaivism) the universal experience of All-Powerfulness.

Ṣaṣ, six.

Śāsana (fr. √*śās*, to order), an order, command; any book or work of authority, scripture, doctrine.

Śāstra (fr. √*śās*, enjoin, teach, instruct), any manual or compendium of rules, any book or treatise, (esp.) any religious or scientific treatise, any sacred book or composition of divine authority (applicable even to the Veda); the word *śāstra* is often found in fine composition after the word denoting the subject of the book, or is applied collectively to whole departments of knowledge, e.g., *Vedānta-śāstra*, a work on the Vedānta philosophy or the whole body of teaching on that subject.

Śāstrin (fr. *śāstra*, q.v.), one versed in the Śāstras; a teacher of sacred books or sciences, a learned man.

Sat (participle of √*as*, to be), being; (in Vedānta) the active condition of the transcendental aspect of the Ultimate Principle (Brahman, q.v.); cf. *asat*.

Śata, one hundred.

Satkāryavāda (compounded of *sat* + *kārya* + *vāda*, qq.v.), the doctrine that the effect exists in the cause; this is the distinguishing feature of the Sāṁkhya system.

Satkāryavādin (fr. *satkāryavāda*, q.v.), an adherent of the doctrine that the effect exists in the cause.

Ṣaṭsampat (fr. *ṣaṭ* used in composition for *ṣaṣ*, six + *sampat*, q.v.), right conduct, which consists of the six acquirements, viz. (1) tranquillity (*śama*, q.v.), (2) self-restraint (*dama*, q.v.), (3) tolerance, (*uparati*, q.v.), (4) endurance (*titikṣa*, q.v.), (5) faith *śraddhā*, q.v.), and (6) mental equipoise (*samādhāna*, q.v.); (in Vedānta) one of the four qualifications listed by Śaṁkara for a student of philosophy, viz. (1) right discrimination (*viveka*, q.v.), (2) right dispassion and indifference (*vairāgya*, q.v.), (3) right conduct (*ṣaṭsampat*), and (4) right desire (*mumukṣutva*, q.v.).

Sattva (fr. *sat*, q.v., + abstract formative *-tva*), being, existence, reality, true essence; (in Sāṁkhya) one of the three constituents (*guṇas*, q.v.) of the Cosmic Substance (*prakṛti*, q.v.), viz. the illuminating aspect of Nature that reveals all manifestations; (in Yoga) the quality of purity or goodness.

Satya (abstract noun fr. *sat,* q.v.), 'truth,' the first of the four ages (*yugas,* q.v.), 'the golden age,' also called the Krita Yuga; its duration is said to be 1,728,000 years.

Siddhānta (compounded of *siddha,* past. pass. participle of √*sidh,* to be accomplished, to succeed + *anta,* end), conclusion; (in Nyāya) an established tenet, one of the sixteen categories and defined as a dogma resting on the authority of a certain school, hypothesis, or implication; the fourth division of a topic (*adhikaraṇa,* q.v.).

Siddharūpa, (in Mīmamsā) an accomplished thing consisting of class, material, number, and the like, and having a visible effect.

Siddhi (present part. of √*sidh,* to be accomplished, succeed), an accomplishment, success.

Śiva (possibly fr. I-E base *keie,* to lie, be at home, be dear; hence, perhaps—euphemistically—'the kindly, gracious, auspicious one'), name of one of the gods of the Hindū Trimūrti or Trinity, viz. Brahmā, 'the creator,' Viṣṇu, 'the preserver,' and Śiva, 'the destroyer'; (among the adherents of Śaivism, q.v.) the Supreme Deity; (in Kāśmīr Śaivism, q.v.) the deity used to represent the static aspect of consciousness in the manifest world, the first tattva (category).

Śivasūtra (compounded of *śiva* + *sūtra,* qq.v.), the aphorisms of the Kāśmīr Śaivism philosophy, ascribed to Vasugupta, q.v., so called because they were supposedly revealed by Śiva to Vasugupta in Kāśmīr; it is classified as an *āgamaśāstra,* q.v.; the literature that followed is classified into two broad divisions, one stressing the doctrines of the *Śivasūtra,* called the *Spandaśāstra,* q.v., and the other emphasizing the philosophical reasons for their support, called the *Pratyabhijñāśāstra,* q.v.

Smṛti (fr. √*smar,* to remember), traditional knowledge as opposed to *śruti,* q.v.

Spanda (fr. √*spanda,* to quiver, throb), 'pulse,' that branch of literature of the *Śivasūtra,* q.v., that lays down in greater detail its doctrines without entering much into the philosophical reasons for them.

Spandaśāstra (compounded of *spanda* + *śāstra,* qq.v.), that branch of literature of Kāśmīr Śaivism that elaborates in greater detail the doctrines of the *Śivasūtra,* q.v., but does not propose to discuss the philosophy upon which they are based; the founder of this branch of literature was Kallata Bhaṭṭa (c. 850–900 A.D.); his treatise is entitled the *Spandasūtras,* generally called the *Spandakārikās.*

Sparśa (fr. √*sparś,* to touch; feel), the subtle element (*tanmātra,* q.v.) of touch; this is a technical term generally translated as Touch and used to mean the sense of feeling as the impression left on the consciousness rather than its tactual meaning; as for example, one is touched by an act of kindness.

Śraddhā (fr. *śrad,* truth, faithfulness + √*dhā,* to put, place, set), faith, trust, confidence; (in Vedānta) one of the six acquirements (*ṣaṭsampat,* q.v.).

Śrauta (fr. √*śru,* to hear), relating to sacred tradition, according to the Veda.

Śrauti, (in Mīmāṁsa) a directly stated prohibition by some text for the performance of a Vedic sacrifice.

Śrutikrama, (in Mīmāṁsā) the order determined by a direct test for the performance of the minor parts of a Vedic sacrifice; see *prayogavidhi.*

Śravaṇa (fr. √*śru,* to hear), hearing, the first stage of self-culture.

Śrotṛ (fr. √*śru,* to hear), one who hears.

Srotra (fr. √*śru,* to hear), the power to hear, one of the five abstract knowing-senses (*jñānendriyas,* q.v.).

Sṛṣṭi (fr. √*sarj,* to let go, discharge, emit), the creation of the universe; (in Kāśmīr Śaivism) the immanent or active phase of consciousness; this phase is also called *ābhāsa,* q.v.

Śruta (past pass. participle of √*śru,* to hear), revealed knowledge transmitted orally by holy men from generation to generation.

Śruti (fr. √*śru,* to hear + abstract formative *-ti*), revealed knowledge, the Vedas; (in Mīmāṁsā) the primary sense of a word or collection of words, not depending upon any other word for its meaning.

Sthāna, (in Mīmāṁsā) when the meaning depends upon the location or word-order.

Sthānakrama, (in Mīmāṁsā) the transposition of a thing from its proper place by reason of being preceded by another thing which is followed by another in the performance of the minor parts of a Vedic sacrifice; see *prayogavidhi.*

Sthūla (fr. √*sthā,* to stand, remain, endure), gross, tangible, material; opposite to *sūkṣma,* q.v.

Sthūlaśarīra (compounded of *sthūla* + *śarīra,* qq.v.), the gross body, the material or perishable body which is destroyed at death; it consists of the five gross elements (*bhūtas*, q.v.); op. *liṅgaśarīra*, q.v.

Śuddha (past. pass. participle of √*śudh*, to purify), pure; (in Kāśmīr Śaivism) the first five categories (*tattva*, q.v.), are classified for the purpose of worship as the Pure Category (*Śuddha Tattva*), viz. *Śiva, Śakti, Sadāśiva, Īśvara,* and *Sadvidyā*, qq.v.; they are called Pure because the dual relationship of subject and object is a single unit, that is, the object is seen as a part of the subject; see also *Śuddhāśuddha* and *Aśuddha*.

Śuddhāśuddha (compounded of *śuddha*, q.v., + *aśuddha*, fr. neg. part. *a* + *śuddha*), pure-impure; (in Kaśmīr Śaivism) the categories (*tattva*, q.v.) from *Māyā* to *Puruṣa* are classified for the purpose of worship as the Pure-Impure Category (*Śuddhāśuddha Tattva*); they are *Māyā, Kāla, Niyata, Rāga, Vidyā, Kalā,* and *Puruṣa*, qq.v.; so called, because they represent that condition in Nature which exists between the world of Pure Unity and the world of Impure Duality; see also *Śuddha* and *Aśuddha*.

Sukha (probably fr. *su*, well + *kha*, axle-hole), 'running swiftly or easily'; pleasant, agreeable, comfortable, happy, prosperous.

Sūkṣma (etymology uncertain), subtle, atomic, intangible; opposite to *sthūla*, q.v.

Sūkṣmaśarīra (compounded of *sūkṣma* + *śarīra*, qq.v.), the subtle body; another name for *liṅgaśarīra*, q.v.; op. *sthūlaśarīra*, q.v.

Sūri (etymology uncertain), a wise man, sage, teacher; used frequently with proper names.

Sūrya (etymology uncertain), the sun or its deity; sometimes an epithet of Śiva.

Suśruta, the author of an ancient work on Indian medicine (*Āyurveda*, q.v.).

Sūtra (fr. √*siv*, to sew), a short sentence or aphoristic rule; any work or manual consisting of strings of such rules hanging together like threads; the term Sūtra is applied to original text books as opposed to explanatory works.

Svabhāva (compounded of *sva*, one's own + *bhava*, q.v.), one's own nature, innate disposition.

Svadharma (compounded of *sva*, one's own + *dharma*, q.v.), one's own duty.

Svāmin (fr. *sva*, one's own + possessive formative *-min*), a spiritual preceptor, holy man; an honorary title used after proper names.

Svarūpa (compounded of *sva*, one's own + *rūpa*, q.v.), one's own form, nature, character.

Tadviṣiṣṭapadārthapara, (in Mīmāṁsā) indicating the order or sequence in the course of laying down certain other things for the performance of the minor parts of a Vedic sacrifice; see *prayoga-vidhi*.

Tadvyapadeśa, (in Mīmāṁsā) the name given to a sacrifice by reason of its resemblance to another from which it derives its name.

Tamas (etymology uncertain), darkness; (in Sāṁkhya) one of the three constituents (*guṇas*, q.v.) of the Cosmic Substance (*prakṛti*, q.v.), viz. the restraining aspect of Nature that obstructs and envelops the other two constituents by counteracting the tendency of Rajas, q.v., to do work and Sattva, q.v., to reveal; (in Yoga) the quality of delusion or ignorance.

Tanmātras (fr. pronoun *tad*, that + *mātra*, element < √*mā*, to measure), 'merely that,' 'thatness,' the Subtle Elements, viz. the essence of sound (*śabda*), touch (*sparśa*), form (*rūpa*), flavour (*rasa*), and odour (*gandha*); they are the subtle objects of the sense powers (*indriyas*, q.v.), the subtlest form of actual matter, without magnitude, supersensible, and perceived mediately only through gross objects.

Tantra (fr. √*tan*, to extend, spread + agential suffix *tra*), that body of religious scripture (*śāstra*, q.v.) which is stated to have been revealed by Śiva, q.v., as the specific scripture of the fourth or present age (*Kali Yuga*, qq.v.), cast in the form of a dialogue between Śiva and his female consort, Pārvatī, q.v.; when he answers the questions, the treatise is called an *Āgama*, q.v., and when she answers the questions, it is called a *Nigama*, q.v.; the Tantras were the encyclopedias of knowledge of their time; the seven marks or topics of a Tantra are (1) creation (*sṛṣṭi*), (2) destruction of the universe (*pralaya*), (3) worship of the gods (*devatānāmārcanam*), (4) spiritual exercise (*sādhanas*), (5) rituals (*puraścarana*), (6) the six 'magical' powers (*ṣaṭkarma*), and (7) meditation (*dhyānayoga*).

Tantrasāra (compounded of *tantra* + *sāra*, qq.v.), 'Tantra-essence,' name of a compilation.

Tantraśāstra (compounded of *tantra* + *śāstra*, qq.v.), name of a work.

Tāntrika (adjective formation of *tantra*, q.v.); a follower of the Tantra doctrine.

Tapas (fr. √*tap*, to make hot or warm), the practice of austerities, penance.

Tarka (etymology ambiguous), confutation, (in Nyāya) one of the sixteen categories and defined as a conjecture for the sake of knowledge of truth in respect to an unknown object by the elimination of all contrary suppositions.

Tarkavidyā (compounded of *tarka* + *vidyā*, qq.v.), 'science of reasoning,' logic, another name used for the Nyāya.

Tatprakhya, (in Mīmāṁsā) a conventional name given to a particular sacrifice, the description of which is given elsewhere in a separate treatise.

Tattva (fr. pronoun *tad*, that + abstract suffix *-tva*), 'thatness,' essence, truth, reality, principle, category; in Sāṁkhya twenty-five are enumerated, in Kāśmīr Śaivism thirty-six are given.

Tattvajñāna (compounded of *tattva*, q.v., + *jñāna*, knowledge <√*jñā*, to know), knowledge of truth, insight into the true principles of philosophy.

Tejas (fr. √*tij*, to be sharp), Fire as an element, (in Vaiśeṣika) the third Eternal Reality (*Dravya*, q.v.); (in Sāṁkhya) the third Sense-Particular (*Mahābhūta*, q.v.), the principle of luminosity, its function is expansion, its Special Property (*Viśeṣa*, q.v.) is Form (*Rūpa*, q.v.), its General Qualities (*Sāmānya Guṇas*, q.v.) are Touch (*Sparśa*), and Sound (*Śabda*), qq.v.

Titikṣā (fr. desiderative form of √*tij*, to become sharp), endurance, bearing heat and cold and other pairs of opposites; (in Vedānta) one of the six acquirements (*ṣaṭsampat*, q.v.).

Trasa (fr. √*tras*, to tremble, shudder), the collective body of living beings.

Trasareṇu (compounded of *trasa*, q.v., + *reṇu*, dust, pollen, atom <√*ri*, to release, be shattered, drip, flow), another name for *tryaṇuka*, q.v., in Vaiśeṣika.

Tretā (fr. *traya*, triple <*tri*, three), the second of the four ages (*yugas*, q.v.); a fourth less righteous and briefer than the preceding, enduring 1,296,000 years.

Tri, three.

Trika (fr. *tri*, three), another name for Kāśmīr Śaivism, q.v.; so called, because it deals with the three-fold principle of God, Soul and Matter; the literature of the system is called *Trikaśāsana*, or *Trikaśāstra*.

Trikaśāsana (compounded of *trika* + *śāsana*, qq.v.), see Trika.

Trikaśāstra (compounded of *trika* + *śāstra*, qq.v.), see Trika.

Trivarga (compounded of *tri*, three + *varga*, division <√*varj*, to turn), the three objects of human pursuit, viz. wealth (*artha*, q.v.), pleasure (*kāma*, q.v.), and virtue (*dharma*, q.v.).

Tryaṇuka (compounded of *tri*, three + *aṇuka*, atomic <*aṇu*, q.v.), a ternary or a form consisting of three variables associated in such a manner that they combine to form an integral whole, operating and functioning as a single system; to produce this form, three lines (*dvyaṇukas*, q.v.) must remain apart and relate themselves on different planes so as not to form a more extended line, e.g. . In this manner they produce an independent unit, operating as a separate system with its own sphere of influence apart from the individual points (*aṇus*, q.v.) from which it is made; this combination of lines gives thickness to the former unit having only length and breadth, and thus produces all visible forms known to us in the objective world.

Tvak (etymology uncertain), the power to feel, one of the five abstract knowing-senses (*jñānendriyas*, q.v.).

Udāharaṇa (fr. preps. *ud*, up, upwards + *ā* + *haraṇa*, carrying <√*har*, to carry), illustration, example, (in Nyāya) the third member (*avayava*, q.v.) of the five-membered syllogism and defined as an object of the perception (*pratyakṣa*, q.v.).

Udāna (fr. prep. *ud*, up + *āna*, breath <√*an*, to breathe), one of the five vital airs (*vāyu*, q.v.) of the inner body; its movement is upwards; its seat is in the throat.

Unmeṣa (fr. prep. *ud*, up, upwards + **mesa*, a winking, opening of the eyes <√*miṣ*, to wink, open the eyes), 'coming forth,' 'becoming visible,' 'appearing'; another term for the manifestation of the universe, cf. *ābhāsa* and *sṛṣṭi*.

Upacāra (fr. prep. *upa*, towards, with, under, down + *cāra*, going, motion <√*car*, to go, move), metaphor, (in Nyāya) one of the three forms of equivocation (*chala*, q.v.).

Upamāna (fr. prep. *upa*, towards, with, under, down + *māna*, opinion, notion, concept <√*man*, to think), comparison, a means of correct knowledge (*pramāṇa*, q.v.), defined as knowledge of a thing derived from its similarity to another thing previously well known.

Upanaya (fr. prep. *upa*, towards, with, under, down + *naya*, leading <√*nī*, lead), application, (in Nyāya) the fourth member (*avayava*, q.v.) of the five membered syllogism and defined as the act of comparison (*upamāna*, q.v.).

Upaniṣad (fr. preps. *upa*, towards + *ni*, down + √*sad*, to sit), 'sitting opposite' the teacher to receive instruction, the philosophical portion of the Veda, q.v., concerned with the nature of man and the universe; the fundamental doctrine is that of the identity of the individual soul or self (*ātman,* q.v.) with the universal self (Brahman, q.v.); the Upaniṣads are regarded as the source of the Vedānta and Sāṁkhya philosophies; they form a part of the Āraṇyaka, q.v., which in turn is a part of the Brāhmaṇa, q.v.; more than one hundred are mentioned, but thirteen are generally listed as the oldest ones, viz. *Chāndogya, Bṛhadāraṇyaka, Aitareya, Taittirīya, Kaṭha, Īśā, Muṇḍa, Kauṣītaki, Kena, Praśna, Śvetāśvatara, Māṇḍūkya,* and *Maitrī;* they date probably from the 8th century B.C.

Uparati (fr. prep. *upa,* towards, with, under, down + *rati,* rest, repose < √*ram,* to make content, bring to repose, calm, stop, rest), tolerance and renunciation of all sectarian religious observances, with the object of acquiring wisdom; (in Vedānta) one of the six acquirements (*ṣaṭsampat,* q.v.).

Upastha (fr. prep. *upa,* towards, with, under, down + *stha,* standing < √*sthā,* to stand), the power to procreate, one of the five abstract-working senses (*karmendriyas,* q.v.).

Utpattividhi, (in Mīmāṁsā) that which lays down a command with a certain object, thereby creating a desire.

Uttara (comparative of *ud,* up, upwards), upper, higher; later, following, concluding.

Uttaramīmāṁsā (compounded of *uttara* + *mīmāṁsā,* qq.v.), 'inquiry into or interpretation of the later or Upaniṣad portion of the Veda'; name of the system of philosophy founded by Bādarāyaṇa (as opposed to *purvamīmāṁsā,* founded by Jaimini, which is an inquiry into the first or Mantra portion of the Veda; *uttaramīmāṁsā* is generally called Vedānta, q.v.

Vāc (fr. √*vac,* to speak), a word, (in Nyāya) one of the three forms of equivocation (*chala,* q.v.); (in Sāṁkhya) the power to express, one of the five abstract working-senses (*karmendriyas,* q.v.).

Vāda (fr. √*vad,* to speak), discussion, (in Nyāya) one of the sixteen categories and defined as the testing of any proposition by means of logic for the sake of arriving at the truth of the proposition.

Vādavidyā (compounded of *vāda* + *vidyā,* qq.v.), 'science of discussion,' another name for Nyāya.

Vādin (fr. *vāda,* q.v.), a speaker, an expounder, or teacher of any doctrine or theory.

Vairāga (fr. pr. *vi,* apart, away, without + *rāga,* q.v.), without desire, absence of worldly desire.

Vairāgya (fr. *vairāga,* q.v.), right dispassion and indifference to the unreal and transitory; this consists of renunciation of all desires to enjoy the fruit of action both here and hereafter; (in Vedānta) one of the four qualifications listed by Śaṁkara for a student of philosophy, viz. (1) right discrimination (*viveka*, q.v.), (2) right dispassion and indifference (*vairāgya*), (3) right conduct (*ṣaṭsampat*, q.v.), (4) right desire (*mumukṣutva*, q.v.).

Vaiśeṣika (fr. *vi-śeṣa*, q.v.), one of the six *Darśanas* (philosophical systems), founded by Kaṇāda (3rd cent. B.C.); so called, because it teaches that knowledge of the nature of reality is obtained by knowing the special properties or essential differences which distinguish the nine Eternal Realities or Substances (*Dravyas*): Earth (*Pṛthivī*), Water (*Āpas*), Fire (*Tejas*), Air (*Vāyu*), Ether (*Ākāśa*), Time (*Kāla*), Space (*Dik*), Self (*Ātman*), and Mind (*Manas*).

Vaiśeṣikasūtra (compounded of *vaiśeṣika* + *sūtra*, qq.v.), the aphorisms of the Vaiśeṣika philosophy, ascribed to Kaṇāda, also called *Mokṣaśāstra* and *Adhyātmaśāstra*, qq.v.

Vaiṣṇavism (fr. *viṣṇu*, q.v.), name of one of the three great divisions of modern Hindūism (the other two being Śaivism and Śāktism, qq.v.); the Vaiṣṇavas identify Viṣṇu—rather than Brahmā and Śiva—with the Supreme Being, and are exclusively devoted to his worship, regarding him as the creator, preserver, and destroyer of the universe.

Vāk, in composition for *vāc*, q.v.

Vākya, (in Mīmāṁsā) when the meaning of a word or collection of words is indicated by the sentence in which it is used.

Vākyabhedabhayāt, (in Mīmāṁsā) the splitting up of a sentence.

Vāma, left; reverse; opposite.

Vāmācāra (compounded of *vāma* + *ācāra*, qq.v.), the 'left' way among the worshippers of Śakti, q.v.; opposite of *Dakṣiṇācāra*, q.v., said to be more monistic than *Dakṣiṇācāra*.

Vāmācārin, one who worships Śakti, q.v., according to the 'left' way; cf. *Dakṣiṇācārin*.

Varga (fr. √*varj*, to turn), a separate division, class, set, or series.

Vārttika (fr. *vārtta* <√*vṛt*, to turn), commentary, an explanatory work, a critical gloss.

Vasugupta, the Father of Kāśmīr Śaivism; author of the *Śivasūtra*; believed to have lived during the end of the 8th century A.D. and the beginning of the 9th century A.D.

Vātsyāyana, the classic commentator on the *Nyāyasūtra*, q.v.; he flourished, perhaps, about 400 A.D.

Vāyu (fr. √*vā,* to blow), Air as an element, (in Vaiśeṣika) the fourth Eternal Reality (*Dravya,* q.v.); (in Sāṁkhya) the second Sense-Particular (*Mahābhūta,* q.v.), the principle of motion, its function is impact, its Special Property (*Viśeṣa,* q.v.) is Touch (*Sparśa,* q.v.), its General Quality (*Sāmānya Guṇa,* q.v.), is Sound (*Śabda,* q.v.); (in Yoga) ten vāyus are given, five known as *Prāṇādi,* belonging to the inner body, viz. *prāṇa, apāna, samāna, udāna,* and *vyāna,* qq.v.; and five, known as *Nāgādi,* belonging to the outer body, viz. *nāga, kūrma, kṛkara, devadatta,* and *dhanaṁjaya,* qq.v.; of the first five, *prāṇa* has its seat in the heart, *apāna* in the anus, *samāna* in the region of the navel, *udāna* in the throat, while *vyāna* moves all over the body; the remaining five perform the respective functions of eructation, opening the eyes, hunger and thirst, gaping or yawning, and hiccuping.

Veda (fr. √*vid,* to know), the generic name for the most ancient sacred literature of the Hindūs, consisting of the four collections (*saṁhitā,* q.v.) called (1) Ṛgveda, hymns to gods, (2) Sāmaveda, priests' chants, (3) Yajurveda, sacrificial formulae in prose, and (4) Atharvaveda, magical chants; each Veda is divided into two broad divisions, viz. (1) Mantra, hymns, and (2) Brāhmaṇa, precepts, which include (a) Āraṇyakas, theology, and (b) Upaniṣads, philosophy, qq.v.; the Vedas are classified as revealed literature (*śruti,* q.v.); they contain the first philosophical insights and are regarded as the final authority; tradition makes Vyāsa, q.v., the compiler and arranger of the Vedas in their present form; the Vedic period is conservatively estimated to have begun about 1500 to 1000 B.C.

Vedāṅga (compounded of *veda,* q.v. + *aṅga,* limb, member, body, subdivision), 'limb of the Veda,' the generic name for six sciences regarded as auxiliary to the Veda, written in the sūtra, q.v., style; they are (1) Phonetics (*śakṣā*), (2) Metre (*chandas*), (3) Grammar (*vyākaraṇa*), (4) Etymology (*nirukta*), (5) Astronomy (*jyotiṣa*), and (6) Religious Ceremony (*kalpa*); they are designed to teach how to recite, understand, and apply Vedic texts.

Vedānta (compounded of *veda,* q.v. + *anta,* end), literally, 'the end of the Vedas,' the popular name of the second part of the Mīmāṁsā, q.v., or third division of Hindū philosophy, technically called *Uttara-mīmāṁsā,* meaning last investigation or examination of the Vedas; because the central topic is the Ultimate Principle or Universal Spirit, called Brahman, the names *Brahmasūtra* and *Brahmamīmāṁsā* are frequently used; another title is Śārīraka

Mīmāṁsā, meaning an inquiry into the embodied spirit; its founder was Bādarāyaṇa, whose date is quite unknown; its central theme is the philosophical teachings of the Upaniṣads concerning the nature and relationship of the three principles, that is, the Ultimate Principle, the world, and the soul, this also included the relationship between the Universal Soul and the individual soul; the various schools that have flourished on the doctrine elaborated in the *Brahmasūtra* of Bādarāyaṇa can be classified according to their interpretation of the Ultimate Principle (Brahman); the three principal schools are *advaita* (non-dualism), founded by Śaṁkara (788–820 A.D.), whose central position is that all is One, only the Ultimate Principle has any actual existence, and everything else is but a reflection; *viśiṣṭādvaita* (qualified non-dualism), founded by Rāmānuja (11th century), who admits that the Ultimate Principle is real and exists, but he qualifies his position by arguing that souls are also real, though their reality is dependent upon this Ultimate Principle; *dvaita* (dualism), founded by Madhva (12th century), who denies that the Ultimate Principle is the cause of the world, and contends that the soul is a separate principle having an independent existence of its own, and is only associated with the Ultimate Principle.

Vedāntasūtra (compounded of *vedānta* + *sūtra,* qq.v.), the aphorisms of the Vedānta philosophy, ascribed to Bādārāyaṇa, q.v., also called *Brahmasūtra*, *Brahmamīmāṁsā*, and *Śārīrakamīmāṁsā*, qq.v.

Vibhatrirūpa, (in Mīmāṁsā) the meaning of a word which is indicated by an affix of a declension.

Vibhūta (fr. pr. *vi,* apart, away, without + *bhūti,* existence, being < √*bhū,* to become, be), the manifestation of great power; (in Yoga) there are said to be eight supernatural powers which one can attain, viz. (1) the power of becoming as minute as an atom (*aṇimā*), (2) the power to become as light as cotton (*laghimā*), (3) the power of reaching anywhere, even to the moon (*prāpti*), (4) the power of having all wishes of whatever description realized (*prākāmya*), (5) the power to expand oneself into space (*mahimā*), (6) the power to create (*īśitā*), (7) the power to command all (*vaśitvā*), and (8) the power of suppressing all desires (*kāmāvasāyitā*).

Vidhātri, (in Mīmāṁsā) that which is indicated by the verb form *liṅ*.

Vidhi (fr. pr. *vi,* apart, away, without + √*dhā,* to put, set, place), order, injunction, command; (in Mīmāṁsā) one of the five divisions under which the contents of the Vedas, q.v., are classified.

Vidyā (fr. √*vid,* to know), knowledge, science, learning, scholarship, philosophy; (in Kāśmīr Śaivism) Limited Knowledge, one of the five Kañcukas, q.v.; it is the power that limits the universal condition of All-Knowledge (*Saravajñatva,* q.v.); therefore, it is the origin of Limited Knowledge.

Vikāra (fr. pr. *vi,* apart, away, without + √*kar,* to do, make, perform), transformation, change of form; (in Sāṁkhya) a product of Nature (*Prakṛti,* q.v.), viz. Cosmic Intelligence (*Mahat,* q.v.), Individuating Principle (*Ahaṁkāra,* q.v.), and the five Subtle Elements (*Tanmātras,* q.v.); from these sixteen other Vikāras are produced, viz. Cosmic Mind (*Manas,* q.v.), five Knowing-senses (*Jñānendriyas,* q.v.), five Working-senses (*Karmendriyas,* q.v.), and five Sense-Particulars (*Mahābhūtas,* q.v.).

Vikāramaya (compounded of *vikāra,* q.v. + *maya* <√*mā,* to measure, form, build), a derivative from Nature (*Prakṛti,* q.v.).

Vikāratva (fr. *vikāra,* q.v., + abstract formative *-tva*), the state of change, transformation.

Viniyogavidhi (in Mīmāṁsā), that which lays down the details of a sacrifice.

Viniyoktrī (in Mīmāṁsa), a word which on hearing one is able to understand immediately the connection of the subsidiary and the principal.

Viṣaya (etymology doubtful), thesis, subject of an argument; the first division of a topic (*adhikaraṇa,* q.v.).

Viśeṣa (fr. pr. *vi,* apart, away, without + *śeṣa,* remainder <√*śiṣ,* to leave over, distinguish), particularity, species, the individual characteristic or special property that distinguishes a particular thing from all other things; (in Vaiśeṣika) the fourth Predicable (*Padārtha,* q.v.); it is by means of the *viśeṣās* or special properties that the Paramāṇus (first four Eternal Realities, viz. Earth, Water, Fire and Air) are distinguished from one another.

Viśiṣṭādvaita (compounded of pr. *vi,* apart, away, without + *śiṣṭa,* past pass. participle of √*śiṣ,* to leave over, distinguish), 'qualified non-dualism,' the doctrine of qualified monism advocated by Rāmānuja, q.v., which admits that the Ultimate Principle (Brahman, q.v.) is real and exists, but he qualifies his position by arguing that souls are also real, though their reality is independent of this Ultimate Principle.

Viṣṇu (probably fr. √*viṣ,* to be quick, speed), name of one of the gods of the Hindū Trimūrti or Trinity, viz. Brahmā, 'the Creator,'

Viṣṇu, 'the preserver,' and Śiva, 'the destroyer'; (among the adherents of Vaiṣṇavism, q.v.) the Supreme Deity; (in philosophy) the principle of preservation.

Vitaṇḍā (fr. pr. *vi,* apart, away, without + *taṇḍa,* of uncertain etymology), cavil, (in Nyāya) one of the sixteen categories and defined as a kind of wrangling in order to heckle the speaker, with no desire to establish any proposition.

Vivarta (fr. pr. *vi,* apart, away, without + *varta* <√*vart,* to turn), 'revolving'; (in Vedānta) an 'appearance,' the forms that manifest in the phenomenal world, regarded as illusions.

Vivartavāda (compounded of *vivarta* + *vāda,* qq.v.), the Vedānta doctrine that the phenomenal world is a mere illusion (*māyā,* q.v.).

Viveka (fr. *vi,* away, apart, without + **veka* <√*vic,* to sift, sever, separate), discrimination, true knowledge; right discrimination between the eternal and non-eternal, the real and the unreal; (in Vedānta) one of the four qualifications listed by Śaṁkara for a student of philosophy, viz. (1) right discrimination (*viveka*), (2) right dispassion and indifference (*vairāgya,* q.v.), (3) right conduct (*ṣaṭsampat,* q.v.), and (4) right desire (*mumukṣutva,* q.v.).

Vivṛti (fr. *vi,* apart, away, without + *vṛti,* enclosure <√*vṛ,* to cover, conceal, surround, prevent), explanation, exposition, gloss, commentary, interpretation.

Vṛtti (fr. √*vart,* to turn, revolve, roll), mode of life or conduct, course of action, behaviour, (esp.) moral conduct; (in philosophy) mode of being, mental state, condition.

Vyakta (fr. pr. *vi,* apart, away, without + *akta,* pref. pass. participle of √*añj,* to anoint), manifest matter; (in Sāṁkhya) 'the evolved or developed,' a product of Nature (*prakṛti,* q.v.); op. *avyakta,* q.v.

Vyāna (fr. pr. *vi,* apart, away, without + *āna,* breath <√*an,* to breathe), one of the five vital airs (*vāyu,* q.v.) of the inner body; its movement is throughout the body.

Vyāpaka (fr. pr. *vi,* apart, away + *āpaka,* obtaining <√*āp,* to reach, attain to, meet), 'pervading,' (in Nyāya) the invariable concomitance, the co-presence of the middle term with the major term.

Vyāpakatva (fr. *vyāpaka,* q.v. + abstract formative *-tva*), 'all-reachingness' or 'all-obtainingness,' (in Kāśmīr Śaivism) the universal experience of All-Pervasiveness.

Vyāsa, 'compiler, arranger,' according to legend, the name of the celebrated mythical sage who is regarded as the one who originally compiled and arranged the Vedas and other portions of Hindū sacred literature; also called Bādarāyaṇa, q.v.

Vyavadhāraṇakalpana (in Mīmāṁsā), interpretation of a sentence according to its context.

Vyudāsa (fr. preps. *vi,* apart, away, without + *ud,* up, upwards + **āsa,* a throwing < √*as,* to throw), throwing away.

Yajurveda, one of the four Vedas, q.v.

Yama (fr. √*yam,* to hold together or back, check, curb, control, restrain), moral restraint, self-control, forbearance; the first prerequisite to the study and practice of Yoga, q.v.); ten rules of conduct (*yamas*) are listed in the classic text, *Haṭhayogapradīpikā,* viz. non-injuring, truthfulness, non-stealing, continence, forgiveness, endurance, compassion, sincerity, sparing diet, and cleanliness; so also *niyama.*

Yathāsaṁkhyapatha (in Mīmāṁsā), 'relative enumeration,' arranging verbs with verbs and subjects with subjects.

Yaugika (in Mīmāṁsā), a derivative word, made up of two or three words, used in the sense conveyed by the component parts of which it is made.

Yoga (fr. √*yuj,* to yoke or join), one of the six *Darśanas,* q.v. (philosophical systems), founded by *Patañjali* (? 3rd cent. B.C.), based on the Sāṁkhya, q.v., system as it applies to the individual; so called, because it teaches the means by which the individual spirit (*jīvātmā,* q.v.), can be united or joined with the Universal Spirit (*Paramātmā,* q.v.); it is defined as 'the restraint of mental modifications'; eight stages are enumerated, viz. moral restraint (*yama,* q.v.), self-culture (*niyama,* q.v.), posture (*āsana,* q.v.), breath-control (*prāṇāyāma,* q.v.), control of the senses (*pratyāhāra,* q.v.), concentration (*dhāraṇa,* q.v.), meditation (*dhyāna,* q.v.); and a state of super-consciousness (*samādhi,* q.v.); the techniques of Yoga are recommended and used by every system of religion and school of philosophy throughout India; the oldest text on its philosophy is the *Yogasūtra* of Patañjali, the most authorative accounts of its techniques are given in the classic texts: *Haṭhayogapradīpikā, Gheraṇḍasaṁhitā,* and *Śivasaṁhitā.*

Yogarūḍhi (in Mīmāṁsā), a compound word which has its own conventional sense.

Yogasūtra (compounded of *yoga* + *sūtra,* qq.v.), the aphorisms of the Yoga philosophy, ascribed to Patañjali, q.v.

Yogin (fr. *yoga,* q.v.), a follower of the Yoga system (usually called Yogī).

Yoginī (fem. of *yogin*), a woman follower of the Yoga system.

Yoni (fr. I-E **ieu-ni* or **iou-ni,* place), a figure representing the female genitals, serving as the formal symbol under which the female power (*śakti,* q.v.) in nature is worshipped, cf. *liṅga.*

Yuga (fr. $\sqrt{}$*yuj,* to yoke, join, or fasten), one of the four ages of the world, viz. (1) Krita or Satya, (2) Tretā, (3) Dvāpara, (4) Kali. The first three have already elapsed and we are now living in the last which began at midnight between the 17th and 18th of February 3102 B.C. The duration of each age is said to be respectively 1,728,000, 1,296,000, 864,000, and 432,000 years of man, the descending numbers representing a similar physical and moral deterioration of men in each age; the four Yugas comprise an aggregate of 4,320,000 and constitute a 'great Yuga' or Mahāyuga.